The Straightforward Guide to
SAFEGUARDING ADULTS

*From Getting the Basics Right to Applying
the Care Act and Criminal Investigations*

Deborah Barnett

Jessica Kingsley *Publishers*
London and Philadelphia

First published in 2019
by Jessica Kingsley Publishers
73 Collier Street
London N1 9BE, UK
and
400 Market Street, Suite 400
Philadelphia, PA 19106, USA

www.jkp.com

Library of Congress Cataloging in Publication Data
A CIP catalog record for this book is available from the Library of Congress

British Library Cataloguing in Publication Data
A CIP catalogue record for this book is available from the British Library

ISBN 978 1 78592 327 2
eISBN 978 1 78450 640 7

Printed and bound in Great Britain

An accompanying PDF 'Safeguarding Adults Training Delivery' is available to download from www.jkp.com/voucher using the code COUCOMO

Contents

Preface

Who should read this book and how to use the information

This book aims to work through safeguarding from the basics to the increasing complexities of multi-agency decision making, and asks the readers to critically analyse the information with others and learn from the discussions. The book is designed to take not only students and academics but also safeguarding practitioners and multi-agency safeguarding leads on a journey through safeguarding adults. It is hoped that the book can instigate topical discussion within both classrooms and safeguarding adults boards. It is my desire to write a book that will spark some lively discussions and debates.

An ideal safeguarding world is one in which routine responses to individuals are challenged and questioned on a regular basis, where preventative measures are favoured over protective measures, and where practitioners understand the importance of information sharing, but do not confuse this with the response to the individual who has care and support needs. It is important to share information and to assess the situation and risks to all persons concerned; however, this does not equate to making decisions about a person, for that person, in response to their needs. The Mental Capacity Act provides the framework for this and is an integral part of all safeguarding work that creates personalised responses to the adult concerned.

In reading this book I would like you to reflect on and identify the difference between our duty to do something set out in legislation and the ethical basis for response to the individual. The Human Rights Act is a foundation Act and is established around the rights of the individual. Our ethical frameworks are based within the constructs of the Human Rights Act. In layman's terms, the Human Rights Act tells us that we can make autonomous decisions as long as we are able to demonstrate that we understand the decision being made (the Mental Capacity Act falls within Article 8, the right to a private and family life, which includes the right to make autonomous decisions) and that in conducting the subsequent actions we are not committing a crime, or harming someone else. To make an autonomous and informed decision we must not have been coerced or intimidated into making that decision. We have a duty to share information for safeguarding purposes, a duty to consider the risks to others and we must consider coercive and controlling behaviours in a domestic situation. We have a duty to share information relating to a potential crime where there is reasonable suspicion of that crime. We also have a duty to maintain the physical and mental wellbeing of the person concerned and to consider their autonomous wishes, only diverging from those autonomous decisions where there is a lawful and recorded rationale.

For the practitioner, enabling a person to take risks is a difficult thing to do. For the person concerned, not being allowed to take risks can feel very restrictive and frightening. In any given scenario where there is a response to the person regarding their health, services or wellbeing, then we must ensure that we are not being overly protective because of our own fears and that we are offering the person the opportunity to take sufficient risks to learn and grow. There is an additional resource that can support safeguarding training that is available to download from www.jkp.com/voucher using the code COUCOMO.

The author

I have worked within local authority adult services for 30 years as a practitioner, social worker, manager and strategic manager. My experience covers all aspects of adult services. In 1994 I worked on the 'Action for Elder Abuse' campaign, beginning my first safeguarding role and sparking an interest. I have chaired a safeguarding adults board. I also chair and author safeguarding adults reviews and am involved in different aspects of safeguarding practice as an independent social worker and consultant. I have a passion for the development of trauma-informed services and hope that in the future both safeguarding adult and children's services will have a greater understanding of adverse childhood experiences (ACEs) and the impact of trauma on a person's life. Addressing the trauma at the time that the traumatic event occurs as part of the safeguarding procedures and having all practitioners 'trauma informed' is something that I aim to achieve.

As well as being a social worker and manager, I have also studied to qualify as a teacher, and training and teaching have been regular aspects of my career. In addition to writing this book I have written some information and guidance for those delivering safeguarding training and who wish to build upon the competencies identified within the inter-collegiate document entitled 'Adult Safeguarding Roles and Competencies for Health Care Staff' (Barnett 2018a). This training information will cover a range of social and health care training considerations and is available online from the JKP website.

Safeguarding and safety

In training when I ask people what safeguarding is all about, one of the first things they say is, 'Keeping people safe.' While you will not find this response very surprising, I want to turn this on its head and ask you to explore this a little. Imagine that there is someone who has the ability to have influence over your life and choices. They come to your door and tell you that they are concerned about you, that they want to keep you safe. What might your anxieties be and what thoughts go through your head?

For me, I start thinking about all the risky but fun things that I enjoy in life: the times that I have smoked, the times that I have drunk too much, gone out without appropriate clothing for the weather, eaten unhealthy food, travelled to places in the world that others may deem risky. Some other examples may be leaving a perfectly safe local authority job to become self-employed, stopping work for a year to write two books and articles on things that I am passionate about and taking a qualification that will mean little or no income. Some of these things define my personality, my sense of adventure, my spirit, my friendships, my drive, my enthusiasm and need to explore and learn new things – my identity.

The difficult times and the happy times – the most potent aspects of my life – are held within the context of risk taking. When someone says that they are going to keep me safe, I immediately start to question what they think safety is and what they would perceive to be too risky, what they would prevent me from doing. None of this sounds good to me. When you tell a person that you may need to make a safeguarding referral, be aware that the person may see this differently from how you might perceive it. Explain what safeguarding is, do not make a statement of safety. Safety is something socially constructed and subjective. It is therefore unhelpful to make assumptions that people will regard you wanting to keep them 'safe' as a positive thing – they may see it as an intrusion.

I would like to explain why I think that 'safety' is a social construct – in other words, an invention of a particular culture, or society, which exists solely because people agree to behave as if it exists, or agree to follow certain conventional rules. To demonstrate this, here are some examples of what safety means to my family members:

Safety is having a community of people supporting you, never feeling trapped or tied to a particular place. It is about tradition, history and culture and having common shared values. Friendships and bonds are really important for your safety. (my maternal grandmother, a Gypsy traveller who lived through the war. She met her Jewish husband in a prisoner-of-war camp)

Safety is about having security, a family and a place to call home. Familiar surroundings and consistent people with consistent messages. Safety is about getting a good education, a good job, being strong, confident and assertive, being able to look after yourself. (my paternal grandmother, a middle-class white female brought up on a farm with tennis courts, ponds, chickens and horses. Her father was a manager in a local coal pit and died in a mining accident when my grandmother was young)

I don't really know what feeling safe is, perhaps having someone that is strong and protective, someone to look after you. (my mother, brought up in child care with numerous foster carers, separated from her brother)

Being safe is making sure that you do everything to protect yourself. You get an education, you make sure that things are secure, you do not make impulsive decisions and you seek information about decisions from others who know more than you do about the decisions to be made. (my father, an ex-police officer, with a good standard of education and prosperous career opportunities)

When I asked a family member who has autism and attention deficit hyperactive disorder, they said, 'Do you mean what being safe means for me, or what you would say being safe was for me?' I clarify, 'What do you think safety means for you?' The reply is amazing: 'It is being safe in life and not just in your environment, because being safe in your environment might be too restrictive. Looking at my end goals in life are far more important to me.'

Each person defines safety from their own experiences and social situations and rejects the perspectives of others. The imposition of someone else's perspective of safety is not only worrying, but might also be overly restrictive due to culture, values, experiences and personal ethics. I am sure that if my family came together they would all agree on some things that they could find common ground on about safety, but in reality, how each person played this out in their lives would be very different.

> Perceptions of safety and danger are 'intersubjective' – products of social construction, collective agreement, and socialization. While objective danger certainly exists, perceptions of danger do not derive directly from observation of the empirical world. The objective environment provides only inconsistent and ambiguous information, permitting ample room for socially constructed beliefs. (Simpson 1996, p.550)

To safeguard a person and help that individual feel safe, the only thing we can possibly do is understand their life narrative, establish what safety means to them and support them to achieve it – anything else is an imposition of our own social construct of safety on another person's life.

I find it interesting that when discussing safety, many people talk about what they know, thus contributing to their feeling of safety. The perspective that knowledge and education help to make us feel safe is replicated in many of my family narratives and was also the perspective of Paulo Freire, a man who studied philosophy, phenomenology and the psychology of language and eventually went on to write *Pedagogy of the Oppressed* (Freire 1970). Giving people the right information to make decisions is an important aspect of making people feel safe.

My philosophy of the learning process in safeguarding

My favourite book is the one mentioned above, *Pedagogy of the Oppressed*, and since first reading this book in 1998, I have used its wisdom to reflect on my own practice as a social worker, manager and teacher. In this book Paulo Freire exposes the faults of a capitalist education and criticises the banking concept of education. The banking concept describes a model where students are taught and the teacher knows everything. The teacher thinks and imparts knowledge and the students are judged on the understanding of the knowledge imparted by the teacher. The teacher talks and the students listen. The teacher defines the programme content and asserts that their beliefs and perspectives are the correct ones, or the only way. The teacher confuses their authority and position of power with knowledge, yet by believing that they have the true knowledge, they establish professional authority and use this in opposition to the freedom and wisdom of the students. Freire (1970) asks us to create a revolution in education where the teacher's efforts coincide with those of the students and engage in critical and reflective thinking. To achieve this, the teacher must trust the students in a mutual quest to humanise the learning experiences together. The teacher of the students poses situations, tools and information, and the students teach the teacher of their experiences of using these tools, models, methods and theories in real-life situations. The students can then challenge the concepts in debate, or reinforce positive aspects of the concepts in a mutual learning process.

This book is based on this type of collective learning and growing within the classroom, training room and conference setting. This joint learning and growing experience invites you, the reader, to also join in, to tell me about what you have discovered since reading this book. The philosophy of the book is also reflective of the type of co-working relationship that needs to be fostered with those who have experienced abuse or neglect. The person in charge of the definition of safety is the person experiencing the abuse or neglect. This life narrative should be not only considered for the capacitated, but also explored sufficiently to ensure actions are taken to establish the life narrative of the incapacitated person and create safety as far as is practicably possible, from their own definition. To achieve this, we must consult with family and friends, exploring their pictures and passions of life.

This book is not an expert sharing of knowledge by which the students must bank the education and follow it without question. It offers some considerations based on legislation, models, methods, theories and research, and asks you to consider, utilise, evaluate and reflect. I am interested to hear your findings.

The ethos of safeguarding practice

Safeguarding is an ongoing learning and reflecting process. There are no safeguarding masters, just people learning from each other: author and reader, teacher and student, practitioner and person requiring our care and support.

I have worked in the area of safeguarding adults for nearly 25 years and throughout this time not a day goes by when someone has not taught me something. Safeguarding is about being humble, open to others' perspectives, and offering appropriate and justifiable challenge and continuous learning. No one practitioner has all the knowledge and critical reflection and produces results on a regular basis. When people analyse your safeguarding work, you learn not only more about your job and your role, how you work with others, but also so much about yourself. I am opinionated but open to challenge, as long as I understand the lawful and ethical justification. I am humble, but can be strong when poor decisions are being made that adversely affect the power and control or safety of others. I am personable, but can directly challenge ill-conceived concepts.

I come across people who say that they know all about safeguarding. This just cannot be true, as no one knows all about the complexities of people's lives and circumstances. There are people who say that safeguarding practitioners should be stern and assertive and exude authority. I would challenge this concept of leadership in safeguarding. I would say that there is a balance of making people feel comfortable enough to share their concerns, but equally comfortable to challenge the barriers. Who are the experts in safeguarding? They are most certainly those who have care and support needs and have manoeuvred the risks and challenges all their lives. These people can teach us the most and we need to listen as equal partners.

If safeguarding practitioners stopped questioning when they say 'Yes, I can help you with that' and started challenging themselves more when they say 'No, I am not accepting that referral', 'No, you cannot take that risk' or 'No, we cannot help you', safeguarding would be more person centred. Consider the consequences of rejecting that referral, stopping a person from taking risks or not providing preventative care and support. Long-term solutions are often the objective of those who use our services.

How much knowledge is enough in safeguarding adults?

The current climate of austerity and the pressures placed on services to deliver in terms of output or outcomes cause us to reflect on the true nature of safeguarding and social work practice. I consider the age-old questions that social work is challenged with:

- How much is enough?

- What constitutes evidence for social workers?

- What affects decision making other than evidence?

- How analytical are social workers (and those safeguarding others) towards their own decision-making processes?

- Is safeguarding true multi-agency work, or is it social work led?

Recently, I have had the privilege to attend a number of Community Care Live events as both a presenter and a participant. These events leave me feeling inspired and proud of my profession. It is the stories of the social workers themselves that inspire me most. Looking towards my very learned colleagues who are presenting at the conference, I see eminent university lecturers, solicitors, barristers, police officers and other key people who interface with social work services, but I learn more from the practitioners themselves and the questions that they pose, driving me to find my own answers.

I enjoy my job and study hard, conducting research every day. I try to listen to individual stories and consider my values and ethics. I am passionate about human rights and breaking down barriers to oppression and discrimination, addressing the fear of being oppressed and discriminated and aiming to avoid misunderstanding and misconceptions. Some of the most devastatingly sad occasions in my career have been when I have not been able to communicate this effectively enough to make a difference.

I love social work practice; there is nothing better than seeing someone achieve something in their life and being there to witness that change in a person. I have had many successes in practice and I love teaching and studying, but, like many other people, I question the expectations that each profession has of safeguarding adults and just how much about these professions the practitioners coordinating responses to safeguarding referrals are expected to know. Shared knowledge and a lack of personal ego are essential tools in safeguarding adults, because no one person has all the answers – it is our combined reflections and suggestions that make a difference. How much do we need to know to open the door to discussion, break down oppressive barriers and challenge linear, stereotypical and service-based decisions?

This book and my previous book on self-neglect (Barnett 2018b) have created a difficult journey for me – one where I explore my own practice and justification for decision making and one where I question just how much is enough.

How much legislation do I need to know?

In conferences, I stand alongside the barristers who challenge us to be legally literate, to understand the law. Star struck, I listen to their amazing descriptions of the law and then try to translate what that means in practice. Over the years, I have come to realise that I am pretty good at this, but interpreting law into practice is never 100 per cent accurate because it is an interpretation. We are being our own judge and jury on a daily basis, reflecting on why we have chosen a course of action. On reflection, I have a good grasp of much of the associated legislation:

- As an adult social worker, I understand the key elements of the Care Act 2014 and the Children Act 1989, enough to have sensible conversations about the application of the law in cases of domestic abuse, forced marriage or other safeguarding-related cases.

- I recognise key elements of the National Health Service Act 2006, the Health and Social Care Act 2014, the Mental Capacity Act 2005, the Mental Health Act 1983 and the Human Rights Act 1998.

- I have studied the Equality Act 2010 in some detail at postgraduate level. I understand the Data Protection Act 1998 and the Freedom of Information Act 2000.

- I understand the common law of negligence and our duty of care, but when it comes to Tort Law I am a little less well versed.

- I understand the Police and Criminal Evidence Act 1984, the Crime and Disorder Act 1998 and the Serious Crime Act 2015. I have both studied and taught Achieving Best Evidence and other elements of supporting vulnerable witnesses in criminal proceedings.

- I know where to look for housing, environmental health, health and safety and other related legislation.

Do I know as much as a judge, barrister, solicitor or someone legally trained in a specific aspect of legislation? The answer to that would be no. I do my very best to interpret relevant legislation in practice, so I may know more about the practical application of that legislation than they do. No one else will tell me how to interpret the law in practice, but they will judge whether I have justified my practice in law.

I try to demonstrate why I have considered the legislation and how I see it applying, and measure this against what the person did or said that made me think it relevant and how proportionate I feel my response to be. I know that in social work I constantly learn, and in safeguarding adults there is an ever-evolving knowledge, where ethical debates are regularly held with knowledgeable colleagues. What I write today will be reconsidered every day and reflected on. No one should be able to say that their practice has stood still; this means your mind, research and skills have frozen in time. Sometimes I hear myself saying that I wished that I had formally studied law, but even if I had I would not be able to study all aspects of the law in sufficient detail. I want to study law because I want to inform my practice, not because I want to be a barrister. I am left with the feeling that no matter how much I know, or what I do, it is never enough. So how much is enough?

The academics of safeguarding

In writing these books, as in my practice, I have considered how academic I need to be. What is it that practitioners are asking for? Is it a good reference, or a way to understand how to put something into practice and defend their decision making? I suspect that practitioners today are required to do both. I remember when I first left university as a newly qualified social worker and went into practice, I could not see how what I had learned or experienced within university translated into what I was doing in practice. Today managers should and are asking for a rationale for the decisions that a professional has made – in other words, what informed their practice. The learning in university is explicitly applied to daily practice and recording.

In times of austerity, with depleted resources, the burning question becomes how much should we be recording to defend our decisions, and how do we balance this with the amount of time that we can spend getting to know the people for whom we are working, those who have care and support needs?

I grapple with this in writing this book from a practitioner's perspective. I have tried to explain something in a simple manner; however, an academic can pull apart what I have said as being overly simplistic, and a barrister could do the same. I came across an excellent example of this when a colleague kindly reviewed my book on self-neglect. I had originally said that as a result of the Care Act, self-neglect is a safeguarding issue and therefore a safeguarding referral should be made to the local authority when the three-part eligibility criteria are met. From an academic perspective, this is inaccurate, as it is the statutory guidance and not the Care Act 2014 that tells us about self-neglect. From a practice perspective in my mind, the Care Act changed the forms of abuse that we consider, and as a result of the legislation and subsequent guidance, I have considered self-neglect as a safeguarding issue. It is the fact that I now know that I must consider self-neglect that is the important factor. How much of a quote am I expected to give in everyday practice? Do I need to quote the guidance, the chapter, the section in my daily recording, is a general awareness sufficient, or do we need some kind of considered reference?

Another example of this presented itself when I was explaining my ten-step approach to information sharing at conference (see Chapter 4). In practice, the *sharing* of information is very different from the *response* to the sharing of information. We can share relevant information about safeguarding concerns where there is reasonable suspicion of abuse or neglect, without a person's consent, if there is a risk to others, public interest issues, potential mental ill-health requiring statutory assessment, domestic abuse meaning that the person may be coerced or intimidated into making a decision, or where there is a potential crime. It is good practice to discuss concerns with the person and their representative. In considering our response, we must consider whether the impact of our actions would be beneficial, or potentially cause further harm. The ethics, values and principles are to be considered in any action taken.

Safeguarding is not just about the victim, it is about all parties involved and wider community safety, and therefore information is shared to get a clear picture, so that all agencies have the opportunity to participate and share their concerns, knowledge and skills. The barrister in the conference was concerned that sharing the information could cause further harm. It is not usually the sharing of relevant information with relevant people that causes harm, it is ill-considered and ill-judged intervention that causes further harm and therefore that would not be safeguarding.

It is very difficult to get a good balance between the knowledge that informs practice (the academic considerations recorded) and the practice (what we actually do and what we have time to write). A busy practitioner often considers a lot of different things, but does not always justify this in every bit of writing to the extent that an academic or barrister might. How academic and how justifiable in law, policies, procedures, models, methods and theories does our practice have to be and how much of this is referenced in our daily recording?

The psychology of safeguarding

I love to understand psychology and I have studied it briefly. In trying to effectively manage safeguarding, I return to the same dilemmas over and over again. Below are a couple of examples of some very brave and amazing people I came into contact with, and I am going to combine their narratives and experiences to demonstrate my dilemma. In safeguarding work, we are often faced with people who have suffered abuse, neglect, trauma, loss and bereavement, and as a result have lost all power and control over their lives. During every training session addressing topics such as domestic abuse, self-neglect, homelessness, substance misuse, sexual exploitation, human trafficking and modern-day slavery, we explore the impact of loss, trauma, abuse or neglect.

In trying to understand the brain, I can also try to understand why people respond the way that they do and why they may present barriers, remain in abusive relationships, become aggressive towards help, and appear capacitated, although they are not able to retain information, and why they present with certain behaviours. I need to understand the impact of abuse and neglect on a person in order to understand the significance of interventions to maintain wellbeing. I am now going to describe two anonymised case studies.

■ When teaching Janet (student social worker) about the Mental Capacity Act 2005 in relation to safeguarding adults, I could see that on occasions her body became tense and her demeanour was almost aggressive. I am teaching about choice, person-centred practice and having a voice or a say in a matter, but this appears to be distressing for her.

Janet challenges, 'A person who is mentally unwell, a person who has suffered abuse or neglect to the extent that it affects their mental health, may be assessed as making a capacitated decision to kill themselves, or neglect themselves until they die, but is that really a capacitated decision?'

I ask whether this person has been assessed by the mental health team and Janet informs me that they have been assessed and are not detainable under the Mental Health Act 1983. I ask if they have engaged with therapy and she tells me that they have not, that they have been offered six weeks of therapy but are too afraid that this may merely open up old wounds, without the time required to heal. They are terrified of talking about the trauma, as they subsequently have severe post-traumatic responses.

The original diagnosis of psychosis was considered in the mental health assessment and the person was considered to be managing it very well; however, they were not managing the impact of the original trauma very well. Janet challenges that the co-morbid impact of trauma and capacity to make decisions as a result of the post trauma on the executive functioning of the brain has not been explored. Janet challenges that they have not ruled this out and could therefore be considered negligent, or not meeting their duty of care. The recognition of trauma and diagnosis has not been considered and could have a significant impact on responses and decision making. Janet continues to challenge, stating that the mental health team have closed the case and do not see grounds for review. While Janet and I have some insight into how trauma affects the brain and brain function, we are not able to help this person without psychological assistance and psychiatric help. Neither the psychiatrist nor psychologist specialise in trauma. Janet returns to her manager, who has even less understanding of trauma and merely tells Janet that as long as she has recorded the capacity assessment and the mental health referral then she has concluded her responsibilities.

Reflecting on Janet's challenge I must agree with her that the impact of trauma on a person's life, particularly when they are displaying such obvious distress that could result in serious harm, or death, must be explored. In defence of social work/health practitioners and their managers, if the psychiatrists and psychologists are not trained to recognise the impact of trauma on the person during their assessments and they miss the signs and symptoms associated with trauma, then access to services becomes difficult. How much are we as social workers or safeguarding practitioners expected to understand (in safeguarding cases) in order that we may try to break down these barriers to services and gain a more insightful understanding of people's trauma responses and potential treatment and therapy pathways?

The wraparound of health and social care response in safeguarding is to prevent further deterioration, to maintain independence, to delay the need for further services and to maintain wellbeing and is therefore at the very heart of safeguarding practice. If a person has suffered trauma, this does not go away, it only grows. The local authority requires psychiatry and psychology services as partners in safeguarding those who have suffered loss, bereavement, abuse and neglect, and recognition of trauma responses if we are to meet our duties under the Care Act 2014.

James sat in my training session on self-neglect and became more and more animated, leading to him disclosing that he had suffered severe neglect as a child and as a result struggled to prevent extreme hoarding behaviours which were affecting his family and his work life. The issues relating trauma to hoarding resonated; however, as he gained more insight, he also became angry about the times that he had presented himself to professionals seeking help and they had not recognised how to help.

When James was talking about his collecting behaviours with professionals, he had not mentioned his childhood of abuse and neglect, and no one had asked. James said that he knew that the collecting and hoarding were as a result of his childhood experiences, but struggled to explain how or why, and could not find a way to stop collecting. James described feeling like a car out of control without any brakes, gathering speed and impetus, and the driver has never been given the manual, or any driving instructions. Randomly and ever frantically, he tries to stop the car, only to find that his efforts exacerbate his difficulties, demonstrating failures at each attempt. James said that if psychology held the key to the brakes, why were services not more observant and why do they not explore the experiences that require the brakes to be applied?

This is a little cryptic as an example, but James was making an analogy that he was feeling out of control, exhausted and frantic but failing in his efforts to stop collecting/hoarding, and that this was replicating experiences and feelings from his childhood. James was angry that professionals did not recognise the symptoms of trauma, loss, bereavement and neglect and were therefore unable to prevent the symptoms that he was displaying and apply the appropriate therapeutic approaches for his presenting difficulties. There is no tablet that can cure hoarding, nor is there a singular therapeutic response. There are, instead, numerous tablets and a variety of responses, depending on the issues presented.

These types of scenarios lead me to question how much psychology a safeguarding practitioner needs to know in order to ask the right questions, or break down barriers to mental health assessment and services.

The sociology of safeguarding

I have studied applied sociology, equality, diversity and criminology at postgraduate level. In managing safeguarding on behalf of the local authority, I reflect on how much the everyday safeguarding response should cover the scientific study of society and societal responses to crime, welfare, mobility, deviance, medical intervention and culture. How far should our sociological analysis go towards informing practice?

To give one example of this, I was researching the responses to safeguarding adults reviews to consider the key themes that arise in practice and to seek to avoid making the same mistakes. I studied approximately 40 cases and created a template of my findings to help assist myself and others during training. The template that I created for self-analysis in cases of self-neglect and safeguarding adults provides a series of questions, guidance and barriers for the practitioner. This ensures that past lessons are learned and that we identify and break down the barriers to effective safeguarding that are repeatedly identified in safeguarding adults reviews. The template identified key themes that arise in most safeguarding adults reviews. What I didn't do was analyse my methodology, identify a control, or consider a mixture of qualitative and quantitative responses to the use of the tool. I determined that people could consider the usefulness in their own practice and use the tool if they found it helpful, or discard the tool if it didn't work for them. Tools are only tools if they suit the work that we are doing and the person is able to benefit from the use of the tool.

I state all this as a defence to professional, analytical and reflective practice; however, I question myself. Would I be able to compete, to achieve, to get some important messages across better if I just conducted the study and demonstrated the scientific and academic application? More people would listen, which would make it more valuable, but would that not make me a sociologist rather than a social worker or safeguarding practitioner?

Another example arose when I was talking about the difference between a person's identity and behaviours and the use of cognitive dissonance to get the person to reflect on the positive aspects of their identity rather than ascribing the negative behaviours as their identity. In studying solution-focused therapy and motivational interviewing, and in the past running practitioner support groups around these methods of intervention, I often supported practitioners to help people move from pre-contemplation of their situation (head in the sand/denial/rejection) to contemplation or consideration of what they are doing and where this will take them. These were interventions that I regularly used to promote a person's contemplation of who they considered themselves to be (identity) and the things that they were doing, such as criminal behaviour, substance abuse and self-neglect/hoarding. Often people would state that it was 'just the way they were', because they felt unable to change what was happening and therefore had ascribed this as part of their identity. But when asked to describe their identity, no one described themselves as a criminal, hoarder or substance abuser. Therefore, identifying the criminal behaviour, hoarding behaviour or substance misusing behaviour as a behaviour rather than an identity means that a person can begin to consider the possibility of change. The next step is to get the person to consider their goals, and the miracle question is used: 'If you were to wake up tomorrow and a miracle has occurred and things have changed for the better, what would you be doing, seeing, feeling, smelling, being?'

In reading what I had written about identity, an academic colleague challenged my statement saying that identity must come from the perspective of the person themselves. I reflected on my sociological learning, and all the different sociological arguments went through my head: labelling theory, the looking glass theory and many other sociological/psychological theories that suggest otherwise. I also considered the development of the self and how nature and nurture affect this. A thousand thoughts passed through my head at this one questioning sentence and, like many practitioners in safeguarding, when challenged, I began to question myself. How much sociological debate do I put into my practice to justify why I have utilised a certain model or methodology?

As a practitioner I have to be proportionate with my recording and it is not always appropriate to write every potential sociological justification for a course of action, in the way that an academic might. I consider the debate and select the course of action that best fits the person and the presenting situation, but I don't always record my working out or rationale for every decision. As a teacher or trainer I often translate these things into tools that I can share for the professional to utilise, or reject, as they see fit. Am I wrong, should I be writing the sociological debate? I am quite capable of achieving this, but when the practitioner goes to their manager and says what do I need to do, how many sociological debates do we expect them to have? How many is enough?

The criminology of safeguarding

I have studied criminology at postgraduate level, I live with an ex-police detective inspector, my father was a police officer, my stepson wants to be a police officer and my son did his degree in criminology.

My life is steeped in the application of justice, keeping the peace and protecting life and property. The maintenance of law and order and the links with safeguarding are of great interest to me, and I shall explore this in more detail within this book because I have an honest belief that people should have equitable access to civil and criminal justice. I would just like to pose a few questions to challenge those in safeguarding work:

- When a police officer attends a safeguarding enquiry and asks if the person has capacity, do you know what they are actually asking?

- What is the difference between a credible witness and a capacitated or incapacitated witness?

- What support can social work offer in interviewing or preparing a person for court?

- What is the connection between police powers of arrest (reasonable suspicion of a crime) and the safeguarding process (reasonable suspicion of abuse or neglect)?

- Why should all those involved in safeguarding be aware of police points to prove?

- How should we support a person to have access to both civil and criminal redress?

- What information should and will be shared with a perpetrator of abuse/crime?

- Should all safeguarding cases receive a crime number?

- When are special measures and additional measures considered?

- What is the witness charter and the victims code of practice?

- What is an evidence-led prosecution?

- Why is it important to not only identify the form of abuse on a safeguarding referral but also whether this is potential domestic abuse?

How many of these questions can you confidently say that you can answer in enough detail to ensure equitable access to criminal and civil justice for those people with whom you work? How many should you know and what should the police know? Where does the knowledge between the police and the safeguarding process begin or end? How much is enough?

The law in safeguarding decision making

I could go on through all the professions associated with safeguarding and ask how much is one person expected to know, to extract enough information to coordinate effective and justifiable safeguarding responses. The answer is that one person is not expected to know all the answers. The safeguarding multi-agency arrangements are in place so that we can coordinate multi-agency responses and use the skills and knowledge of our police, psychiatrists, psychologists, health care professionals, solicitors, barristers, occupational therapists and other associated professions.

As a safeguarding practitioner, I am not going to have all the answers, but what I do need is enough information to open the door to discussion and challenge the barriers to safeguarding the person, in a person-centred manner that reflects the safeguarding principles. Safeguarding must create an identity of its own in case law and case reflection and not one that comes from differing perspectives, but one that comes from a reasonable practice perspective, where lessons learned are lessons learned in practice, that can be practically applied in a manner that the relevant agency or practitioner can understand. The Human Rights Act 1998 should be utilised across all agencies for this purpose in everyday practice.

The Care Act 2014 is both ambitious and aspirational and has been presented at a time when local authorities are short of resources and there is growing social care need (Mandelstam 2017). The Griffiths (1988) report began the law reform that resulted in the Community Care Act 1990, which was the predecessor of the Care Act 2014. The report suggested that it would not be acceptable to allow ambitious policies to be embarked upon without appropriate funds. Recent cases presented in court have identified the challenges faced by local authorities to make financial provision to meet needs, while trying to lessen obligations. The Care Act 2014 aims to address this by emphasising the need for preventative action, use of existing community resources that do not require a charge or fee and use of family care provision to meet need. The emphasis on preventing or delaying the need for services directs practitioners to consider long-term goals and not merely short-term measures; however, services are struggling to manage the critical matters and therefore move away from preventative or long-term measures.

Mandelstam (2017) identifies a number of ways in which local authorities try to manage the pressures with the limited resources available and warns of reckless or excessive use of escape routes. One such way that is frequently identified in safeguarding is the misapplication of eligibility criteria, where eligibility is not applied to its fullest extent, or is altered or mutilated, or additional threshold criteria are applied. The three-part eligibility criteria for safeguarding will be explored in further detail later in this book, addressing some of these concerns.

The Care Act 2014 (Section 79) permits local authorities to enable others to carry out certain functions on its behalf. This includes conducting enquiries on its behalf, where they are the most relevant and appropriate people to take the lead. The Care Act 2014 aims to ensure that the local authority has overall responsibility for the oversight and guidance involved in safeguarding adults. This means that the local authority will remain liable for any delegated functions undertaken, or omitted. This may be subject to judicial review, but it means that the local authority maintains some responsibility for ensuring that appropriate action is taken, even when others lead an enquiry. I wonder how achievable this is in practice, given the low threshold for safeguarding.

The courts are largely concerned with the methodology rather than the professional judgement or conclusion, so they will therefore consider the decision-making process, the working out, rather than the final answer. Someone may disagree with your final outcome, but as long as you can demonstrate what you have considered and why, what you have ruled out and why, or the exploration of potential hypotheses, then the court will see your work favourably. Schwehr (2018), in talking about common problems with the Care Act 2014, considers the ambiguity of definitions, exploring when a want becomes a need. Instead of asking how much is enough, Schwehr asks how much is not enough, and determines, 'The stance of what's "adequate" can't go so low as to strike the administrative Law Court as so unreasonable that no public body could possibly think it enough.'

There are some basic expectations regarding professional standards, ethics, values and principles and the application of legislation.

Figure P.1 shows some examples of things that may be considered poor safeguarding practice.

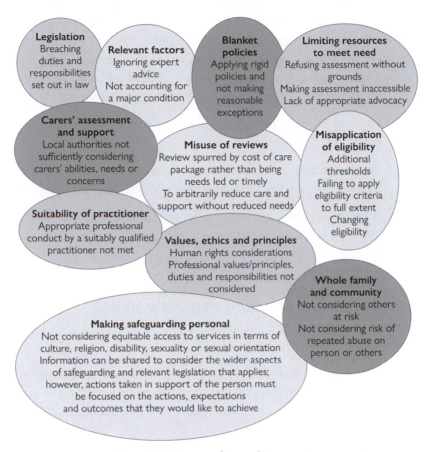

Figure P.1: Poor safeguarding practice

Within this book, we shall explore the things that we must consider in making safeguarding arrangements, and defensible or justifiable decision making in practice.

Safeguarding adults operates within a context of uncertainty, ambiguity and indeterminacy. The role of the safeguarding lead is one of coordination, delegation and hypothesis development, to explore the evidence and create defensible and justifiable outcomes based on the wishes and feelings of the person concerned. The outcomes expressed by the person are not based on empirical evidence, but what works for them. In addition to this, the safeguarding lead cannot merely think about the person who is reported to have suffered abuse or neglect, they must also think about others who may be affected, the potential perpetrator and their rights, and balance the ethics involved. In this type of context, we must ask the question about whether strict empirical and theoretical knowledge in itself is effective enough. We are operating within a mixed paradigm of practice and face legal and media scrutiny, so in interpreting laws into policies and procedures we may need to guide practitioners about the tripartite between:

- the law, models, methods, theories and research (empirical evidence)

- the things the person said that they wanted and the things that the practitioner observed the person doing (rational evidence)

- proportionality – justifying a proportionate response to the above potentially conflicting issues, based on the balance of credible evidence.

How do we make decisions as practitioners?

As practitioners, we grapple with the practical experience of our profession in decision making as we:

- reflect on lessons that we have learned, personally, as a team and an organisation, through our encounters and acting in a way that we feel is the correct and most sensitive manner

- need to justify a course of action via legislation, models, methods, theories or research

- provide evidence for a hypothesis from evidence gathered from the person, others who know the person, and other professionals

- define why we have acted proportionately in any given situation.

While we try to gather the empirical evidence and make sense of the knowledge base available to us, considering concepts and theories, we must also apply these to different people, within different families and different communities with differing values. Munro (2011) argued that procedural compliance and dominant organisational cultures are in conflict with the development of reflective learning and transferable skills in complex family and community situations. Such approaches fail to consider the wider complexities of the person within their given ecological and environmental context, and to address much more than a singular aspect or component of a much wider complex and interconnected system. Baumann *et al.* (2011) suggest that the mapping and illustrating of influencing factors and the processes of judgement and decision making can support the various nuances for further analysis. To be reflective as practitioners we must consider a model which expands rather than limits the scope of reflection.

This book is not designed to be an oracle for safeguarding, it is not designed to be a safeguarding manual and I am not an expert in my field. I am just an everyday practitioner offering examples and experiences to other practitioners for contemplation. It is merely legislation, models, methods, theory and research that I am proposing you become aware of, consider and then decide whether these are applicable to the situation that you are presented with in practice, or not. My aim is to share and reflect on practice and not to be a barrister, academic, police officer, sociologist or psychologist; my aim is to be the best safeguarding practitioner I can possibly be and to support others with my experiences along the journey. I love to hear your stories, analyse them in training together and find potential solutions, reflecting on what went well and what didn't, and learning from this process. I hope that this book offers you the opportunity to do the same. Safeguarding adults boards and practitioners, please ask yourselves, how much is enough to maintain defensible decision making and good practice?

KEY POINTS

In the current climate of austerity measures and social policies, how much is enough? How justifiable do my responses need to be? How much is any one practitioner expected to know of any discipline? How do we ensure resilience in an increasing population of people who have care and support needs? How do we ensure that every person is safeguarded in a meaningful way, not just now but into the future? Here is an example for you to consider.

Kay-Lee is 18 years old, has a learning difficulty and has been drinking excessive amounts of alcohol over a two-year period. Kay-Lee self-harms, cutting her legs and arms. Recently she has changed her group of friends and has been spending time with older boys and men more than twice her age. Kay-Lee claims one man in his forties is her boyfriend and he gives her presents.

Services are aware of this man, as there have been a number of allegations of rape and sexual exploitation made but all witnesses have refused to give evidence before arriving at court. Kay-Lee says that she loves this man. Kay-Lee's parents have become more and more distressed by her behaviours within the house and have eventually asked her to leave the family home. Kay-Lee says that she is staying with friends; however, the property is owned by the person she regards as her boyfriend and a number of other women reside in or regularly visit the same address for parties. You speak with Kay-Lee and she appears to understand your concerns for her, but she refuses any intervention.

Should a safeguarding enquiry be conducted? Provide a rationale.

- What are your concerns for Kay-Lee?

- Who else are you concerned about?

- What risks does this man pose to others?

- Who are the other boys/men and what risks might they pose?

- What led Kay-Lee to self-harm before meeting these people?

- What support and psychological help might Kay-Lee require?

- What capacity assessments may be required?

- What legislation may be applied and how does this work?

- How do we maintain contact and communicate with Kay-Lee?

These and many other questions need to be answered as part of the enquiry and part of the multi-agency response. How much would you need to know to challenge any agencies who are unwilling to provide their time and resources?

CHAPTER 1

Introduction
An Overview of the Process

The safeguarding adult procedures in each local authority differ to accommodate staffing structures, demographics and existing processes. The structure and process of receiving a safeguarding referral can also differ. Some local authorities will triage safeguarding adult referrals through the single point of access and require basic information for referral purposes, seeking further information through the enquiry process. Some local authorities have a safeguarding team, a multi-agency safeguarding hub (MASH) or duty system and will expect practitioners to have risk assessed the concern and conducted part of the enquiry process and response prior to making the referral. Some local authorities have a combination of the two methods.

The local authority can make enquiries itself, or in some circumstances it may determine that other agencies are better placed to conduct enquiries. The decision will be based on the nature of abuse and neglect and the knowledge and skills necessary to conduct the enquiry. While the local authority provides oversight and guidance for safeguarding adults, any agency can be involved in the referral, the enquiry or the decision-making process. The local authority safeguarding team (or equivalent) will support and coordinate responses and ensure that positive outcomes for the person at risk of, or suffering, abuse and neglect are met. Potential responses could be:

- advice and guidance and signposting to relevant services

- an assessment of need and a care and support plan or the review of a care and support plan

- actions identified for a number of agencies to conduct in relation to the victim, potential perpetrator and others involved (capacity, consent and legislative frameworks considered)

- a police-led enquiry.

Or they could be a combination of any of the above. All of the tools described in this book can be used prior to making the referral, to open discussion during the referral and throughout the enquiry process. Consideration must be given at any stage to potential crime and working with the police and other emergency services. In asking questions and assessing the situation, the practitioner involved must be careful not to ask leading questions where there is reasonable suspicion of abuse or neglect and must refer to the police as soon as there is reasonable suspicion of a crime.

The core purpose of adult care and support is to help people achieve the outcomes that matter to them in their life. To achieve this, the Care Act 2014 introduced the 'wellbeing principle'. Wellbeing is at the heart of safeguarding adults and is broadly defined as:

- maintaining personal dignity (including treating the individual with respect)

- physical, emotional and mental health and wellbeing

- protection from abuse and neglect

- control by the individual over day-to-day life (including the care and support provided) and the way it is provided

- participation in work, education, training and recreation

- social and economic wellbeing

- domestic, family and personal wellbeing

- suitability of living accommodation

- the individual contribution to society.

This places a duty on all care and support staff to meet needs and achieve wellbeing. To achieve this, staff will be creative in their approaches to safeguarding adults. A wide range of family and community support/services, aids and adaptations, assistive technology and the person's own access to technological solutions can be used in the safeguarding plan.

Central to the process must be the:

- need to identify risks and protect people from abuse and neglect (beginning with the assumption that the individual is best placed to judge their own wellbeing)

- individual's expectations of the process

- individual's views, wishes and feelings

- importance of preventing or delaying the need for care and support and the importance of reducing needs that already exist

- need to ensure that decisions are made that have regard to all the individual circumstances

- importance of the individual participating as fully as is possible

- importance of achieving a balance between the individual's wellbeing and that of any friends or relatives who are involved in the caring of that individual

- need to ensure that any restriction on the individual's rights and freedom of action is kept to a minimum and is the least restrictive option.

The core purpose of adult care and support is to help people achieve the outcomes that matter to them in their life, and this is described through the wellbeing principle. All safeguarding interventions will need to have regard to the wellbeing principle.

In safeguarding training, I introduce the wellbeing principle and I ask the opening question, 'What is safeguarding and what does it mean?' Dry wipe sheets are placed in front of groups who are sat around tables and they write on the paper. Figure 1.1 is a typical example of what is written.

During my training sessions, I tend to use 'Socratic questioning', which is a way of questioning people to uncover assumptions, get to the truth of things, explore more complex ideas and distinguish what is known from what is not known. I seek clarification, probe assumptions, reasons and evidence, and question viewpoints and understanding. Below are some of the questions and answers that I receive. Please read through the questions considering how you would answer. Many complex safeguarding matters are covered in a half-day, or a day's, training session, and in some cases via an e-learning package with little practical follow up. People learn the key safeguarding words, but rarely have an opportunity to fully explore what those words mean in practice. When questioned about the meaning of commonly used safeguarding language, many practitioners find that they have limited understanding of the application of the wellbeing principles and how the Care Act suggests we should work to keep people safe and well. Here are some of my questions and typical anwers:

Q: Do we just protect people, or do we prevent abuse from occurring too?

A: We prevent abuse and neglect too.

Q: Who prevents abuse or neglect from occurring?

A: Everyone.

Q: How do we prevent abuse and neglect?

During the course, I give the participants some time to consider this last question and ask them to write their answers on flipchart paper. Some typical answers can be found in Figure 1.2.

Figure 1.1: Q&A – What is safeguarding and what does it mean?

Figure 1.2: Q&A – How do we prevent abuse and neglect?

I probe a little further: 'So if you are recognising and reporting abuse and neglect and following your safeguarding procedures, does that mean that you have a suspicion that abuse or neglect has occurred? Is that not protection rather than prevention of abuse and neglect?'

Following my interjection, the answers become more detailed:

- *Care planning* – All aspects of a care plan count as prevention from abuse and neglect. If we do not provide care and support to people who would not be able to conduct the task themselves then they are being neglected. Providing the support ensures that we prevent neglect from occurring. This means that when this goes wrong and someone does not get the necessary care and support, they are in need of safeguarding.

- *Recognising restrictions and restraints* – Identifying when we are being overly restrictive is preventing abuse, because we should not be doing things that restrict a person unnecessarily.

- *Capacity and consent* – Determining whether a person is able to consent to a course of action and could potentially make unwise decisions, or whether they are not able to consent and we must make a best interest decision for them, is preventing abuse and neglect from occurring, because we cannot provide care services or treatment without valid consent. If care services or treatment was provided without valid consent, that would become a safeguarding matter.

- *Anti-oppressive practice* – Considering oppression and discrimination is preventing abuse and neglect from occurring, because if we discriminate or are oppressive we are abusive.

- *Everything that we do* to provide care, support, treatment or services to someone who would suffer if the services were not provided is prevention of abuse.

The aim of adult safeguarding is to ensure that (for those people aged 18 or over):

- harm is prevented and risks of abuse and neglect are reduced for adults who have care and support needs

- individuals are safeguarded in a way that supports them in making choices and having control in how they choose to live their lives

- the person's experience of safeguarding is the best possible and practitioners have a focus on positive outcomes perceived by the person concerned.

Those who need safeguarding help are often older and frail, living on their own in the community, or in care homes. They may be people who have physical or learning disabilities and people who have mental ill-health or other care and support needs. They are people at risk of suffering harm both in organisations and in the community.

Safeguarding means protecting an adult's right to live in safety, free from abuse and neglect. It is about people and organisations working together to prevent and stop both the risks and experience of abuse or neglect, while at the same time making sure that the adult's wellbeing is promoted, including having regard to their views, wishes, feelings and beliefs in deciding on any action. We must also recognise that adults sometimes have complex interpersonal relationships and may have mixed, contradictory, unclear or unrealistic feelings about their personal circumstances.

All organisations should work to promote the adult's wellbeing in their safeguarding arrangements. Professionals should work with the adult to establish what being safe means to them and how that can be best achieved. Being safe is only one aspect of a person's life; safety without enjoyment, or opportunity to grow, is something that we would not choose for ourselves.

Local authorities must cooperate with each of their relevant partners, as described in the Care Act 2014, and those partners must also cooperate with the local authority, in the exercise of their functions relevant to care and support, including safeguarding functions and those to protect adults.

There is a duty to share information for safeguarding purposes. When abuse or neglect is reported to a local authority, it has a duty to make enquiries (or cause enquiries to be made) and determine the response required to prevent abuse or neglect, or to protect from abuse or neglect. Many people who have care and support needs can experience difficulty maintaining physical and mental wellbeing following abuse or neglect and the safeguarding process should support the person to maintain wellbeing and gain equitable access to criminal justice. If the person has substantial difficulty being involved in any aspect of the process, then an advocate or appropriate family representative may be required to provide support.

Section 42 of the Care Act 2014 describes a safeguarding enquiry and identifies that a local authority must make (or cause to be made) whatever enquiries it thinks necessary to enable it to decide whether action is required. The enquiries are to be conducted when the adult (aged 18 or over) meets the three-part eligibility test for safeguarding and there is reasonable cause to suspect that the adult in the local authority area (irrespective of whether they are ordinarily resident there or not):

- has needs for care and support (whether or not the authority is meeting any of those needs)

- is experiencing, or is at risk of, abuse or neglect

- as a result of those needs, is unable to protect themselves against the abuse or neglect or the risk of it.

The referral for safeguarding does not just relate to the individual, but to all parties affected or involved: victim, potential perpetrator(s), family members including children, neighbours and community members. The local authority must have oversight of safeguarding procedures, but can request another agency to make enquiries on its behalf, or chair multi-agency meetings for safeguarding purposes where it is independent from the abuse/neglect. For example, in a case of self-neglect where someone is hoarding, the housing provider may have greater knowledge of the person and services involved, and the person may not have been formerly known to the local authority. It may be more beneficial for the housing provider to carry out enquiries or conduct a multi-agency meeting. Information and outcomes must be shared with the local authority. It may be that you have determined that the person hoarding has suffered severe trauma and that a psychology-led enquiry and coordination may be required.

If a person is capacitated and able to make a particular decision, they are entitled to make an unwise decision for themselves, as long as it does not have an adverse effect on others. All parties have an obligation to ensure that actions taken are proportionate and in line with safeguarding principles: empower, prevent, protect, proportionate, partnership and accountability.

This chapter does not address the variety of responses and interventions required throughout the enquiry and safeguarding process. The enquiry seeks to identify gaps in knowledge and identify suitable services or resources to meet these gaps and provide support around the person. The range of responses can be as varied as the range of needs and the complexity of individuals involved. To achieve this, capacity, consent, legislation, risk and the needs, wishes and expectations of the person concerned must be explored through a dynamic multi-agency process placing the person concerned at the centre of their own care and support, while considering the potential for civil or criminal redress.

The forms of abuse and neglect identified within the Care Act 2014 have extended the remit of safeguarding, and the eligibility criteria encompass anyone who has needs for care and support. You as a reader could be eligible for safeguarding should you, for example, find yourself in hospital unwell and unable to protect yourself from abuse or neglect. If you could not provide or get access to your own food or water and the hospital does not provide this, then you have care and support needs and, as a result, you may not be able to protect yourself from neglect. The response to you may be very different to someone who has complex health conditions, care is identified as being provided by a family member, and the person suffers domestic abuse including physical and financial abuse, and has no means of communicating with others.

Safeguarding could be about a person with a mental health condition groomed for suicide bombing, or a person from a different ethnic, religious or cultural background forced into marriage and told that they are being dishonourable if they do not marry a particular identified person. Each form of abuse and each person contextualised within their family or community requires the involvement of different services, different responses and different legislation, and they may be capacitated or incapacitated in each decision to be made. There is not a form, policy, guidance procedure or process that could accommodate the variation. It is a challenge to understand how to work with the support of agencies and within legislative frameworks and maintain the person at the centre of their care while protecting others involved and considering potential criminal acts. This challenge requires that everyone works together in assessing the person within the context of the situation to prevent oppression, discrimination, restrictive practice and negligence. This supports us in preventing, identifying, reporting and responding to abuse and neglect, and improves services provided to people who have care and support needs.

KEY POINTS

Safeguarding is every bit as much, if not more, about prevention as protection. We cannot ascribe rigid policies and procedures to a set of circumstances that are as diverse as safeguarding matters. Safeguarding identification, reporting, enquiries and actions are everyone's responsibility.

Joan lives in older persons' residential care. She cannot feed herself or drink without assistance. One day, two paid care providers do not arrive for their afternoon shift and Joan is not provided with food or drink.

To feed someone and support them to drink is to safeguard the person, preventing neglect when they cannot manage to feed themselves, or access fluids themselves. If the food and drink were to be regularly forgotten, this would affect the wellbeing of the person and become a safeguarding matter for further enquiries to take place. The eligibility criteria define all these things as safeguarding matters.

Preventing physical and mental deterioration, or providing appropriate services to those who cannot provide them for themselves, is all safeguarding. The care home usually provides the safeguarding response by supporting Joan to eat and drink. There may be clinical commissioning group (CCG) leads, or a practice development lead, who challenge practice in certain environments that would add the additional scrutiny to safeguard the people affected. The safeguarding team may eventually get involved if concerns are escalating. The local authority must assure itself that all safeguarding measures are in place and working to maintain wellbeing. The local authority does not necessarily provide the safeguarding response.

Eligibility means that the person:

- has **needs for care and support** (whether or not the authority is meeting any of those needs)

- is experiencing, **or is at risk of**, abuse or neglect

- as a result of those needs, is **unable to protect** themselves against the abuse or neglect or the **risk of it**.

We must ensure a response to safeguard the individual; however, this does not mean that safeguarding is a separate entity from daily practice to act in a person-centred manner, keep people safe and maintain wellbeing.

CHAPTER 2

The History – From *No Secrets* to the Care Act 2014

My first safeguarding role was in 1994 and came about as a result of the Action for Elder Abuse campaign and social policy documents such as *No Longer Afraid* (Tomlinson 1993) and was later influenced by the work of Bradley (1996) and Brammer (1996) in considering the impact of elder abuse. Shortly after my initiation into safeguarding work in older people's services, I began work in learning disability services and was asked to take a lead in receiving reports of abuse or neglect involving people who had learning disabilities. The late 1980s and early 1990s saw a recognition of abuse affecting those people who had learning disabilities, older people, people who had mental ill-health, or other disabilities affecting their ability to both prevent abuse and neglect and protect themselves from abuse or neglect. My early years in the safeguarding field were filled with frustration, barriers and lack of insight into the issues impacting on those suffering abuse and neglect. By 2000, a national policy guidance became available and provided some direction for safeguarding services.

The *No Secrets* policy guidance (Department of Health and Social Care 2000) identified a remit for safeguarding adults. Wales and the Welsh Assembly produced a similar document called *In Safe Hands* (National Assembly for Wales 2000), and in Scotland statutory legislation developed in the Adult Support and Protection Act 2007. In addition to these, there were guidance documents such as *Safeguarding Adults* (Association of Directors of Adult Social Services 2005) that provided further direction and guidance for local authorities. These documents provided some assistance and enabled greater coordination; however, when the political climate changed, perspectives on health and social care provision changed and these documents required a revision.

The House of Commons Health Select Committee Inquiry into Elder Abuse in 2004 made recommendations to expand the remit of safeguarding adults to move away from local authority social work eligibility criteria to a more encompassing definition.

> The 'No Secrets' definition of elder abuse should be expanded to include those individuals who do not require community care services, for example older people living in their own homes without the support of health and social care services, and those who can take care of themselves. (Health Committee 2004, p.9)

This definition was intended to be broad and take into consideration not only those in receipt or eligible for social care services, but also those in receipt of housing and health, and those who may not be involved in housing, health or social care but unable to manage the impact of abuse or neglect within their own home. It is within this scrutiny of eligibility and definition forming that the first consideration of domestic abuse and safeguarding began to evolve and that the concept that someone may be vulnerable, for example as a result of being older and in a domestic abuse situation, was developed.

In a chapter in *Good Practice in Safeguarding Adults*, Fitzgerald (2008, p.21) identifies the need for 'intelligent intervention that ensures the appropriate use of strategies'. Fitzgerald highlights a key point: 'The victim should not have to demonstrate a dependence in order to access adult protection support...and should get no less support if channelled through safeguarding procedures than alternate procedures.'

The consultation into *No Secrets* considered the changing climate of social policy and explored a safeguarding vision, to:

- increase the independence, choice and control of service users

- access meaningful community empowerment and safer housing in the wider society

- improve access to criminal justice for all.

The review of *No Secrets* illuminates the direction of social policy travel in relation to safeguarding adults and provides insight into the development of the Care Act 2014 and the interpretation of the wording used within the Act.

The *No Secrets* guidance recognised a public duty that required the formal cooperation of a number of agencies to safeguard effectively; however, without key legislation this cooperation was often disregarded, or poorly understood. Joint working was inconsistent and there was no universal system for safeguarding. With many local authorities applying the social work eligibility criteria, safeguarding became a hit and miss system. Someone safeguarded in one local authority may not meet the eligibility criteria for safeguarding in another local authority. The consultation and review of *No Secrets* highlighted this, stating:

> Implementation was slow and inconsistent; joint working was patchy and some partners were unwilling to 'come to the table'. There were no dedicated resources and no specific legislation associated with *No Secrets*. While the guidance was an important leap forwards it did not lead to a strong and effective universal system for preventing, recognising and responding to adult protection issues. (Shareweb.kent. gov.uk 2009)

The need for further clarity in safeguarding being the business of everyone in the community was also highlighted within the stakeholder feedback during the *No Secrets* Review, which states:

> These messages suggest the need for a more integrated safeguarding framework, making safeguarding everybody's business. This would need to address safeguarding in both regulated and unregulated care; to define safeguarding roles for housing officers, nurses, advocates, social workers and police officers; and to integrate guidance on hate crime, vulnerable witnesses, community safety, domestic abuse, safeguarding children and forced marriage. (Shareweb.kent.gov.uk 2009)

The report identified the need to be consistent with the Equality Act, which was at the time being proposed as the new Single Equality Bill. In addition, consideration of greater equality within safeguarding highlighted the poor reporting of safeguarding issues from people of black or ethnic minority backgrounds, and the lack of culturally sensitive approaches and appropriate advocacy. The Mental Capacity Act 2005 also provided a strong focus for change and for safeguarding to become more person centred.

At the beginning of the century (2000–2010) there was a strong focus on health and social care services increasing people's independence and promoting inclusion within communities. The White Paper *Our Health, Our Care, Our Say* (Department of Health 2006) demonstrated that services needed to be reformed to become more personalised, with choice and control over the services that they receive. The *Putting People First* paper (Department of Health 2007) identified the need for collaboration between the sector's professional leadership, the providers and the regulators. The agenda defined practice that considered the required outcomes of service users and carers and transformed the experiences of localised support services. The White Paper *Communities in Control: Real People, Real Power* (Communities and Local Government 2008) aimed to place the power back within communities and empower all citizens to take an active role within their own communities. Highlighting that community empowerment goes hand in hand with community safety, the White Paper considers unlawful exclusion and undemocratic processes that disempower certain people within the community. Hate crime and discriminatory abuse are highlighted.

The review of *No Secrets* placed a strong focus on the need to have equitable access to criminal justice and also highlighted the need for joint working with the police and the courts. Recognising the difficulties of people who have disabilities, illness or are intimidated to access criminal justice, the report identifies the need to support access and facilitate special measures. The need for all partners to not just recognise and report abuse but to prevent abuse from occurring and put safeguarding strategies in place is a central theme to the review. Serious case reviews identified that people who had a number of co-morbidities or low-level issues were not being safeguarded, and the review considered the need to change this situation.

Today the key safeguarding themes that local authorities struggle with include the following:

- Who is eligible for safeguarding?

- What does care and support needs mean?

- What do we mean by prevention?

- What is a Section 42 enquiry and how much is enough to determine an enquiry has been made in low-level cases?

- How do we ensure person-centred safeguarding and what does this mean in practice?

- How do we get equitable access to criminal justice for people who have disabilities, illnesses or are intimidated?

- What are the local authorities' responsibilities and what are the responsibilities of other agencies?

- What can the local authority do in cases of domestic abuse? Do all cases of domestic abuse, homelessness and self-neglect result in safeguarding?

- How do I manage my safeguarding services with such an extensive agenda?

These questions have been around since the *No Secrets* policy guidance in 2000, and despite much safeguarding evolution, the same questions remain today. It is not because local authorities and their partners do not understand the legislation. It is because they do not know how to manage the legislation with the resources and budgets that they have at their disposal. The answer is that social policy has changed the role of the local authority from one of being largely a provider of services, to one of breaking down barriers of oppression and discrimination, problem solving and negotiating, coordination and delegation. It is therefore a combination of commissioning, governance and quality assurance.

The role of safeguarding defined by the consequentialist nature of the Care Act 2014

Quality safeguarding services are defined by the outcomes and expectations of the person and how well these outcomes are met by services supporting that person. This means that the Care Act 2014 is largely situated within the ethics of consequentialism and that the consequences of our actions and the morality of the situation are determined by the narrative of the person receiving our support and/or their carers, family and representatives. In other words, whether we have done a good job safeguarding the person or a bad job safeguarding the person is determined by how they feel about the process and outcomes.

While this is important, the Human Rights Act 1998 is a foundation law coming largely from a deontological perspective and informs us of what the law states is right and wrong; therefore, while we must always strive for positive outcomes for the person, the human rights of the individual and others must be considered throughout safeguarding and we cannot violate anyone's human rights. Commissioning, governance and quality assurance must therefore be considered within the ethical structure of safeguarding.

Strategic safeguarding structures

NHS England (2018) defines commissioning as 'The process of planning, agreeing and monitoring services'. The Care Act defines what wellbeing looks like and what we should do in terms of creative use of existing resources, community resources or commissioning to meet the needs and outcomes of eligible people and their carers. There is a governance role in order to manage effectively and control processes in line with relevant legislation, duties and obligations. There is a quality assurance process to ensure that we understand what the people who require care and support and their carers want and whether we are sufficiently meeting needs and outcomes (productive quality). Safeguarding falls into this world, and the local authority has responsibility for oversight and guidance, to conduct enquiries or cause enquiries to be made to ensure that abuse and neglect are prevented by providing appropriate least restrictive or intrusive services that meet the individual's needs. We have an obligation to ensure that services are in place to meet need, or are commissioned appropriately to prevent abuse or neglect and protect the person from abuse or neglect in the future. We have an obligation or duty to ensure that we have oversight of and guidance for the process in line with legislation (governance) and that the outcomes and expectations of the service users are met (quality control).

The safeguarding conflict between methodology and funding arises because of limited public sector resources. The anticipated cohesive communities with local resources providing specialist services to local people did not transpire in a way that bridged the gap left by removing social service provision in the community. Meeting basic needs within the community is difficult enough with limited resources; however, meeting complex needs with limited community services becomes incredibly expensive. Cheaper but less appropriate options may be sought, with cost-busting exercises deployed by local authorities. Local authorities are not alone in these cost-saving endeavours. The police, health, housing and other agencies all have methodologies for cost saving that do not necessarily support those who may fall into minority groups, underprivileged groups, difficult-to-reach groups and those most vulnerable to abuse or neglect, as these groups of people may be regarded as resource intensive and the services often do not reach the outcomes that they are seeking.

Care is returned back to family support and maintaining care within the family for as long as possible. Families try to meet the needs of the individuals in their care, but all too often are not made aware of the meeting of a care need becoming a duty to provide care or to inform services where this duty fails. In utilising family resources (to meet an assessed and identified need) we must ensure that the needs of the individual are met effectively and that the family member is aware of their responsibilities and reporting duties and that this is part of the planned care response. This means that the governance arrangements are about governing not only service providers to meet quality standards and legislative obligations, but also family members in meeting identified need.

Expectations and outcomes are defined by a person's limited experience and knowledge of what is available. This could be very limiting if choice is not thoroughly explored and the person is not supported to understand the potential that the options provide. The quality assurance processes could limit development if not appropriately exercised in the manner described in the Mental Capacity Act 2005, to maximise a person's understanding and choice.

The operational safeguarding team/practitioners acting within a multi-agency dynamic

Rather than explaining the complexities of commissioning, governance and quality control to other agencies in among coordinating a potential crime, or complex family and community dynamics, the safeguarding practitioner often feels it is easier to take on the bulk of the work and chair the meetings, organise the outcomes for the care plan and meet with the family to discuss their needs and caring responsibilities.

The safeguarding practitioner will often become involved in supporting the victim in a criminal case because they understand the issues affecting access to criminal justice. In doing this work and bridging the gaps in service, they are not able to manage the volume. If someone refuses to conduct a capacity assessment, it is easier for the safeguarding practitioner to conduct it than argue against established protocols within other organisations. In pulling together a multi-agency meeting to coordinate responses to self-neglect, neglect or abuse, it is often easier to organise and chair the meeting than to persuade a partner organisation that they are best placed to conduct the meeting.

With an increasing population of people who are older, or who have autism, learning disabilities or mental ill-health, we must share safeguarding responsibilities and establish the appropriately skilled practitioner to lead the enquiry. This could be a nurse, occupational therapist, mental health worker or other relevant professional. The professional would have support, oversight and guidance from the local authority. Without a focus upon preventative work and work supporting a person to address trauma as a result of the abuse, referrals will continue to increase. Earlier intervention targeted by the correct people and overseen by the local authority will meet the aspirations established by the Care Act 2014 and the statutory guidance. Strong governance holding agencies accountable for safeguarding enquiries (when most appropriate), meetings and responses is required along with an escalation of concerns where cooperation is lacking.

KEY POINTS

The local authority has responsibility for oversight and guidance and ensuring positive safeguarding outcomes; however, it is the agencies themselves that should be doing the safeguarding. All agencies need to break down barriers to access, ensure that the person is central to the process, conduct capacity assessments, share information with each other as appropriate and cooperate in safeguarding people at risk of or suffering abuse or neglect. This means conducting multi-agency meetings, making enquiries, working alongside the police, conducting and coordinating capacity assessments, understanding legislation and not ascribing these tasks to the local authority. Remember that there must be independence to the enquiry process, and therefore any agency involved in the safeguarding incident should not be making the enquiries.

CHAPTER 3

Indicators of Abuse and Neglect, Including Indicators of Trauma

When considering the roles and responsibilities of safeguarding adults, the first topic that most people identify as a responsibility is the need to recognise the indicators of abuse or neglect and how to report concerns when there is reason to suspect abuse or neglect is taking place. Many people are now familiar with these indicators of each of the forms of abuse or neglect, but it is less clear whether the impact of abuse or neglect is being recognised and the person provided with care and support to meet identified needs in relation to trauma.

The impact of abuse or neglect: trauma

It is important in all cases of abuse or neglect to consider the impact of the trauma on the person and to seek help and support. Many people can feel overwhelmed by traumatic histories and, after suffering years without appropriate support or assistance, they stop talking about their trauma and present with specific problems such as accommodation, space issues, financial or benefit problems, substance misuse, physical or mental health problems, and family or relationship breakdown. Some people may talk about their histories as if they are insignificant, as they cannot cope with imagining the magnitude of the things that they have endured. Others may have suffered childhood abuse, or such terrible abuse that they have disassociated from the experience and have little memory of the trauma itself. Others may be afraid to talk of the trauma for fear of triggering symptoms that they cannot control.

Can you imagine being dependent on someone for care and support, at their mercy to provide you with food, essential medication, drinks and social contact, and then they abuse or neglect you? Consider how you might feel in these circumstances. Many cases of organisational abuse or neglect have hit the media headlines; however, I rarely read about the work conducted to address the impact of such terrible things happening to older people, or people who have disabilities, mental ill-health or learning disabilities. It is bad enough to suffer the distress of a carer harming you, but when abuse occurs within the community and is a family member, this becomes domestic abuse. The pain and loss experienced by being abused or neglected by your child or loved family member must be horrendous.

There are three types of traumatic experience: the single experience which may be a life-threatening or significant event, ongoing non-life-threatening issues that accumulate or the trauma experienced by terrorism or war. The *Diagnostic and Statistical Manual of Mental Disorders IV* (American Psychiatric Association 1994) considers post-traumatic stress disorder associated with a specific event such as a car accident, witnessing violence, natural disaster, rape and war, while the *Diagnostic and Statistical Manual of Mental Disorders 5* (American Psychiatric Association 2013) considers complex trauma and describes how children's exposure to multiple or prolonged traumatic events impacts on development. Subsequent research has identified that prolonged experience of trauma also has a significant effect on the brain function of adults (Maynard 2017).

The types of experiences that may be classed as traumatic events include the following (though this is not an inclusive list):

- *Community violence* – predatory violence, including robbery, shootings, rapes, beatings, stabbings and other conflicts between people who are not family members.

- *Domestic violence* – an incident or pattern of incidents of controlling, coercive, threatening behaviour, violence or abuse between those aged 16 or over who are, or have been, intimate partners or family members regardless of gender or sexuality. This can include forced marriage, honour-based crime and female genital mutilation as well as psychological, physical, sexual, financial and emotional abuse. A child witnessing domestic abuse may also suffer trauma.

- *Physical abuse* – including assault, hitting, slapping, pushing, misuse of medication, restraint and inappropriate physical sanctions.

- *Sexual abuse* – including sexual exploitation, childhood sexual abuse and the sharing of sexual images on social media.

- *Psychological abuse* – including emotional abuse, threats of harm or abandonment, deprivation of contact, humiliation, blaming, controlling, intimidation, coercion, harassment, verbal abuse, cyberbullying, isolation and unreasonable or unjustified withdrawal of services or support networks.

- *Neglect* – including ignoring medical needs, emotional or physical care needs, failure to provide access to appropriate health, care and support or educational services or the withholding of the necessities of life such as medication, adequate nutrition and heating. Consider the potential of childhood neglect such as being brought up in an environment with parents who hoard, or where there is excessive substance misuse.

- *Organisational abuse/system-induced abuse* – where someone has been neglected or suffered restrictive, intrusive or abusive practice within an institution or care setting. This can also include childhood traumas such as being separated from siblings in the care system, traumatic foster placements, removal from parents or parental home, multiple placements or inappropriate provisions.

- *Financial abuse* – this can be particularly distressing when the amount of finances lost enforce homelessness or substantial lifestyle changes.

- *Human trafficking and modern-day slavery* – including child trafficking, forced labour and debt bondage, forced marriage, sexual exploitation, domestic servitude and organ or egg harvesting.

- *Discriminatory abuse* – including hate crime and mate crime.

- *Serious accident, illness, medical procedure or loss of abilities* – including older people experiencing significant loss of physical or mental ability, status and personal feelings of value. It also includes unintentional injury, accident and severe physical illness, and experiencing painful and prolonged medical procedures or life-threatening procedures.

- *Natural or manmade disasters* – natural disasters may include the effects of hurricanes, volcanic explosions affecting the home environment or loss of life, major floods or fires. Manmade disasters may be where people have created something that posed significant risk or harm.

- *War, terrorism or political violence* – including incidents such as bombing, stabbings, shootings, decapitations, rapes and looting, or incidents that are a result of terrorist control and activity.

- *Traumatic grief and separation* – including the death of a parent or main caregiver, sibling or grandparent. Accidental deaths, homicides, suicides, premature death or unexplained death can be particularly traumatic.

- *Being a witness to extreme forms of abuse or neglect identified above* – this can be particularly disturbing for a child.

We cannot be judgemental, or create a hierarchy of traumatic events. It is important to explore the person's own experiences with them and understand the impact that the trauma has had on their life. Herman (1992) writes that the traumas experienced by war veterans or prisoners of war can be comparable in their psychological effects to ongoing domestic violence or sexual trauma. To provide appropriate and targeted measures to end homelessness, hoarding and self-neglect, to address the impact of trauma on people who have experienced being trafficked, used as a slave or sexually exploited and to prevent further trauma being placed on displaced people or those experiencing the atrocities of terrorism or war, or the abuse and neglect of children, we must relabel these services. These labels place the blame with the victim of trauma.

Where a person is severely self-neglecting and refusing services or where:

- substance misuse is impacting on a person's physical and mental wellbeing

- motivation seems to be missing

- there is anger or resentment and the person does not trust services

- the person repeatedly enters harmful relationships, or places themselves in danger

- the person cannot resolve homelessness

- the person appears withdrawn, lost or shut down

- self-harming behaviours are present and the person seems unable to stop despite mounting risk

- no matter what you do it doesn't seem to be working

...at some point, someone must consider that these just might be responses to trauma and loss. Surely these symptoms of trauma displayed in front of us cannot be ignored? We continue to blame and denigrate those who have suffered, maintaining them in a cycle of increasing trauma response with decreasing support and services. This is put into context when you consider the mounting resource costs and misdirected services: the social workers, nurses, housing workers, homeless services, substance misuse services, hospital discharge delays and associated resources all misdirecting their time, money and energy to fixing that which they cannot fix:

- the clutter

- the homelessness

- the drinking or drug taking

- the self-harm

- the self-neglect.

We cannot *make* a person address these things any more than we can make someone gain weight, or lose weight, without their dedication to the cause. If a person has suffered trauma, the only thing that will cure the symptoms of trauma, such as misuse of substances, homelessness, hoarding and self-neglect, self-harm, increasing mental and physical health problems and risks to the person and others, is by addressing the cause, addressing the trauma and the trauma symptoms. In many cases, this will require multi-agency intervention and close links between psychiatry, psychology and social work to address the presenting trauma symptoms medically and psychologically.

The responsibility of labelling someone with mental ill-health falls within the ethics and values of having a label. The benefits of being diagnosed with a mental health disorder must outweigh the negatives. Giving the person labels that are not helpful, or that do not provide access to treatment or therapy, can have negative consequences for that person. Another consideration in favour of a diagnosis is to better understand or determine a person's capacity to make specific decisions. This does not mean taking choice or control away from the person, this just means that appropriate and proportionate person-centred support can be provided when required.

In response to a person's experience of trauma, other services will be required to support the person with issues that arise, such as physical health concerns, establishing housing, occupational therapy or physiotherapy input, cleaning services or clearing services, once the person decides that it is the right time for them. The cost of addressing the real issues is significantly lower than throwing money at things that will not and cannot work; however, to achieve this we must be vigilant to the indicators of trauma and create access to psychiatry and psychology to address the trauma and presenting co-morbidities.

The statutory guidance for the Care Act 2014 identifies that local authorities should not limit their view of what constitutes abuse or neglect, as this can take many forms and the circumstances of individual cases should always be considered, as long as the three-part eligibility criteria are met. I shall explore this in more detail in relation to trauma while considering the different forms of abuse and the care and support required from health and social services in addition to the criminal aspects and working with the police.

Financial abuse

The Care Act 2014 statutory guidance identifies financial abuse:

> Financial abuse is the main form of abuse investigated by the Office of the Public Guardian both among adults and children at risk. Financial recorded abuse can occur in isolation, but as research has shown, where there are other forms of abuse, there is likely to be financial abuse occurring. Although this is not always the case, everyone should also be aware of this possibility. (Section 14.24)

Potential indicators of financial abuse include:

- change in living conditions

- lack of heating, clothing or food

- inability to pay bills/unexplained shortage of money

- unexplained withdrawals from an account

- unexplained loss/misplacement of financial documents

- the recent addition of authorised signers on a client or donor's signature card

- sudden or unexpected changes in a will or other financial documents.

This is not an exhaustive list, nor do these examples prove that there is actual abuse occurring. However, they do indicate that a closer look and possible investigation may be needed.

Crosby *et al.* (2008) define financial abuse to include but not be exclusive to:

- inadvertent mismanagement of funds

- opportunistic exploitation

- deliberate and targeted financial abuse

- scams – telephone contests and get-rich-quick investment schemes

- internet scams

- phishing

- distraction burglary/doorstep crime

- consumer fraud.

The statutory guidance to the Care Act identifies similar financial abuse, stating, 'Most financial abuse is also capable of amounting to theft or fraud and would be a matter for the police to investigate' (Section 14.27). The statutory guidance warns of the sophisticated and convincing methods used by scammers.

The Care Act 2014 statutory guidance states that we should not underestimate the potential impact of financial abuse and asks us to consider other aspects of abuse where financial abuse is identified. Domestic abuse may also be a factor to consider.

Financial scamming is becoming more prevalent and scammers often target the more vulnerable people within society. The Office for National Statistics (2015) estimates that there were 5.1 million incidents of fraud and 3.8 million adult victims in England and Wales; however, it recognises that those reported are the tip of the iceberg and many more scams go unreported. The Office of Fair Trading (2006, p.12) defines scams as: 'Misleading or deceptive business practice where you receive an unsolicited or uninvited contact and false promises are made to con you out of money'. The Financial Conduct Authority (2017) identifies things that people can do, or advice that you can give to help people avoid scams:

- Treat all unexpected calls, emails and text messages with caution. Don't assume they're genuine, even if the person seems to know some basic information about you.

- Don't be pressured into acting quickly. A genuine bank or financial services firm won't mind waiting if you want time to think.

- If you're buying a financial product such as a loan, insurance, investment or pension, only deal with a Financial Conduct Authority-authorised firm.

- Always double-check the URL and contact details of a firm in case it's a 'clone firm' pretending to be a real firm, such as your bank or a genuine investment firm.

- Go to the Financial Conduct Authority website and check the list of unauthorised firms and individuals where complaints have been received. If the firm isn't on the list, don't assume it's legitimate – it may not have been reported as yet.

The Financial Conduct Authority also advises that advance payments, bank account details or pin numbers should not be given to anyone unknown and the validity of advanced payments should be questioned. Websites or information with poor graphics, misspelled words or poor grammar may be suspect. If people use the telephone, they may install a call blocker system or a telephone preference service. All financial arrangements should be given in writing in advance of any transaction and you should have time to consider the transaction. People should not deal with any cold callers, and anyone, whether it be on the telephone, in the street or online, should have valid credentials that are checked out. All offers should be thoroughly researched. Practitioners should support the public to understand these safeguarding measures.

Two people considering a financial transaction, particularly a large transaction, are better than one. If the person is interested in a product and has a neighbour, friend or family member who lives close by, they can ask the person selling the product to return when they have that other person with them. Some people carry a card requesting sellers to contact the support person identified on the card, if they wish to sell them something. If the seller becomes pushy or agitated, this is an indication that they may not be genuine, and if the person feels that they are in danger they should contact the police.

The potential for call handlers to help safeguard

A major concern is the ability for domestic financial abuse that can be facilitated as a result of call handlers untrained in the Mental Capacity Act 2005. Organisations such as banks, Personal Independent Payments, Attendance Allowance and the Department for Works and Pensions (DWP) have a poor system for dealing with confidentiality and financial transactions. Below is a short case study about Anthony and his mum Jane (real names have been changed):

> ■ Anthony is a 19-year-old man who has been diagnosed with autism, attention deficit hyperactivity disorder, speech and language disabilities, dyspraxia, dyslexia and suspected deficits in attention, motor control and perception. Unfortunately, due to the nature of his disability, Anthony is unable to understand some detailed correspondence enough to make complex or new financial decisions and complex health decisions. Anthony's mum (Jane) is supporting him to become independent and holds an appointeeship but as yet has not applied for a court appointed deputyship because she hopes that he will continue his journey towards independence over the next couple of years.
>
> Jane has major concerns about the way that communications with banks, building societies, NHS helplines, the DWP, student finance, health care plans for college and university, applications for repeat prescriptions and similar services are handled.

Jane explains that:

- the disability of the person is often considered rather than the capacity

- the person with a disability is asked to speak on the phone to consent, without being supported to understand what they are consenting to (e.g. Anthony has been asked for consent to talk to his mother about his Personal Independence Payment going into her bank account instead of his. Anthony has no concept of what this means, but says yes)

- the person with a disability saying 'yes' acts as consent and the call handler does not ask questions to determine whether they understand what they are consenting to

- there is often misunderstanding about what a person can use an appointeeship for and when a court appointed deputyship is required

- there is often misunderstanding about when a court appointed deputyship or lasting power of attorney can be applied and when it should not be applied

- no consideration of an advocate or family support is added to the account or decision making

- capacity assessments are not conducted or recorded, and in some instances people are held accountable or culpable for actions that they did not understand in the first place

- reasonable adjustments under the Equality Act 2010 are not considered

- letters are sent that the person cannot understand, and passwords and access criteria are applied to accounts that the person will not recall. For example, on some occasions, Anthony has been asked to say the third and sixth letter of his password – something that he would find impossible to do without support. Jane says that when she tried to support him, the call handler said that they could hear someone prompting Anthony and therefore they could not allow access to the account.

Jane recognises that call handling is a fast and interactive service that should not be arduous, but she feels that call handlers for associated health and financial services should be in a better position to understand the appropriate legislation and identify potential safeguarding concerns.

While Jane is caring, focused on Anthony and responsible in her interactions, she has concerns that some significant medical and financial decisions could be made easily by her for her own benefit rather than Anthony's (if she was unscrupulous), and using the current systems this would not be questioned. Safeguarding should be something embedded within financial institutions and regimes and should be considered in every health intervention.

Financial abuse and trauma

Victims of financial crime may feel the impact of trauma in much the same way as victims of violent crime (Deem 2000). In the aftermath of Robert Maxwell's Mirror Group pension fraud, victims were described as suffering anxiety, stress, fear and depression, with some identifying that they felt the scam had attributed to their partner's death (Spalek 1999, 2006). James and Graycar (2000) agree with Spalek (1999), claiming that financial abuse causes fear, lack of trust and acute and chronic anxiety, and can be a life-threatening event. Increased depression and social isolation, and vulnerability to further financial exploitation, affect many older and vulnerable people who often have the additional difficulty of being unable or not in a position to replace lost funds (Walsh and Bennett 2000).

Physical abuse

The Care Act 2014 statutory guidance identifies physical abuse as including:

- assault
- hitting
- slapping
- pushing
- misuse of medication

- restraint

- inappropriate physical sanctions.

Physical abuse may include rough handling, forcible feeding or withholding food, and making someone purposefully uncomfortable such as removing blankets, leaving windows open and removing warm clothing. Potential indicators may include:

- no explanation for injuries

- inconsistent accounts for marks, bruising, injuries

- grip marks

- loss of hair, bruising, cuts, marks, burns, scalds

- frequent injuries

- unexplained falls

- failure to seek medical advice or attention

- signs of neglect

- a change in behaviour, particularly around a specific person.

Physical abuse and trauma

Some years ago, a good friend of mine was subject to a severe assault that changed him physically and emotionally forever. The attack left my friend with a shattered cheekbone, and although he had formerly been keen on boxing, keeping fit and martial arts, issues about his ability to protect himself had an impact on his self-esteem. The scars left on his face were significant, but the scars on his emotions, feelings and identity were so much greater. My friend left his secure job and went travelling in a van – not a converted van, just a van with a mattress. He lived in this van for many years, with few belongings, and disengaged from a lot of his friends. It is painful to see someone that you care about remove themselves in this way. He had a journey that he had to make to find himself again, and eventually it seems that he did just that. It has taken nearly 30 years and I guess that he will never return to the confident, self-assured person that he was. He now has a gentler quality about him, and I can see him exploring life with his partner and son and finding a new direction.

Domestic abuse

The Care Act 2014 statutory guidance identifies domestic violence as including psychological, physical, sexual, financial and emotional abuse as well as so-called honour-based violence (this includes forced marriage).

There are many reasons why people who suffer abuse or neglect won't, or feel they can't, make a disclosure, so it's important to build trust to enable a possible future disclosure. Always be alert to the possibility that an individual is experiencing abuse or neglect and be prepared to offer support.

Be aware of signs that could indicate abuse is taking place, such as physical injury (inconsistent explanations for bruises or other injuries, frequent bruises or injury), controlling behaviour (partner always present during appointments, won't allow person to talk for themselves, person has limited access to money) and environmental indicators (holes in doors/walls, broken furniture, a tense atmosphere in the home).

Ensure professional interpreters are used, and never use family members, children or friends where abuse is known or suspected. Only ask questions about abuse or neglect when victims are on their own and in a private place.

A considerable proportion of safeguarding adults work relates to the abuse or neglect of people with care and support needs who are living in their own homes. Domestic abuse is perhaps most commonly thought of as violence between intimate partners, but it can take many other forms and be perpetrated by a range of people.

In 2013, the Home Office announced changes to the definition of domestic abuse:

> Incident or pattern of incidents of controlling, coercive or threatening behaviour, violence or abuse...by someone who is or has been an intimate partner or family member regardless of gender or sexuality.
>
> - Includes: psychological, physical, sexual, financial, emotional abuse; so called 'honour' based violence; female genital mutilation; forced marriage.
>
> - Age range extended down to 16.

Many people think that domestic abuse is about intimate partners, but it is clear that other family members are included and that a lot of potential to safeguard those who have care and support needs at home is missed. The Care Act confirms that domestic abuse approaches and legislation can be considered safeguarding responses in appropriate cases. Legal frameworks are to be considered.

Where a person (over the age of 16) who has care and support needs is abused or neglected by a family member, or person of the same household as themselves, they are eligible for safeguarding, but this also constitutes domestic abuse. Domestic abuse referral pathways and legal responses should be considered in all community safeguarding matters concerning family members and individuals of the same household – for abuse, and/or where the person who has care and support needs has been neglected. This will include situations where coercive and controlling behaviours have been used to intimidate the person and prevent access of services to the person, resulting in harm to their physical and mental wellbeing.

What do I need to consider?

The Duluth Wheel of Power and Control (Domestic Abuse Intervention Programs (DAIP) 1984; see Figure 3.1) can be really helpful in assessing domestic abuse. Working within substance misuse services I used this wheel in discussion with people when they began to disclose events. Initial disclosure was often about finance, or a physical attack. We would explore aspects of the wheel at a person's own pace. Some people were able to consider the whole wheel and identified various things that had happened to them. Other people needed more time to consider each element and so discussion was broken into sessions. When the person was able to recognise that what was happening to them was domestic abuse, I was able to begin the discussion about talking to someone from domestic abuse services. I found this a gentler way of allowing the person to explore the impact of what was happening to them and their family and speak to someone about it. Working in this way, every person accepted support, although not everyone wanted to leave or prosecute as soon as they recognised abuse. Engaging with others to talk about things affecting them and their relationships is a big step, and a step towards considering their own safety and that of their children and family members. For some people, it can take a long time before they are ready to move on.

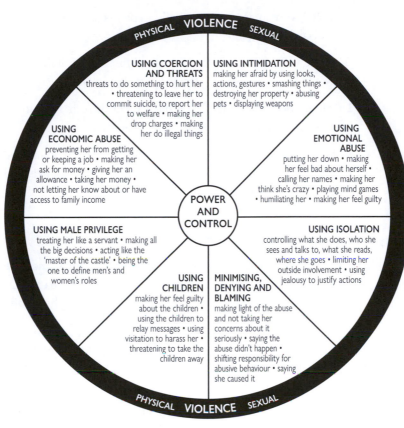

Figure 3.1: The Duluth Wheel of Power and Control

The wheel describes domestic abuse of women, but men can also suffer from domestic abuse. The challenges to find appropriate support for people of same-sex relationships and the lesbian, gay, bisexual and transgender (LGBT) community is huge. Responding to individual needs and life stories is the key to personalised safeguarding responses. The prevalence of domestic abuse perpetrated against people who have care and support needs is currently under-reported and yet studies still identify higher statistics than those who do not have care and support needs.

Research commissioned by Women's Aid in October 2007 and published on the Domestic Violence London website (2019) identifies that:

- 50% of disabled women have experienced domestic abuse compared with 25% of non-disabled women.

- Disabled women are twice as likely to be assaulted or raped as non-disabled women.

- Both men and women with a limiting illness or disabilities are more likely to experience intimate partner violence.

- Disabled women are likely to have to endure it for longer because appropriate support is not available.

- A study of women who access mental health services identified between 50% and 60% had experienced domestic violence, and up to 20% were currently being abused.

Honour-based violence (HBV)

HBV is a form of domestic abuse where the perpetrator feels that the family member has acted dishonourably. To break honour means that certain rules of conduct or status have not been applied by the family member. Examples include the following:

- A person who has a disability or mental ill-health can be seen as bringing dishonour to the family, because they are not regarded as fit or healthy.

- A person having a same-sex relationship or having a partner from a different cultural or religious background may be seen as dishonourable.

- A person rejecting a forced marriage.

- Pregnancy outside marriage.

- Seeking to leave the marriage.

- Dress or makeup seen as inappropriate.

- Public displays of affection.

HBV can exist in any culture or community; some examples may include but not be exclusive to: Turkish, Kurdish, Gypsy/Travelling community, Jewish, South Asian, African, Middle Eastern.

Forced marriage

Arranged marriage with the free consent of both parties is lawful. Forced marriage is against the law. A forced marriage is one where there is no consent and the marriage is performed under duress. Victims of forced marriage may be subject to abuse, neglect and serious crimes like rape and murder.

Female genital mutilation (FGM)

FGM refers to a variety of procedures where female genitalia are removed. FGM often is conducted during puberty; however, there are children who have been forced to have genitalia removed and it has been conducted on many adult women. There are four broad categories of FGM (World Health Organization 2008):

- Type 1: Clitoridectomy – partial or total removal of the clitori, and/or clitoral hood.

- Type 2: Excision – partial or total removal of the clitoris and the labia minora, with or without excision of the labia majora (tissue around the vaginal opening).

- Type 3: Infibulation – narrowing of the vaginal orifice with creation of a covering seal by cutting and placing together the labia minora and/or the labia majora, with or without excision of the clitoris. (Cutting the skin around the vaginal opening and placing it together to form a cover over the vaginal opening, stitching the skin together and leaving a small hole to urinate and menstruate from.)

- Type 4: Unclassified – all other harmful procedures to the female genitalia for non-medical purposes, for example pricking, piercing, incising, scraping and cauterisation.

Often these procedures are conducted in insanitary conditions and using non-sterilised instruments such as razor blades, parts of tin cans and broken glass. The risk of infection is very high, and childbirth can be very painful and problematic, causing risks to both the mother and the child. Girls are seperated from their family and can often be alone, afraid, in pain and bleeding. The psychological consequences can be significant. It is estimated that every year two million women will undergo genital mutilation, often without consent. To be taken from your home in Britain to another country to have this procedure is against the law, even when the procedure is undertaken abroad. It is a safeguarding matter and must be reported.

It is essential that we consider the possibility of domestic abuse in safeguarding situations. Domestic abuse is the leading cause of morbidity for women aged 19–44 – greater than cancer, war and motor vehicle accidents. Two women a week die in domestic abuse situations (World Health Organization 2008). When people have disabilities or mental health problems, perpetrators of domestic abuse can use the needs of the individual to put them down, control them or humiliate them (Local Government Association and Association of Directors of Adult Social Services 2015).

The following boxes outline safeguarding and domestic abuse considerations.

Consider the connection between safeguarding and domestic abuse	Consider the impact of domestic abuse
• Follow safeguarding procedures • Understand the links between domestic abuse and safeguarding and use resources/legal frameworks for both • Consider patterns of coercive and controlling behaviour (crime) as well as incidents of abuse/neglect • Take into account gender, sexuality and intergenerational issues • Do you know whether the person has care and support needs? Seek advice from your local authority • Do you know what domestic abuse resources and legal frameworks could be used? Seek advice from domestic abuse services	• What is the impact of abuse on children – children's services referral/advice/guidance? • Are there any other people who may have care and support needs? • What is the potential for neglect? (Consider wilful neglect) • Consider the person's mental health – referral for assessment • What is the risk to others?

Consider the barriers and challenges

- Can you recognise a person who may need safeguarding?

- Can you recognise domestic abuse?

- Do you understand why a person may not leave an abusive relationship?

- Are there any ethnic, cultural (including age-related) or religious barriers?

- Do you feel comfortable routinely asking people about their safety?

- Is there accessible information about services to signpost people to?

- Are workers given time to build trust with people to assist the person in disclosing information?

- Is the person dependent on the potential perpetrator to provide key aspects of care?

- Has the person's previous experience of services become a barrier for them?

- Is it possible that people are making assumptions about the person and their needs, wishes and perspectives or have they asked the person?

Mental capacity

- Does the person have capacity to understand that they may be suffering abuse/neglect?

- Does the person have capacity to consent to referrals or are best interest decisions required?

- Do staff recognise why a referral would be made without the consent of a capacitated person or in the best interests of a non-capacitated person?

- Is an unwise decision potentially the result of coercion or controlling behaviour?

- Have you considered the use of an independent mental capacity advocate (IMCA), an independent domestic violence advocate (IDVA) or an independent sexual violence advocate (ISVA)?

- Do staff recognise that they can make a safeguarding referral when the person has capacity and does not consent to the referral, and do staff know what the circumstances are?

Safety

- Follow the principles of safe enquiry

- Is the environment safe?

- Does the person have contact details and a safe way for you to contact them?

- Are there any high-risk factors?

- Has referral to a multi-agency risk assessment conference (MARAC) been considered? Consent is not required

- Remember that even when a person does not wish to disclose abuse or neglect, the conversation assists in developing rapport and letting the person know that you are willing to listen

- Ask direct questions until there is reasonable suspicion of abuse

- Keep good records reflecting what the person said and any interventions used

- Take immediate protective measures that the person considers will keep them safe

- Safety plan for the future

- Follow local policies and procedures

- Do a continuous risk assessment

- Be aware that staff often look for the good in people and place undue confidence in the ability of families to care effectively and safely (the rule of optimism)

- Use risk assessment forms and tools to aid judgement, not as an end in themselves

- Ensure person-centred practice

The law

- Remember to keep safeguarding personal

- Consider places of safety and support services for both the short term and long term

- Consider the types of legal actions and responses that can be used in safeguarding and domestic abuse

- Know where to get good legal and professional advice

- Give information and advice to the person

- Consider legal frameworks: Mental Capacity Act, Human Rights Act, Equality Act, Domestic Violence, Crime and Victims Act

- Consider case law, such as *R v Brown* – cannot consent to assault

- Consider police evidence-led prosecution

- Consider new laws regarding coercive or intimidating behaviour

- Consider all Care Act and safeguarding adults/children duties

- If someone is abusive and they themselves have care and support needs, make sure that they have access to information, advice, assessment and support

- Consider confidentiality and share appropriate information

Domestic abuse and safeguarding safety planning

Supporting the person to make plans for their own safety is very important. Power and control are being taken away from the person on a regular basis as a result of the abuse they are experiencing and so you must ensure that your practice is person centred. Safety is what the person perceives it to be, as long as they are making informed decisions that are free from coercion and intimidation.

Multi-agency risk assessment conference (MARAC)

A MARAC is a meeting to share information and talk about how to help domestic abuse victims at high risk of murder or serious harm. A number of specialist agencies talk about the victim, perpetrator and family and share information. An action plan is written for each victim. The SafeLives website identifies how to make a referral, when to make a referral and how to respond to emergency situations (SafeLives.org. uk 2018). You can speak with local domestic abuse services who will provide you with more information about access to MARACs. The SafeLives website will also provide information on local MARACs. There are also specialist independent domestic violence advocates (IDVAs) who can support victims of domestic abuse.

Domestic abuse and trauma

Trauma in cases of domestic abuse is presented in much the same way as trauma experienced as a result of neglect, war and abuse, and I shall describe the impact of trauma in some detail within the following self-neglect section of this chapter, so please read through the signs and symptoms of trauma that are explained. In relation to domestic abuse, the blame for a person returning to an abusive relationship is often identified. Practitioners say, 'Well, we tried to help her, but she just keeps going back, she is making a choice.' The consideration of the impact of the abuse on the person is often disregarded, rarely considered as part of the reason for their responses. Trauma can be so significant that post-traumatic stress can be triggered. This is a serious mental health matter and can become debilitating (Herman 1992).

Why would a person who is humiliated, denigrated, financially abused and physically assaulted and sometimes sexually abused want to remain with someone who might eventually end their life?

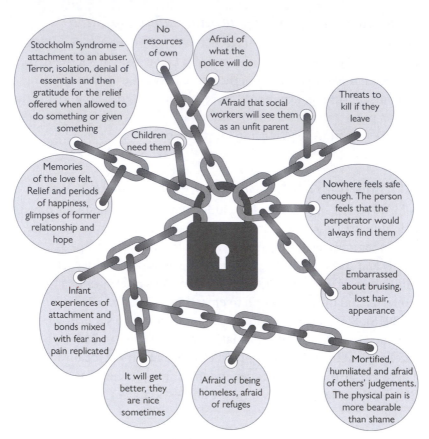

*Figure 3.2: Locked in to abuse – the 13 chains
that lock a person to their abuser*

As illustrated in Figure 3.2, there are many reasons why a person may choose to remain in a relationship that is abusive. Most of these reasons relate to either past experiences of trauma, abuse and neglect, recent trauma experiences or the person's ability to analytically rather than emotionally process the risk information, or a combination of these. Dealing with the intensity of domestic abuse can lead a person to remain frozen in a fear response, unable to make choices or decisions. When people are dependent on their abuser for care and support, these emotions can be exacerbated. In addition, the lack of recognition of domestic abuse in safeguarding cases means that the appropriate support is not there. This may be as a result of people making assumptions about the nature of relationships in older people, or people who have disabilities, or it may be a lack of awareness around domestic abuse and the interface with safeguarding. According to Knight and Hester (2014), in cases of domestic abuse involving a person who has dementia, safeguarding referrals are made, but the involvement of domestic abuse services is rarely considered.

Self-neglect and hoarding

The Care Act 2014 statutory guidance identifies self-neglect:

> This covers a wide range of behaviours, neglecting to care for one's personal hygiene, health or surroundings and includes behaviour such as hoarding. It should be noted that self-neglect may not prompt a Section 42 enquiry where other means are more appropriate, for example a person who has a physical disability, mental ill-health and/or learning disability and cannot manage to care for their personal hygiene, health or surroundings may require an assessment of need and planned intervention to meet those needs. (Section 14.17)

An assessment should be made on a case-by-case basis. A decision on whether a response is required under safeguarding will depend on the adult's ability to protect themselves by controlling their own behaviour. There may come a point when they are no longer able to do this without external support, and complex multi-agency responses are required. The Self-Neglect and Hoarding Risk Assessment Tool (see Chapter 5) may assist you in determining the risks and making a decision about the need for safeguarding, but do remember that this is just a tool and not a substitute for professional judgement.

Self-neglect and trauma

Severe self-neglect, including hoarding, is often linked with traumatic experiences, current, recent or childhood abuse/neglect, loss and bereavement (Frost, Steketee and Tolin 2011). Braye, Orr and Preston-Shoot (2014) also identified similar reasons for self-neglect and relayed some of the experiences that people who were self-neglecting disclosed:

> These included stories of being orphaned, of childhood physical and sexual abuse, of incest, and traumatic wartime experiences. At least one person had a lifelong struggle with sexual orientation. Some suffered from mental illness, while others were caregivers to loved ones with severe mental illness. One survived a murder attempt by

a mentally ill spouse. Seventy-five per cent of those who were self-neglecting revealed one or more of these experiences, while fewer than 25 per cent of controls spoke of such experiences. The researchers concluded that these traumatic histories and life changing events appeared to be associated with, and could possibly lie on the causal pathway to development of, frank self-neglect. (Braye *et al.* 2014)

Braye and colleagues also considered behaviours presented in a variety of cases of self-neglect and identified symptoms including:

- social isolation

- attachment to animals or objects

- memory difficulties or poor concentration

- retention of goods including bodily fluids

- anger

- poor sleep patterns

- alcohol or drug use

- poor self-care or ability to plan

- guilt

- anxiety

- fear about germs or contamination

- lack of motivation

- depressed or changeable moods

- disinhibited behaviour or attention-seeking behaviour

- panic attacks

- disassociation

- bodily aches and pains with no apparent reason (somatisation).

The list above describes symptoms that would not be unusual to see in a person who has suffered a great trauma or loss. It may even be symptomatic of someone suffering post-trauma after life-threatening experiences or intense fear. Most self-neglect is therefore a symptom of trauma.

The *Diagnostic and Statistical Manual of Mental Disorders 5* (American Psychiatric Association 2013) identifies hoarding disorder as a distinct disorder in its own right and eligible for mental health intervention. The problem is that treatment pathways have not yet been explicitly identified. My recent experiences of working with a psychologist, psychiatrist and social worker have produced outstanding results when they have addressed the 'trauma' in connection with the 'hoarding disorder' and other presenting co-morbidities such as anxiety, depression, dementia, paranoia, psychosis and other mental health concerns. Once treatment pathways are identified for the wide-ranging co-morbid mental health issues associated with trauma, then psychological and medical interventions can be found to support the person. The diagnostic element of the capacity assessment is met and then the functional elements can be explored. The psychological approaches are 'trauma informed' – the aim is to not re-traumatise the person and to enable them to maintain all control relating to decision making where possible. Eventually the person will begin to heal and they will want to change their environment. Working with the person to help them organise and sort belongings, provide motivation and practical support throughout the process and engaging with occupational therapy and social work with an aim to build upon the person's strengths and make connections within the community ensures that the person re-engages with people and develops a sense of purpose and belonging.

Hoarding disorder is defined as the excessive acquisition of and inability to discard objects, resulting in debilitating clutter. The person diagnosed with hoarding disorder may have deficits in cognitive processing and maladaptive behavioural patterns. Behavioural patterns associated with hoarding disorder may include impaired attention, impaired verbal and non-verbal recall, and impaired categorisation and decision making. Maladaptive beliefs may include beliefs about perfectionism, making wrong decisions, being wasteful and losing something important, as well as emotional or anthropomorphic (describing the objects as if they were in human form) attachment to objects. Poor insight and avoidance of decision making is often evident in people who hoard, contributing to the resistance to engaging with support services. Other potential reasons for lack of engagement will be explored later.

Tolin *et al.* (2012) researched the attachment that people with hoarding disorder had to objects and found anomalies or abnormalities in their brain function. These abnormalities could be found in the frontal cortical region and the anterior cingulate cortex areas of the brain, which are involved in executive decision functions, such as remembering things, categorising things, attachment, impulse control and the motivational significance of stimulus.

The body responds by sending increased blood supply, breathing regularity and temperature changes when stressed. Tolin *et al.* (2012) measured these responses and used neurological imagery to see where the brain stimulus occurred. Considering the role of the amygdala and the mid-anterior cingulate cortex, the research identified that when people who have a hoarding disorder were asked to discard something that did not belong to them, there was less of a response than the control group, or the group of people who had a diagnosis of obsessive compulsive disorder. In fact, the response was so significantly low that Tolin *et al.* (2012) compared this to the kind of response expected of someone who has an autism spectrum disorder. This may identify why a person who has a hoarding disorder may have significant difficulty with decision making, categorising things and placing things in an order, or difficulties with impulse control and attachment. Saxena *et al.* (2004) had similar findings in an earlier study.

The anterior cingulate cortex plays a critical role in complex cognitive and attentional processing and it has been hypothesised that it plays a primary role in making selections when faced with streams of information, and in response selection and the correct response selection, or inhibition of response selection. Having an impairment, or severely low stimulus response, may mean that inattention, impulsivity as well as memory are affected and there appears to be some link to attachment issues. The same regions of the brain become hyperactive in people who have hoarding disorder, a pattern often seen among patients with anxiety disorders. Hyperactivity in this area of the brain can lead to a greater sense of outcome uncertainty and therefore hamper the decision-making process (Badgaiyan and Posner 1998). In patients who have had traumatic experiences and suffer from post-traumatic stress disorder, the same exaggerated responses occur in relation to stress triggers, and these can also be seen in patients who have autism (Hamner, Lorberbaum and George 1999). If confirmed in future research, this could have important theoretical and treatment implications because it may mean that the experiment conducted by Tolin and colleagues was merely triggering stress responses, stemming from previous trauma. It may also explain why people who have autism can easily become hoarders. Baron-Cohen (1989) and Snowdon, Pertusa and Mataix-Cols (2012) identified commonalities between the behaviours displayed by people who have autism spectrum disorders and those who have problems with hoarding. The link between attention deficit hyperactive disorder and hoarding disorder has also been considered (Frost *et al.* 2011).

In analysing the impact of trauma, Adshead (2000) identifies that the impact of a trauma on a person will be affected by things such as early fear experiences and insecure attachments and resilience factors such as self-esteem. Dodge *et al.* (1997) identifies that early fear experiences may be significant in terms of later capacity to manage threat. It may well be important, therefore, to consider early childhood experiences as well as any traumatic events in the life of a person who self-neglects or hoards.

Barlow *et al.* (1986) argue the importance of making clear the existing relationships among syndromes, rather than simply listing all the diagnoses for which a patient is eligible. Spitzer (1984) identifies the need for skilled clinical judgement to establish the functional relationship among various symptom clusters in any given patient. Van der Kolk *et al.* (1996b) describes how in trauma patients there is a recognition of a high degree of co-morbidity and that describing individual symptoms does not give the full extent of the person's suffering. People continue to suffer the symptoms of trauma long after the original impact, and this may be missed by clinical practitioners faced with someone self-neglecting or hoarding, as the predominant and obvious factor is the clutter, or the personal state of the patient. Relating back to the trauma symptoms Van der Kolk *et al.* (1996b) identified, 'In those patients clinicians are liable to miss the association between their patients' current symptomology and their past histories of trauma.' Braye *et al.* (2014) also describe similar complex co-morbidity in people who self-neglect.

In focusing specifically on the hoarding or self-neglect, practitioners may be missing the historical context of the trauma that precipitated the subsequent self-neglecting or hoarding behaviours, and this detracts from the exploration of co-morbidities and prime diagnosis. If trauma was the original instigating factor, then self-neglect is a symptom of trauma. Perhaps the services should be called 'trauma services' rather than self-neglect services? This would focus the attention away from blaming the person for their behaviour to supporting them via legitimate mental health routes. This would also seek to differentiate between those self-neglecting because they have a disability, mental ill-health or learning disability and cannot self-care and those who self-neglect as a result of trauma and loss.

Making the connections between misdiagnosis or co-morbidity and trauma would refocus professional intervention and support, and would:

- distinguish between those who self-neglect because they cannot manage as a result of mental ill-health or disability and who require an assessment of need and a care plan and those who have deep-rooted bereavement, loss, grief, abuse or neglect issues and require mental health intervention

- identify those who might require a Section 42 safeguarding enquiry and those who need social work intervention

- move the focus away from blaming the person, labelling them as aggressive, lacking insight or eccentric, to considering the presenting symptoms of potentially long-term trauma response

- consider the executive brain functioning problems experienced by people who hoard or self-neglect as potential symptoms of trauma

- consider the hypersensitivity arousal experienced by people who self-neglect and hoard as a response to trauma

- consider the attachment to objects rather than people as a response to trauma

- consider the compulsions and impulse control issues as a result of trauma

- consider the changeable moods, lack of sleep and lack of social interaction as a response to trauma

- consider the retention of objects and/or bodily fluids observed in people who self-neglect or hoard as a response to trauma

- consider the squirrelling of goods as a response to trauma

- consider the enclosing of the person into a tight space with barriers around them as a response to trauma

- consider the guilt, self-degradation and lack of self-worth as a response to trauma

- consider the inability to sort, organise and plan (including self-care) as a response to trauma

- consider the memory impairment or distraction as a response to trauma

- consider appropriate treatment pathways for attachment and motivation the presenting symptoms rather than clearing of clutter and methodologies that create further harm

- enable appropriate treatment routes through mental health services

- focus on capacity assessments – trauma has a physical impact on certain areas of the brain that cover certain functions: the hippocampus, the amygdala and the frontal cortex of the brain. A person may in conversation appear to have capacity and be highly intelligent, but the impact of stress on the hippocampus may mean that the person is unable to learn new things and may struggle to retain information, or stay on track with a conversation

- provide reasons why a person responds with quick-fix solutions (getting another makes me feel happy). The impact of the trauma on the amygdala and the frontal cortex may mean that the person struggles with rational thought and favours automatic habits and knee-jerk responses

- identify why people who hoard can also misuse substances

- correlate the tendency to hoard in people who have impulse control disorders, autism spectrum disorders and a hoarding disorder with the similar aspects of the brain stimulated in response to trauma

- consider whether the person is re-enacting elements of the trauma.

Maynard (2017), in talking about post-traumatic stress and other 'stressor'-related disorders, identifies exactly the same areas of the brain affected by post-traumatic stress as those that Tolin *et al.* (2012) identified in people with hoarding disorders. Maynard (2017) identifies that:

> Both the amygdala and the mid-anterior cingulate cortex become over-stimulated when a person suffers with post-traumatic stress disorder. However, the hippocampus, right inferior frontal gryus, ventromedial PFC [prefrontal cortex], dorsolateral PFC, and orbitofrontal cortex all become hypoactive, some to the point of atrophy.

When feeling threatened, the amygdala stops its usual processes to consider the threat and begin the stimulation of senses, affecting the formation and storage of information and chronologies – timelines no longer exist and everything is in the current context. This affects fear conditioning and memory consolidation. When there is nothing to tell the person that the threat was in the past, the person becomes stuck in constant preparedness for threat. Relating this to the study by Tolin *et al.* (2012) looking at hoarding disorder, perhaps it was the threat of removing the goods that caused the reaction in this part of the brain and stimulated feelings associated with the original trauma.

Maynard (2017) identifies the role of the mid-anterior cingulate cortex in monitoring conflict and emotional awareness, registering physical pain and regulating heart rate and blood pressure. When affected by trauma, a person may have a stress response to conflict resolution, as they are sensing a significant threat that warrants a fast response and thus increases the heart rate. Memory consolidation is also affected by trauma, and what becomes a long-term memory in those not suffering the impact of trauma may not become a memory for those suffering trauma. The hippocampus and in particular the ventromedial PFC have a role in personal and social decision making, which can also be significantly affected. This may mean that the person sounds very capable, bright, intelligent and credible, but they may have significant impairment of memory, chronology and insight into risks.

The orbitofrontal cortex seems to be involved in sensory integration and expected rewards and punishments, regulating emotion and decision making. This aspect of brain function is less well known, as the correlation between its functions and our responses is complex; however, we recognise that those suffering stress respond to sensory triggers or threat triggers. The prefrontal cortex is also interconnected with many brain functions, including memory and sleep patterns, which become affected as a result of trauma experience. While a great deal of research regarding the brain functions of those suffering hoarding disorder and those suffering as a response to trauma is required, research has already made the clear link demonstrating a large majority of hoarders as having suffered a past trauma, or as having a disorder that creates similar patterns of activity/inactivity in the same areas of the brain.

Research into the impact of trauma and research into the behaviours displayed by someone hoarding explored within this book demonstrate many commonalities, suggesting that we may need to become more trauma aware and go back so far as to explore any adverse childhood experiences. For further potential psychological considerations, the 'Power, Threat, Meaning Framework' provides insight into the co-existing issues that may be affecting the person and their behaviours (see Bps.org.uk 2018). To achieve a greater understanding of the links between the behaviours and the symptoms, I shall explore:

- attachment
- guilt responses
- the re-enactment of trauma patterns
- social isolation and social deprivation.

There are different types of hoarding behaviours – some are identified as chaotic with mounds of what appears to be rubbish, and some are very ordered and organised. The prime consideration is about the attachment to objects – is the person really attached to the things/objects or are they having difficulty managing the stuff that they have in their home? Is it that the person just cannot manage to sort and organise or are they both unable and unwilling to let go of this support mechanism? The next consideration is the person's response to trauma and the impact that this has had on their behavioural responses.

There are many misconceptions about how we think we would respond when faced with real danger. If asked how you would respond if there was a terrorist attack on a hotel that you were staying in, most people would say that they would run and hide; however, we know that people do not all run and hide. Some people play dead, some freeze and cannot move, some run, and a small few may try to attack the attacker. This fight, flight, freeze, flop scenario is part of our body's natural defence mechanisms to help us deal with danger. All our body's energies go to heightening our senses to protect ourselves, and so the incident is played out in front of us in a series of sensory stimulus-inducing scenes. The individual's perception that the world is safe becomes shattered as they recognise how unpredictable, fallible and dangerous things really are. A small percentage of these people retreat into psychosis and the rest struggle to find a way of seeing the world as safe once more, in order that they can function.

Lodrick (n.d.) describes how some people disassociate and therefore remove their contemplative self from the scenario and others will look for some aspect of the incident for which they can blame themselves: 'It would not always be like that, I made a mistake that I can now avoid and therefore it is not that the world is not safe, it is because I did something wrong.' A rape victim may say things like 'I should have fought harder' or 'I shouldn't have gone down that dark lonely pathway alone.' Someone who has cared for a relative who has died may say things like 'I should have been there when they died' or 'I should have insisted that they saw the specialist sooner.' Some people may feel guilty for not recognising the intentions of an attacker sooner. This guilt reinstates the necessary illusion that the world is safe and predictable.

> If the individual can ascribe some responsibility to him/herself then this horrific happening was not an 'act of random bad luck' (a concept that human beings cannot tolerate as it creates unendurable levels of anxiety), it was something that could have been predicted and should have been predicted. (Lodrick n.d.)

If we relate this to those people who hoard as a result of trauma, the guilt that they may be experiencing is as a result of what they perceive to be a choice that they now regret. If the person feels that they made some poor choices, then they experience guilt; however, if the person feels shame, they are considering themselves as a 'bad' person. Considering yourself as 'bad' attacks your identity, and considering yourself as having made some poor decisions is about your behaviours. It is infinitely easier to help a person change behaviours rather than their perceived identity. Treatment, however, will be required for the two elements – the sense of self/identity in relation to the trauma and the symptoms which are maintaining the stress response, and the actions around the presenting behaviours such as impulsive acquisition and attachment to objects. The feelings of guilt present a barrier to treatment as the person is afraid to either admit their guilt and add shame and personal blame to the devastation that they are feeling or to open up and accept that it was not their fault. The latter without therapeutic support can cause further traumatic difficulties of which the person may be quite afraid.

This guilt is added to when people hoard and can be observed when they talk about the volume of goods and in their responses to the cluttered environment. The person has not been able to stop acquiring goods, often to their dismay when they return home and have nowhere to put the objects, resulting in feelings of guilt. 'I shouldn't have bought that book. I have the paperback version already.' Over the years, people have pointed out the clutter and have asked the person to change this situation that they feel frozen within. Feeling helpless, this turns the guilt into shame and the person tells you, 'This is just the way I am', turning behaviours into an identity and also reflecting the original guilt and shame patterns experienced through trauma. Montminy *et al.* (2017) identify this process, stating:

> It is common for persons with a history of trauma to find themselves re-enacting traumatic patterns... Such re-enactments can contribute significantly to their general levels of stress, trigger reminders of previous trauma and the re-experiencing of symptoms. An example of a pattern of re-enactment is the following cycle: feeling isolated, longing for rescue, feeling let down or abused, retreating into isolation and feeling alone and neglected.

In addition to the fight, flight, freeze or flop trauma responses, a fifth response may be considered, and this is the 'friend' response (Ogden and Minton 2000; Porges 2004). This response becomes operational from birth, with the baby crying for the attention of the mother to meet their needs, and relies on their cry to illicit help in the same way an adult may shout for help when in danger, hoping for rescue. When a child becomes ambulant they may move toward caregivers for support and protection, and when they begin to speak, they also begin to negotiate their way out of danger. Porges (1995) calls this the social engagement system, and Lodrick (n.d.) likens it to the child who smiles or laughs when being chastised, suggesting that it is an attempt to engage socially with the person causing the fear. If the child is unsuccessful in engaging the caregiver, they will become agitated and may display symptoms of anxiety or depression (Porges 1995). In earlier social contact, the child or younger adult may have tried to deal with distress, trauma or conflict by trying to engage the perpetrator. If their attempts failed, this will affect self-esteem, create anxiety around other social contact and perhaps cause the person to feel as if they cannot be loved or are not deserving of others' attentions.

During the 1950s and 1960s an American psychologist called Harry Harlow (Harlow and Zimmerman 1958) conducted a series of experiments using rhesus monkeys. The baby monkeys were isolated from birth, having no contact with each other or anyone else. Control groups were kept for three, six, nine and twelve months before being placed back with the other monkeys. Not having any opportunity to form attachments to significant others, the monkeys held their own bodies and rocked compulsively. Initially they were afraid of the other monkeys but eventually became aggressive towards them. They were unable to communicate or socialise and the other monkeys bullied them. The result was that the isolated monkeys self-harmed, tearing out their own hair, scratching and biting at their own arms and legs. The extent of the abnormal behaviour in the monkeys reflected the length of time spent in isolation, with those left in isolation for a year never recovering. While this was unethical and had only limited value in understanding humans, the possible implication is that social isolation can lead to self-neglecting and self-harming behaviours.

The research by Steptoe *et al.* (2013) aimed to determine the correlation between loneliness and social isolation and whether these are associated with increased mortality. A large study involving 6500 men and women aged 52 or older found significant evidence that mortality was directly linked to social isolation. Although both social isolation and loneliness impair the quality of life and wellbeing, efforts to reduce isolation are more likely to be relevant to mortality. Early intervention to support the person hoarding to re-engage with people and the community may therefore have significant benefits.

As part of early childhood development, the child learns to separate themselves from their mother by use of objects such as cuddly toys or special blankets to provide comfort, rather than always comfort seeking from mother. These are termed transitional objects and they not only provide comfort but also solace, predictability and constancy, representative of a stable and predictable world. We have already explored how trauma can shake the stability, safety and predictability of the world experienced by the person suffering the trauma and how a person may isolate themselves from the risks posed by people. Perhaps the attachment to objects presents safety, as objects cannot harm the individual and can provide some comfort?

Brenner (2004) argues that transitional objects are used throughout the course of our lives, providing solace and memories, and more importantly they define a state of presence in the world. If a person has lost trust in people and feels lonely and socially isolated, the attachment to the objects may provide comfort. Trauma can also cause disassociation and feelings of disconnectedness. Perhaps the attachment to the objects defines the person's state of presence in the world – a real-life reminder that they exist and are present. Bowlby (1969) identified that attachment is a biological function that is indispensable for both reproduction and survival. Research has demonstrated that disturbances of attachment bonds have long-term neurobiological consequences and biopsychosocial effects and cause biological changes; for example, the capacity to regulate emotions, difficulty in learning new skills, alterations in immune competency and an inability to engage in meaningful social relationships (Courtois and Ford 2009; Van der Kolk *et al.* 1996a).

To further explore the relationship between attachment to people and attachment to objects, Harlow and Zimmerman (1958) conducted a second experiment with eight rhesus monkeys separated from their mothers immediately after birth. They were placed in cages with two objects: a wire surrogate mother and a surrogate mother made of soft terry towelling cloth. Four monkeys could get milk from the wire mother and four from the cloth mother. Both groups spent more time with the cloth mother even when the cloth mother had no milk, so there was preference shown for the softer and more tactile object. The monkeys only went to the wire monkey when hungry, returning to the cloth mother for the rest of the day. If a frightening object was placed in the cage, the baby monkeys took refuge with the cloth mother. The monkeys recognised this cloth item as a safe base, and as such it represented something which could alleviate fears.

Harlow and Zimmerman (1958) found that the monkeys who grew up with objects as surrogate mothers were more timid, easily bullied and had difficulty forming relationships and mating; however, the surrogate mother objects provided a more stable environment than having nothing at all. Social deprivation affected the monkeys but not as badly as maternal deprivation. There may therefore be some benefit to a person attaching themselves to objects that are available to touch and feel safe around, and hoarding may represent a need to have these objects to feel the sense of safety and security. Removing these objects could have a significant detrimental effect on the person unless they are first supported to engage with other people.

I am not a psychiatrist or psychologist; however, once I have pointed out these links, psychiatrists and psychologists have been able to clearly understand the interventions required. There remains a barrier to this, and that is the reluctance of some services to open that 'can of worms' without financial support.

An American study considered the prevalence of hoarding disorder in individuals seeking help from eviction intervention services and found that almost a quarter of individuals met the criteria for hoarding disorder (Rodriguez *et al.* 2013). While this was a relatively small sample size, the anecdotal stories from social work practice suggest many people suffering from hoarding disorder are faced with eviction for non-compliance with tenancies. For some individuals faced with eviction, mental health problems are cited (Crane *et al.* 2005). Given the correlation between mental ill-health, trauma and hoarding, the housing provider would have been required to assess the person's capacity to understand the tenancy agreement and any other offered housing interventions, make suitable referrals for appropriate mental health assessment and intervention if not already involved, make a safeguarding referral and make reasonable adjustments due to the nature of the condition.

The consideration of the human right to autonomy (private life) and peaceful enjoyment of possessions needs to be considered. A person cannot be held culpable for something that they do not understand, or were incapable of achieving, due to mental or physical ill-health. Large-scale clear-ups and/or eviction will only serve to further traumatise the person and create more negative trust issues with providers and services. Once offered a property the person will find that the problems begin again unless the original trauma is addressed. The cost of clearing and repairing properties is significant. It must be better to help the person recover from trauma and support them to get the property cleaned when they are ready. This way the tenancy is maintained and the risks minimised.

Homelessness and safeguarding considerations in relation to trauma

While homelessness is not specifically identified as a form of abuse, neglect or self-neglect in the Care Act 2014 or the statutory guidance, the links with trauma and potential co-morbid mental ill-health/ substance misuse are widely reported and therefore should be considered in relation to meeting the three-part eligibility test.

The Glasgow Homeless Network carried out research into homelessness in 2002 and produced a report that identified clear links between homelessness, trauma and loss. Many studies into the kinds of trauma that homeless people experience have been conducted. Speak to any worker in services for homeless people and they will be familiar with matters of childhood abuse, neglect and exploitation. Experiences of domestic abuse, and other forms of abuse or neglect such as rape or physical violence, are well recorded and the media have regularly reported the prevalence of war veterans living on the streets. A study of homeless women revealed high rates of childhood physical and sexual abuse, domestic abuse and family violence, and many participants displayed symptoms of post-traumatic stress disorder (Davis 2008).

The trauma responses described in the previous section relating to self-neglect and hoarding apply to all experiences of trauma. The impact of trauma on the brain's ability to organise, sort, plan, prepare, manage stress, assess risk, control impulse, self-care, manage anger and aggression and manage attachment must be considered in relation to rough sleepers or homeless people's responses, if we are to provide a solution to the revolving door of homelessness. Ignoring the links between homelessness and trauma will only lead to increased need for more intensive mental health, physical health and social care responses later down the line. By making referral to a 'trauma service' or psychological services when eviction, hoarding, self-neglect, self-harm, substance misuse or sexual exploitation is identified and the person is displaying symptoms of trauma, we can address the cause and not the symptom. Trauma services are moderately rare at the moment. Many sexual abuse referral centres will be available to support a person dealing with the impact of trauma from sexual abuse. The Havens in London not only supports the impact of trauma on a person, but also the criminal aspects of trauma and how to assist the person in giving more credible evidence (Smith and Heke 2010). The Trauma and Homeless Team covering Glasgow and the Clyde consider the impact of trauma on the homeless person and work on therapeutic interventions.

The development of a safeguarding-led and multi-agency response to trauma and crime would ensure that everything we know about prevention, protection, empowerment, proportionate response, accountability and working in partnership can be utilised to develop more specific mental health-led approaches in safeguarding adults. This would support both recovery and equitable access to criminal justice for those who have suffered trauma. Effective safeguarding of those who are homeless, self-neglecting and suffering from trauma will not only be hugely beneficial to the person, who is able to find recovery pathways by addressing the mental health issues, but is also cost effective in preventing the need for intensive future services. Homeless services would benefit from having this mental health-led approach too.

Sexual abuse and sexual exploitation

The Care Act 2014 statutory guidance identifies sexual abuse as including:

- rape

- indecent exposure

- sexual harassment

- inappropriate looking or touching

- sexual teasing or innuendo

- sexual photography

- subjection to pornography or witnessing sexual acts

- indecent exposure

- sexual assault

- sexual acts to which the adult has not consented or was pressured into consenting.

Sexual abuse/sexual exploitation and trauma

In all cases of abuse or neglect it is important to be vigilant to and assess for the potential impact of trauma on the person. In cases of sexual abuse or exploitation it is recognised that the impact of sexual trauma on a person can equate to other traumatic events such as natural disasters and road traffic accidents (Smith and Heke 2010). People who have been raped or sexually assaulted are extremely susceptible to developing post-traumatic stress disorder. Rothenbaum *et al.* (1992) reported that 65 per cent of victims displayed symptoms of post-traumatic stress disorder one month following the rape or sexual assault. Capauzzo, Heke and Petrak (2007) have similar findings, with 64 per cent of victims displaying symptoms after one month.

Sexual abuse, domestic abuse, homelessness and trauma

Consider the post-traumatic symptoms expressed and displayed by the woman in the case study below, who suffered extreme domestic abuse, including rape. In addition, consider the difficulties this woman might have giving a statement for criminal conviction, and in daily self-care and housing arrangements. Think about the impact of trauma described previously. Does she meet the eligibility criteria for safeguarding?

■ My partner beat and raped me. I tried to escape by climbing out of the upstairs window, but he got a cord and pulled it around my neck, dragging me back into the room. I was choking and afraid, my heart was beating fast and a taste of bile came into my throat. I grabbed for the phone but he kicked it away and stamped on it; the shards of glass glistened on the carpet and I could see part of my face in one – it was shattered and broken. I could hear his son crying in the next room. We bought our house together in the days when it was rosy; back then I didn't realise the reasons why his wife had left him and was too afraid to take her son. I was proud of my first house, my friends were there, family nearby and it was home. A home shattered by meals thrown at me for not being good enough, drunken rape that lasted hours as he became increasingly angry with me for not being good enough to make his penis hard. I tried to escape and he dragged me back up the stairs by my hair, pulling handfuls of hair out as I banged up each step. He ripped my clothes and said that he would rather kill me than see me leave, and he punched into my face. The blood felt warm and comforting to some degree and I watched it drip onto the new carpets that we had bought. I decided to placate him and tell him it would all be alright, we could try again. He began to calm down after a while and I made a run for the door. I lost one shoe on the way. He started to chase me and I stumbled, but I managed to get away.

Walking the three miles in the freezing cold with bruises all down my face from his punches, a sore throat from the cord around my neck, hair missing and bare skin showing where my clothing had ripped, I was too afraid to go to the police. I couldn't deal with that, and anyway I would have felt bad. That's how ingrained it was that I was to blame. The police stopped me and asked if I was alright and I said yes and walked on. I got to my friend's house and she was out. Her partner heard my tale and decided it was a good time to have sex with me. I became pregnant and homeless, wandering the streets, afraid to stop in case I was at risk from others. I was terrified of everything. I couldn't sleep, I couldn't eat, I couldn't tell anyone, I felt so ashamed.

He, my friend's partner, offered that I could stay at his house for a week or two as long as I got a termination of the pregnancy. I went to hospital alone and left alone haemorrhaging and homeless once again. I went to the local pub disorientated and confused and I collapsed, waking up in hospital, but it wasn't long before they discharged me. I became anaemic from constant blood loss, very tired and very distressed. I was walking into gambling clubs, casinos and strip clubs, anywhere that was warm and had lights. I sat by supermarket air vents that blew hot air outside and sometimes I had to ask if people had money for me. I hated this but my partner had made me leave my job to look after his son, so they told me that I was not eligible for benefits. Without a fixed address, it seemed as though I wasn't eligible for anything.

Sat in cold doorways struggling to stay clean, warm and fed, I could see the looks on people's faces as they passed. 'She must be on drugs', they said. 'Look at how thin and pale she is.' I wasn't taking drugs, but would you really blame me for wanting a bit of escapism? 'She could just go to the refuge', they said. 'It's her choice', but they didn't know that I was afraid of the people in the refuges. I had a job, a house, a career and an education and I made judgements about who 'they' were. In my mind, 'they' were something different from me, this didn't happen to people like me, I was just weak. I should have been stronger.

The people passed by me on the streets and threw things at me, belittling me and reinforcing the things that he had said about me being rubbish, incapable and dependent. I often put my head in my hands and wished that he had strangled me to death.

I finally got the courage to go to services for help and they gave me a food package, but the next day there was none left. They told me that I needed to make appointments, but I had nowhere to write them down. I didn't know the month, let alone the day of the week or time, and my memory didn't seem to be working any more. They blamed me for missing appointments and they closed the case. I went to housing and they offered me a flat in a very rough area away from everyone that I once knew. I went to look at the flat and on the back of the door there were seven locks, nails all down the walls and graffiti. The smell in the flat was appalling and through the walls I could hear the neighbours arguing. This was my identity, my worth now: fear, dirt, locks, bars on the windows and aggression. I was trapped in something that felt like hell, with no way out. I shivered, remembering the last attack that I experienced and the sounds that my neighbours might have heard, and I told the housing man that I was sorry but I could not accept the property. I was more afraid of that lifestyle than being frozen in the wilderness of homelessness. 'You can't really be homeless' he said, 'cos you only get one chance'.

Battered and bruised, rejected by everyone, with my trust for human kindness shattered, I found myself crying, or shouting whenever I interacted with people. They said that I had no diagnosable mental illness, it's just behavioural, and there was no treatment that they could offer me for that. I eventually stumbled through the doors of a strip club and they gave me a job and a shared house to live in. I can't tell you the rest just now, but I escaped two years later and have never mentioned it until now.

I hear them in the services – they assess me now, and they say she was homeless and became a prostitute. They talk about a person that I don't identify with and I don't understand. They tell me that I have dissociative seizures, but I am not really sure what it's all about and they say that I can have six weeks of counselling. Six weeks of counselling will only open up wounds – who is then going to help me heal them? I am not mad, I am not bad and I was never this sad. None of this is me, I am someone who bought their own house, had a job, friends and a family – all the rest was just surviving.

For this person, family relationships had broken down due to domestic abuse and her abuser isolated her from others. Real friendships were difficult to maintain among the jealousy and intimidation. Once homeless, all contact with significant people was lost. This social isolation, lack of meaningful contact, lowered self-esteem and the traumatic experiences impacted on the brain in terms of trauma, exacerbating and reinforcing the original traumatic experiences. She once again went into survival mode and the brain shut down the ability to plan, prepare, self-care and organise in favour of creating the defence against attack, heightening stimulus responses. She talks of the sensations, smells, sounds and sights, indicating that she was experiencing survival mechanisms. She refers to her inability to maintain information and her difficulty with recall. Her ability to trust others has become affected and self-esteem is low, making her vulnerable.

The consequences of the traumatic events in a person's life result in the person trying to avoid any stimulus associated with the trauma. In this case, the locks on the door, bars at the windows and shouting may have replicated the feeling of abuse experienced. The person fled without gaining accommodation and was further blamed for the effects of trauma. These things were outside her control as her brain had decided that survival mode was required.

The clinical definition of trauma describes the persistent symptoms of increased arousal, being overly alert to sensory stimulus indicating danger and having problems sleeping, controlling anger and organising things. This results in significant impairment of occupational and social functioning. The emotional impact of trauma can create the mistrust of people and lack of motivation and has a huge effect on a person's self-esteem and self-belief.

Safeguarding provides the care and support around a person to prevent the need for future services, to maintain physical and mental wellbeing. In the case example, domestic violence was the immediate cause of homelessness. The person became socially isolated as a result of the domestic abuse, had little or no access to funds, no control over bills, mortgage or tenancy agreements, and therefore references were problematic. The National Alliance to End Homelessness (2017) identifies that on a single night in January 2016 12 per cent of the overall homeless population, making up to 70,000 people, reported having experienced domestic violence at some point. It cites that research in New York has identified that one in five families experience domestic violence in the five years before entering a homeless shelter, and 88 per cent reported that the domestic abuse significantly contributed to their homelessness. Statutory homeless statistics show that domestic violence is consistently reported as the main reason for loss of last settled home for around 13 per cent of the people applying for accommodation as a homeless person. One study found that domestic violence accounted for as much as 30 per cent of all those accepted as homeless within one large local authority (Davis 2008). Supporting the person suffering sexual or domestic violence early may prevent long-term physical, psychological and financial difficulties.

The family fleeing domestic abuse is suffering trauma; they have been attacked, controlled and violated. They leave behind all their possessions, family connections and support and must try to settle in a new area. The lack of support networks, the move from the family home to a refuge and/or temporary accommodation and the lack of services to support the family can exacerbate the feelings of worthlessness and trauma. The loss of the relationship, home and possessions adds to the difficulty of resettling. People become concerned that the perpetrator may find them when in permanent accommodation, leading to periods of homelessness and disruption (Jones, Pleace and Quilgars 2002).

In this case study, the sexual abuse, domestic abuse and resulting trauma exacerbated difficulties in finding suitable housing. It is clear that the woman was being held accountable for reactions that are the body's natural responses to protect and keep a person safe. Discrimination occurs when errant judgements about worthiness are assigned to differentiate between those accepted as 'homeless' and those seen as 'intentionally homeless' and therefore not offered another housing opportunity. Consider the support, multi-agency responses and coordination of services that might be required to ensure that there is 'social justice' for this person who all too frequently is rejected as undeserving. What is the safeguarding role here and what is the social work role?

Psychological abuse

The Care Act 2014 statutory guidance identifies psychological abuse as including:

- emotional abuse

- threats of harm or abandonment

- deprivation of contact

- humiliation

- blaming

- controlling

- intimidation

- coercion

- harassment

- verbal abuse

- cyberbullying

- isolation

- unreasonable and unjustified withdrawal of services or supportive networks.

Psychological abuse and trauma

The impact of psychological abuse can be significant and lead to long-term mental ill-health. In my experience, psychological abuse tends to be part of a referral with other forms of abuse; however, it is even rarer to see a safeguarding referral for psychological abuse on its own. This may be because where there is psychological abuse there is a likelihood of other forms of abuse, or it may be that psychological abuse is not recognised.

Mary, a 65-year-old woman who had a stroke some years previously, described how she felt:

> I thought that domestic violence was about people hitting you. I wouldn't have considered that my miserable existence was called domestic abuse. I was married to him for 32 years and he was fine until I had my stroke. He didn't want to help me, he would call me stupid and tell me that I was losing my mind; he would do things, or move things, to make me think that I was too.

I would ask him to get some shopping and I needed certain things because of my health issues. He would not buy food that I could eat and would just cook for himself. I would hurt myself trying to get something that I could eat. I cut myself, burnt myself, but he never moved to help. He said that he would find someone capable of having a relationship with, unlike me. He wouldn't help me to dress and wouldn't let me call someone to come and help, so I often just sat day and night in my wheelchair. My neighbours worried, but I didn't want to get him in trouble. It was my fault I had become unable to look after him the way that I always had.

Mary was blaming herself for her disability and was becoming extremely depressed; she eventually confided in a neighbour, who contacted social services. Mary was involved in a meeting and said that she would like to leave her husband and move into more suitable accommodation with support. Mary requested that things be put in place so that she didn't have to see her husband, or speak with him again. Family, friends, social services and domestic abuse services supported her to achieve her goals. Mary is now divorced, has her own money and lives in her own accommodation with support. Carers help Mary to dress and prepare food and she has made friends where she lives. Mary says that she feels sad that her marriage ended; she believed in her vows and wanted to remain until death parted them. Mary went on to say, 'I think that it might have been my death that parted us, sooner rather than later, if Joan, my neighbour, had not helped me.'

Modern slavery

The Care Act 2014 statutory guidance identifies modern slavery as encompassing:

- slavery

- human trafficking

- forced labour and domestic servitude

- traffickers and slave masters using whatever means they have at their disposal to coerce, deceive and force individuals into a life of abuse, servitude and inhumane treatment.

People who have limited opportunities, a lack of education and unstable social or political backgrounds, people from war-torn countries or those displaced as a result of war, and people who are vulnerable, such as those with learning disabilities, autism or mental ill-health, can be coaxed into situations where they are trafficked and used as slaves. The Modern Slavery Act 2015 makes provisions for victims and creates a defence for those who commit an offence as a direct consequence of their slavery, meaning that they will not be treated as criminals by the justice system. Modern slavery is defined as the recruitment, movement, harbouring or receiving of children, women or men through the use of force, coercion and abuse of vulnerability, deception or other means for the purpose of exploitation. It is a crime under the Modern Slavery Act 2015 and includes holding a person in a position of slavery, servitude and forced or compulsory labour, or facilitating their travel with the intention of exploiting them soon after.

Some common occupations that can be involved in modern slavery include but are not exclusive to:

- nail bars

- hand car washes

- tarmacking/block paving

- fast-food, take-aways, restaurants

- care work

- sex industry

- food packing

- hospitality.

There are some common signs:

- *Isolation* – victims may rarely be allowed to travel on their own, seem under the control and influence of others, rarely interact or appear unfamiliar with their neighbourhood or where they work.

- *Poor living conditions* – victims may be living in dirty, cramped or overcrowded accommodation and/or living and working at the same address.

- *Physical appearance* – victims may show signs of physical or psychological abuse, look malnourished or unkempt, or appear withdrawn.

- *Few or no personal effects* – victims may have no identification documents, have few personal possessions and always wear the same clothes, day in, day out. What clothes they do wear may not be suitable for their work.

- *Restricted freedom of movement* – victims have little opportunity to move freely and may have had their travel documents retained, such as passports.

- *Unusual travel times* – victims may be dropped off and collected for work on a regular basis either very early or late at night.

- *Reluctant to seek help* – victims may avoid eye contact, appear frightened or hesitant to talk to strangers and fear law enforcers for many reasons, such as not knowing who to trust or where to get help, fear of deportation and fear of violence to them or their family.

Properties may have bars at the windows, or permanent coverings, for example curtains or blinds may always be shut. There might be closed-circuit TV over entrances and exits. The letterbox may be sealed to prevent use, and power lines may be tacked from other properties or sources. There may be overcrowding issues at the property, and access to certain rooms may be blocked. Properties are badly cared for and could be sublet. People within the property may wear unsuitable clothing for the weather or for the job that they say they are doing.

Modern slavery and trauma

People being trafficked are promised better things, a better life, job and housing prospects where these may seem particularly difficult. The terrible realisation that they have been taken as a slave and the abuse suffered as a result add to any previous traumas experienced. This may cause a number of mental and physical health problems.

Salway and Such (2017) conducted research into slavery and public health and identified that:

Modern slavery is a human rights violation and has severe consequences for the health and wellbeing of survivors. It is an exploitative crime that impacts on physical and mental health and has public health implications. The role of public health in addressing modern slavery has not been fully articulated in the UK.

In developing a public health response to slavery they identified the four Ps:

- *Prevention* – this covers the recognition and reporting of slavery, the development of community awareness and capacity to resist situations that give rise to slavery, and changing global systems and policies to reduce the demand for the supply of exploited labour. In the widest sense, this is prevention of the impact of trauma, such as appropriate treatment for mental ill-health as well as physical health symptoms.

- *Protection* – access to appropriate care and security, with health and social care responses. This includes victim-centred approaches, and breaking down the stigma and mistrust of law enforcement and statutory services.

- *Prosecution* – having access to special measures in court, and supporting the health and communication needs of the victim to enable this.

- *Partnership* – the coordinated multi-agency approach.

Discriminatory abuse

The Care Act 2014 statutory guidance describes discriminatory abuse as including forms of harassment, slurs or similar treatment because of race, gender and gender identity, age, disability, sexual orientation and religion.

Read *Discrimination: Your Rights* (Gov.uk 2018) for further information.

Hate/mate crime

Hate crime is a crime committed against someone because of their gender, disability, identity, race, religion, belief or sexual orientation.

Hate crimes can include:

- threatening behaviour

- assault

- robbery

- damage to property

- inciting others to commit hate crimes

- harassment.

Mate crime is when someone pretends to be friendly with a person and purports to be their friend. They select a person deliberately because they have a disability or mental ill-health, or they may be old and frail or have substance misuse problems. People chosen for mate crimes are often quite socially isolated and keen to develop friendships. Unfortunately, the person initiating the friendship has no intention of being a friend, they just want to abuse and exploit the person. The person who is subject to abuse and exploitation may be willing to accept more than most would in the pursuit of friendship, and many observers may perceive the relationship as friendly. Family and professionals may be happy for the person to have friends and may encourage the relationships without questioning the imbalances.

Some potential indicators may be:

- bills not being paid, lack of money, loss of possessions

- will changes or lasting power of attorney/court appointed deputyships drawn up under suspicious circumstances

- new people visiting

- increased noise and rubbish, more people at the person's home

- changes in behaviour and routine

- secret mobile phone or internet use

- disengaging from existing friendships and family contact.

Housing providers are in a good position to spot and report any anti-social behaviour that could potentially be identified as hate or mate crime (Parry 2013).

Discriminatory abuse and trauma

Targeted hate and mate crime can have a profound effect on the person and their family. The person may become socially isolated, afraid to go out, afraid of making friends and even afraid of social media connections. Trauma associated with the hate and mate crime will affect the person's ability to manage daily tasks and their confidence in social situations. Therapeutic support may be required.

Organisational abuse (formerly known as institutional abuse)

The Care Act (2014) statutory guidance identifies organisational abuse as including:

> Neglect and poor care practice within an institution, or specific care setting such as a hospital or care home, for example, or in relation to care provided in one's own home. This may range from one-off incidents to on-going ill-treatment. It can be through neglect or poor professional practice as a result of the structure, policies, processes and practices within an organisation. (Section 14.17)

Incidents of abuse may be one-off or multiple, and affect one person or more. Professionals and others should look beyond single incidents or individuals to identify patterns of harm, just as the clinical commissioning group, as the regulator of service quality, does when it looks at the quality of care in health and care services. Repeated instances of poor care may be an indication of more serious problems and of what we now describe as organisational abuse. In order to see these patterns, it is important that information is recorded and appropriately shared.

Organisational abuse and trauma

The person moving into residential care and the family of that person place a lot of trust in the fact that the family member will at least be safe and well cared for. When this trust is broken, all parties feel the impact. Look for signs of the impact of abuse on the person and consider this in carers' assessments too.

Neglect and acts of omission

The Care Act 2014 statutory guidance identifies neglect and acts of omission as including:

- ignoring medical, emotional or physical care needs

- failure to provide access to appropriate health, care and support or educational services

- the withholding of the necessities of life, such as medication, adequate nutrition and heating.

Neglect and trauma

As with all other forms of abuse, neglect can have a serious impact on a person's mental and physical wellbeing. Look for signs of trauma.

KEY POINTS

It is very important to recognise the indicators of abuse and neglect to report and address the concerns. It is equally important to recognise the impact of the abuse and neglect on the person and continue looking for signs of distress or trauma. To maintain wellbeing, we must provide support as soon as possible to prevent deterioration of mental and eventually physical wellbeing, as a result of trauma. This will not only support the individual, but also contribute to lessening the need for future services. Early identification of trauma will assist us in lessening the impact and therefore the associated trauma responses that leave a person struggling to cope, resulting in, for example, self-neglect, hoarding, sleeplessness, anxiety, homelessness, flashbacks, poor eating habits, poor memory, substance misuse or alcohol abuse, and other associated difficulties.

A coordinated psychology and safeguarding response to trauma, addressing any co-morbid mental health issues, will prevent deterioration of the person's wellbeing and the need for more crisis-driven services in the future.

CHAPTER 4

Capacity, Consent and Information Sharing

Can I make a safeguarding referral when the person is capacitated and does not consent?

Any initial discussions or enquiries about safeguarding matters should involve the person and any appropriate representative, unless it is clear that this would pose further risk to the person. Part of ensuring that the person is fully involved in the whole process is to give them information and advice about what they can expect, what can happen and what choices they have, and to discuss their desired outcomes and expectations. This is an ideal time to talk with the person about the rights that they have to be involved in the process and to have the same access to civil and criminal redress. Communication should be clear and not full of jargon; it should describe the care and support that could be considered and the benefits of any safeguarding intervention.

The initial consent to share information for safeguarding purposes should be discussed with the person unless there are lawful reasons to share the information anyway. The General Data Protection Regulation (GDPR) identifies that we must seek explicit consent to share data unless we have a lawful basis to share without the person's consent (Information Commissioner's Office 2018). To have explicit consent you must ensure that you:

- have checked that consent is the most lawful basis for processing
- have made the request for consent prominent and separate from your terms and conditions
- do not use pre-ticked boxes or any other type of default consent

- use clear and plain language that is easy to understand

- specify why you want the data and what you are going to do with it. This means that on first meeting, and whenever appropriate, people using your services and their carers will have to be reminded that you can share information where there is reason to suspect a crime (abuse or neglect), there is reason to suspect coercive or controlling behaviours and therefore not autonomous informed consent, if the person's mental health deteriorates warranting assessment under the Mental Health Act or where it is in the public interest to do so (explicit risk to others)

- give the person options to consent separately to different issues

- identify people with whom the information will be shared

- tell people that they can withdraw consent at any time during the process

- make people aware that they can refuse consent without detriment when capacitated to do so and there are no other lawful considerations

- do not make consent a precondition of a service

- remember that consent applies to people over the age of 16, although the courts may consider the capacity of those younger who appear to understand enough to make their own decision

- record when and how you got consent

- record what the person was told and what they said every time consent is required

- regularly review consent to check that there are no changes

- have processes in place to refresh consent

- make it easy for people to withdraw consent and act on this as soon as you can.

Please note that the GDPR specifically bans pre-ticked consent options. The GDPR also identifies that consent is only valid if you can offer a person a real choice and control over how you use their data, and want to build their trust and engagement. If you cannot offer genuine choice, consent is not appropriate. If you would still use the data without consent, asking for consent is misleading and inherently unfair. If you are using the data then you must have a lawful basis. Public authorities and people in a position of power should avoid relying on consent, and unless they can demonstrate that it is freely given, they must use other lawful reasons for using the person's data (Information Commissioner's Office 2018).

The lawful reason for using the data is when you are obliged to process the personal data to comply with the law. For example, the Care Act states that we have a duty to share information. Section 14.69 of the statutory guidance identifies that:

> When an employer is aware of abuse or neglect in their organisation, then they are under a duty to correct this and protect the adult from harm as soon as possible and inform the local authority, CQC [Care Quality Commission] and CCG [clinical commissioning group] where the latter is the commissioner. Where a local authority has reasonable cause to suspect that an adult may be experiencing or at risk of abuse or neglect, then it is still under a duty to make (or cause to be made) whatever enquiries it thinks necessary to decide what if any action needs to be taken and by whom. The local authority may well be reassured by the employer's response so that no further action is required. However, a local authority would have to satisfy itself that an employer's response has been sufficient to deal with the safeguarding issue and, if not, to undertake any enquiry of its own and any appropriate follow up action (for example, referral to CQC, professional regulators).

In addition to this, Section 45 of the Care Act 2014 identifies that:

> (1) If an SAB [safeguarding adults board] requests a person to supply information to it, or to some other person specified in the request, the person to whom the request is made must comply with the request if –
>
> (a) conditions 1 and 2 are met, and
>
> (b) condition 3 or 4 is met.
>
> (2) Condition 1 is that the request is made for the purpose of enabling or assisting the SAB to exercise its functions.

(3) Condition 2 is that the request is made to a person whose functions or activities the SAB considers to be such that the person is likely to have information relevant to the exercise of a function by the SAB.

(4) Condition 3 is that the information relates to –

(a) the person to whom the request is made,

(b) a function or activity of that person, or

(c) a person in respect of whom that person exercises a function or engages in an activity.

(5) Condition 4 is that the information –

(a) is information requested by the SAB from a person to whom information was supplied in compliance with another request under this section, and

(b) is the same as, or is derived from, information so supplied.

(6) Information may be used by the SAB, or other person to whom it is supplied under subsection (1), only for the purpose of enabling or assisting the SAB to exercise its functions.

In other words, where there is reason to suspect abuse or neglect, then you must conduct enquiries, as a duty under Section 42 of the Care Act 2014, and if you know that this information is going to be shared for this purpose then you should not seek consent, but inform the person what information will be shared, with whom and for what purpose (see the ten steps later in this chapter). The person/family/carers should have already been made aware of this during former assessments or meetings and this should not come as a surprise. Action taken for the individual (not wider safeguarding matters) can only be made with informed consent, or where the person lacks capacity to make that particular decision at that specific time (assessed and recorded) in their best interests (without being risk averse). The response to the sharing of information is different from the assessment to determine whether information should be shared.

You must determine a reliable basis for sharing the information without consent. You must therefore consider whether:

- the legislation used is appropriate to the situation

- you have considered your responsibility to protect the individual's interests

- you have conducted an assessment of the situation and recorded justification for the sharing of information

- you have identified relevant aspects of legislation or guidance relevant to the situation

- you have checked that there is not a less intrusive way that would achieve the same result

- you are confident that on balance the person's autonomy and individual interests do not override (you may need to consider all the potential capacity assessments required to determine this)

- you have tried to reduce the impact on the person of sharing the data.

In addition to the general guidance within the Care Act 2014 and statutory guidance, you can also consider other more reliable and explicit aspects of the law and our duties to protect the public, our duties to protect those who do not/cannot provide informed consent due to coercion, intimidation, impairment of the functioning of the brain or mind, or where there is criminal behaviour. The information sharing must be:

- necessary – if you can address concerns without sharing personal data then you have no lawful grounds for sharing without consent

- documented to identify the lawful purpose of sharing data without consent.

It is important to identify the law or appropriate source of advice or guidance that clearly sets out your obligation. In all situations, please remember the ethics involved in information sharing and actions taken. The sharing of information should be to prevent harm and should not cause further harm or distress to an individual. All information shared must be proportionate to the situation presented to address lawfully the concerns. Information should therefore be specific to the safeguarding circumstances and there should be justification about why the sharing of information was appropriate and proportionate.

Please consider the ten steps to information sharing set out in Figure 4.1 and the text below.

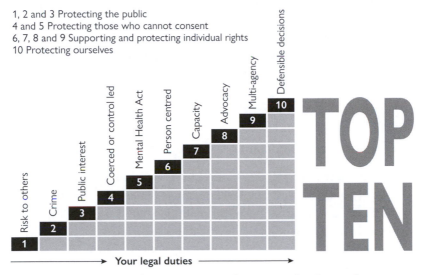

1, 2 and 3 Protecting the public
4 and 5 Protecting those who cannot consent
6, 7, 8 and 9 Supporting and protecting individual rights
10 Protecting ourselves

Figure 4.1: The ten steps to information sharing and decision making in safeguarding adults

Step 1

You do not need consent to share relevant information with relevant people, in a proportionate manner, where there is reasonable suspicion of *a risk to others*. The safeguarding enquiry will need to consider whether there are any children at risk, other adults who have care and support needs at risk, or whether the person is in a care and support role and could pose a risk to others (Social Care Institute for Excellence 2018).

Step 2

You do not need consent to share relevant information with relevant people, in a proportionate manner, where there is reasonable suspicion of *a crime*. You can find further guidance relating to disclosure of information and potential crime in Sections 17A and 115 of the Crime and Disorder Act 1998.

Step 3

You do not need consent to share relevant information with relevant people, in a proportionate manner, where it is in the *public interest* to do so. This could include public health risks such as fire, vermin and toxic or explosive substances. The Caldicott Guardian website provides further guidance within its *Information Governance Review* (Department of Health 2013).

Step 4

The cross-government definition of domestic violence and abuse is:

> Any incident or pattern of incidents of controlling, coercive, threatening behaviour, violence or abuse between those aged 16 or over who are, or have been, intimate partners or family members regardless of gender or sexuality. The abuse can encompass, but is not limited to:
>
> - psychological
>
> - physical
>
> - sexual
>
> - financial
>
> - emotional.
>
> Controlling behaviour is a range of acts designed to make a person subordinate and/or dependent by isolating them from other sources of support, exploiting their resources and capacities for personal gain, depriving them of the means needed for independence, resistance and escape. Coercive behaviour is an act or pattern of acts of threat, assault, humiliation, intimidation or other abuse used to harm, punish or frighten the victim. (Home Office 2015)

In safeguarding situations where a family member is providing the care and support and there is reason to suspect that they may be coercing or controlling the person who has care and support needs, the enquiry must rule out coercive and controlling behaviour. The person may be too threatened or intimidated to access care and support. This falls under Section 76 of the Serious Crime Act 2015, which identifies coercive and controlling behaviour as a crime.

A capacitated person can make autonomous decisions; however, where a decision may be influenced by a domestic abuse situation, it cannot be said to be an autonomous decision, and therefore any enquiry must consider that a person may be stating that they do not consent to actions due to the fear or threat of harm. You therefore do not need consent to share relevant information with relevant people where there is reasonable suspicion of coercive or controlling behaviours.

Step 5

You do not need consent to share relevant information with relevant people where the person's decision making may be affected by severe mental ill-health, requiring an assessment under the Mental Health Act 1983. If a person is deemed to be at serious risk of harming themselves or others, an assessment will take place. The police have powers to enter a person's home for this purpose under Section 135 and can take a person to a place of safety from a public space under Section 136. Relatives or professionals can ask for a Mental Health Act assessment where there are significant concerns about a person's mental health and how this affects their ability to make use of any help, support, advice or guidance offered. An enquiry should rule out potential mental ill-health affecting the person's ability to accept care, services or treatment.

Step 6

After the duty to protect the public and our ability to protect those who cannot consent have been addressed, we must consider the identity, culture, history, rights, needs, wishes, expectations and outcomes that the person wishes as a result of safeguarding. After ruling out the first five steps, all decisions should be made with the person central to the decision making. The capacity of the person to make each decision should be considered. There is an assumption of capacity; however, where unwise decisions are being made and there are circumstances that suggest questionable judgement, a capacity assessment should be conducted, in an open and honest fashion. If the person has capacity to make decisions and does not consent to a course of action relating to themselves, or information to be shared about themselves, then they should have their wishes respected.

Step 7

Safeguarding Adults (Association of Directors of Adult Social Services 2005, p.4) states, 'Everyone has a right to follow a course of action that others judge to be unwise or eccentric, including one which may lead to them being abused.' However, it goes on to state, 'Where a person chooses to live with a risk of abuse the safeguarding (care and support) plan should include access to services that help minimise the risk.' Section 11 of the Care Act 2014 builds on this, suggesting that an assessment of need and safeguarding arrangements can be considered even without the compliance of the person concerned should they lack capacity to make the decision and it is deemed to be in their best interests, or where significant risk of abuse or neglect may be identified.

If a person does not have capacity to make a decision (they don't understand sufficiently the aspects of the decision identified in the capacity assessment), they cannot consent to a course of action. If care, services or treatment is given without assessing capacity and determining that it is in the best interests of the person, then this may not be defensible. Please ensure that if you doubt a person's capacity to make a decision you assess and record their ability using the guidance below, if you are the person requiring consent to carry out care, services or treatment. Every occasion where a professional is offering care, services or treatment to an individual and they are concerned that the person does not understand what is being offered, the professional must assess the capacity of that person to consent or decline. The professional offering the care services or treatment understands the course of action being offered and therefore is best placed to determine whether the person understands it too.

Any safeguarding enquiry may have a variety of agencies involved in the care and support of the person and their family. The alerts or concerns must be considered throughout enquiries and responses to those concerns coordinated. There will be many occasions where the person's capacity to consent to a course of action may also require assessment, by a variety of agencies for a variety of topics. This will need action planning and coordinating throughout the enquiry process.

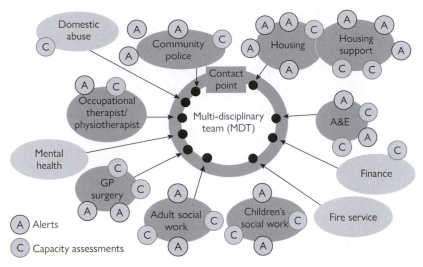

Figure 4.2: The multi-agency coordination of capacity assessments

Figure 4.2 demonstrates an example of the number of agencies involved, the number of capacity assessments required by each agency and the need to coordinate these assessments via safeguarding arrangements.

MENTAL CAPACITY ACT 2005

The Act sets out a single, clear, two-stage test for assessing where a person lacks capacity to take a particular decision at a particular time.

- Stage 1 – Is there an impairment of, or disturbance in, the functioning of the person's mind or brain? It does not matter if this is permanent or temporary.

- Stage 2 – Is the impairment sufficient to cause the person to be unable to make that particular decision at the relevant time?

A person is unable to make a decision if they cannot:

- understand the information relevant to the decision to be made

- retain that information for long enough for the decision to be made

- use or weigh that information as part of the decision-making process

- communicate their decision.

BEST INTERESTS CHECKLIST

The following factors need to be taken into account when determining if what is being done is in that person's best interests. The Mental Capacity Act Code of Practice also contains a best interests checklist.

1. Consider all relevant circumstances.

---

2. Determine if the decision can be put off until the person regains capacity.

3. Permit and encourage participation, for example find appropriate means of communication or use other people to help the person participate.

4. Give special considerations for life-sustaining treatment.

5. Consider the person's wishes, feelings, beliefs and values.

6. Take into account the views of other people.

7. Take into account the view of an IMCA, if appointed.

8. Consider if there is a less restrictive alternative or intervention that is in the person's best interest.

Step 8

Under Section 68 of the Care Act 2014 the local authority must provide an independent advocate where appropriate family support is not available and the person would have substantial difficulty being involved in the process. Substantial difficulty is described as difficulty in one or more of the following:

- Understanding relevant information.

- Retaining that information.

- Using or weighing that information as part of the process of being involved.

- Communicating the individual's views, wishes or feelings (whether by talking, using sign language or any other means).

This means that advocacy must be available throughout the safeguarding process.

Step 9

The local authority must consider who should be involved in the safeguarding process. This may include agencies currently involved and agencies which could provide relevant information.

Step 10
Defensible decision making

- Person centred:
  - Record what the person said that led you to make this decision (the 'I' statements).
  - Record the person's actions that led you to make this decision (observations).
  - Summarise information about the person that led you to make this decision (history).
  - Record information, advice, guidance and support offered, to enable and empower the person to make this decision.

- Legislation used:
  - Record legislation used.
  - Record models, methods or theories used.
  - Record policies or procedures used.
  - Record research used that led you to make this decision.

- Proportionate:
  - Record what was ruled out and why.
  - Record why you considered this to be the least intrusive and the least restrictive intervention.
  - Record why you believed this intervention to be a proportionate response.

Defensible decision making always follows the word 'because' and is the justification for the level, extent and course of action taken. I chose this action because... I ruled this out because... What you have ruled out in an enquiry is as important as what you have chosen. Many enquiries begin with a number of hypotheses to explore through evidence, so it is important that these considerations are recorded and transparent.

The information may need to be shared with others where there is reasonable suspicion of abuse or neglect and the person lacks capacity to make the decision (and it is in their best interests to share the information), where there is a risk to others, or public interest issues, where there is a potential crime, where the person may be suffering domestic abuse and there is reason to suspect coercive or controlling behaviours, or when the person requires statutory assessment under the Mental Health Act 1983. The purpose of an enquiry is to consider the person's capacity to make a variety of decisions and the impact of abuse on the person and their decision making, to provide support and guidance, to identify the gaps in knowledge and to make enquiries to fill those gaps.

The alleged perpetrator has a right to know that allegations have been made against them and public law means that we must act without bias, enabling the person to set out their case. If it is deemed to be a risk to the person or others for information to be shared with the potential perpetrator, this must be justified and recorded.

KEY POINT

Do not be afraid of sharing information for safeguarding purposes – there is more concern about the lack of information sharing. The GDPR clarifies that we should not be seeking consent to share information if we are going to share it anyway. We should only seek consent where there is no other lawful reason to share the information. There are numerous reasons to share information cited within law, including the duty to share information for safeguarding purposes under the Care Act 2014. If we do seek consent, we must try to help the person understand what information will be shared and why.

In training I often ask, 'What is consent for safeguarding? What does this mean?' I think that this is key. If you are doing a capacity assessment about whether a person has the capacity to consent to safeguarding, what are you going to ask the person? You are faced with someone who has care and support needs and there is reasonable suspicion of abuse. You are asked by your manager to go and assess this person's capacity to consent to safeguarding. Plan your capacity assessment.

Is consent for safeguarding consent to share information with the local authority? Is consent the consent to share information with the police? Is it to provide safeguarding responses such as specific care, support and services, or is it consent to assess? We need to be more specific about what we need consent for. It is only those who do not understand the time and issue-specific nature of capacity and consent, safeguarding practice or the 'Making Safeguarding Personal' agenda that would seek a broad and sweeping response to a very personal and specific course of action, based on the person's wishes, values and outcomes. What one person defines as their outcomes to feel safe and well will be different to the next. It is only when the person expresses their specific outcomes that we can determine what safeguarding means to them, and the enquiry process will coordinate any capacity assessments required in relation to each desired outcome when necessary.

In some situations, we may not need consent to share information with the local authority, because there are, for example, other people at risk. We may not need consent to share information where there is reasonable suspicion of a crime; however, we would need consent in relation to any actions relating to a person's needs, unless they are assessed as lacking capacity to make a particular decision and a best interest decision is therefore made. There are too many potential variables to know or describe what safeguarding means prior to initial enquiries taking place about risk to others, potential crime, capacity in relation to each aspect of safeguarding requiring consent, potential for domestic abuse and coercive and controlling behaviours, or whether the person's mental health is so severely affected that they require detention and assessment under the Mental Health Act.

CHAPTER 5

Safeguarding Eligibility Criteria

The three-part test

The eligibility criteria are a three-part test where to be eligible for safeguarding a person must:

- have needs for care and support (does not need to be eligible for local authority services)

- be experiencing or at risk of abuse and neglect

- as a result of those care and support needs be unable to protect themselves from either the risk of or the experience of abuse or neglect.

This is illustrated in Figure 5.1.

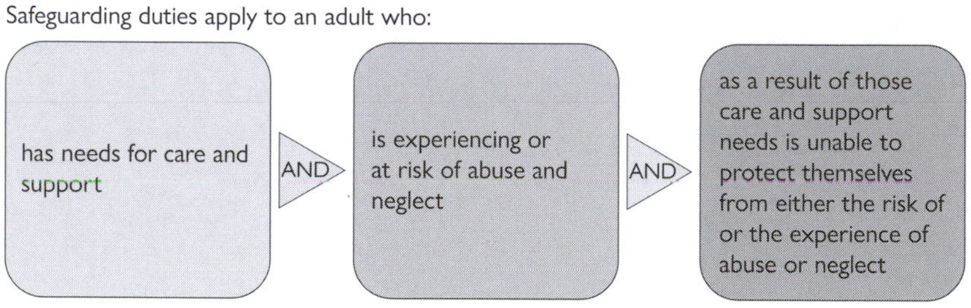

Safeguarding duties apply to an adult who:

| has needs for care and support | AND | is experiencing or at risk of abuse and neglect | AND | as a result of those care and support needs is unable to protect themselves from either the risk of or the experience of abuse or neglect |

Figure 5.1: The three-part eligibility test

The Care Act 2014 guidance tells us that, to achieve these aims, it is necessary to:

- ensure that the roles and responsibilities of individuals and organisations are clearly laid out

- create a strong multi-agency framework for safeguarding

- enable access to mainstream community safety measures

- clarify the interface between safeguarding and quality of service provision.

Who meets these eligibility criteria?

To explore who meets these eligibility criteria we must consider the review of *No Secrets* (Department of Health and Social Care 2000) and the development of the Care Act 2014. Under previous *No Secrets* policy guidance, to be eligible for safeguarding a person must have community care needs, and local authorities interpreted this as the need for social work intervention, applying the criteria of Fair Access to Care as social work eligibility criteria. Fair Access to Care criteria were applied differently in each local authority, and therefore someone with low needs would be eligible in some local authorities, while a person had to have substantial or critical needs in other local authorities to have access to safeguarding. The Law Commission recognised that someone safeguarded in one local authority area may not be safeguarded in another area and deemed this unacceptable (Department of Health 2009). Many serious case reviews highlighted the inadequacies of this system, resulting in vulnerable people being abused, neglected and killed because they did not meet the high thresholds for services.

An example of this was 'Adult A' from Stockport, described as a vulnerable young man whose life was cruelly cut short at the age of 22, murdered by other vulnerable young people. 'Adult A' did not enjoy a stable family life and was looked after by Stockport Local Authority until the age of 21. It was believed that he had a mild learning disability and reports alluded to mental ill-health and potential autism spectrum disorder, although nothing was formally diagnosed. 'Adult A' had difficulty sustaining tenancies and on one occasion was homeless; he became estranged from his family and marginalised within society. Children's services recognised his vulnerability; however, 18 months after children's services' statutory obligations towards him ceased, he was killed. Adult services had identified that he was not eligible for their services and a referral was not made for adult safeguarding.

To prevent this postcode lottery of access to services and the high threshold for safeguarding, the Law Commission recommended that the needs for care and support should be more encompassing than the high eligibility criteria for local authority services. Under *No Secrets*, safeguarding meant that when a person met local authority eligibility criteria they were referred to a safeguarding team, or for safeguarding support. Under the Care Act 2014 'needs for care and support' does not refer to local authority eligibility criteria, but to *any* needs for care and support, and is explicit that local authority eligibility criteria for services do not apply.

In the Law Commission's scoping report (2008) it was identified that, unlike Scotland, England and Wales did not have an existing legal framework for safeguarding adults. The aim of the scoping study was to identify a framework that would identify local authority powers and duties. The requirement to safeguard adults and responsibilities of adult protection were clearly identified within the Law Commission's report on adult social care (Assets.publishing.service.gov.uk 2011). A consultation process informed this document, and the Law Commission defined safeguarding and adult protection, stating:

> Safeguarding relates to the prevention of abuse and has a broad focus that extends to all aspects of a person's general welfare, adult protection refers to investigation and intervention where it is suspected that abuse may have occurred. Safeguarding, considered in this context, is properly part of the general approach to be taken to assessment and the delivery of services. (Assets.publishing.service.gov.uk 2011)

The three-part eligibility criteria relate to safeguarding duties encompassing adult protection and therefore apply to all aspects of prevention as well as protection. Local authorities should consider all safeguarding concerns and determine the level of response required. In the past, adult protection was called safeguarding, but now the definition of safeguarding is considered as all aspects of prevention including the provision of daily care and support. It is only when the person is not safeguarded that *adult protection* is required (safeguarding team or similar coordinated multi-agency response). There is a duty to share information with the local authority for the purpose of safeguarding. The local authority will determine the way forward considering whether the following are required:

- An adult protection response coordinated by the local authority.

- An adult protection response coordinated by health, housing or a relevant profession.

- A social work assessment, review or planned care to maintain wellbeing.

- A professional response by one or more agencies where actions will be requested by the local authority and outcomes will be monitored.

- A safeguarding response to prevent the risk of abuse or neglect. This may be signposting to services, offering advice and guidance or seeking therapeutic support.

The care and support statutory guidance, issued under Section 14.13 of the Care Act 2014, identifies that 'The nature of the intervention and who is best placed to lead will be, in part, determined by the circumstances. For example, where there is poor abusive, neglectful care or practice, then a clinical response may be more appropriate.' This means that while there is a duty to share information with the local authority for safeguarding purposes, the local authority must effectively make enquiries and ask questions to sufficiently establish the risks and gain enough of a picture to triage and assign responsibility for the response. The local authority can therefore cause others to make enquiries on its behalf. The majority of safeguarding cases do not meet eligibility criteria for local authority services; however, safeguarding duties still apply. Other agencies should not impose the impossible burden of managing all safeguarding responses on the local authority.

The responsibility of the local authority falls within the statutory duties identified within the Care Act 2014, including the duty to make enquiries (or cause enquiries to be made), share information, cooperate with others and ensure the wellbeing of the individual. An enquiry may be as simple as a telephone call to the referrer, or as complex as a full police investigation, or a variety of things in between. When asked 'Whose responsibility is it to safeguard?', the answer received in safeguarding training is 'Everyone'. When asked what that means, people say things such as 'Recognising and identifying abuse or neglect and reporting it to the local authority, which would take responsibility for the case and coordinate the response, often via a multi-agency meeting chaired by a safeguarding team member'. Many cases that meet safeguarding eligibility criteria do not require this level of response. Many cases are not in need of social work intervention, and many cases would be better supported by other individuals within other professions. The local authority acts as a signposting service and provides guidance and support in safeguarding cases. The safeguarding response is now clearly defined as everyone's responsibility to not only report, but also to respond. Where safeguarding has failed and cases become adult protection cases, it is very likely that they will meet eligibility for local authority services. The local authority still has a duty to consider safeguarding responses to prevent abuse and neglect from occurring and maintain wellbeing within an ongoing continuum of safeguarding, care and support provision from the low-level cases to the more complex cases. Promotion of preventative measures within community services should form part of any local authority safeguarding advice and guidance.

Section 14.24 of the Care Act 2014 statutory guidance identifies that:

> Adults with care and support needs are potentially less likely to be able to protect themselves from the risk of abuse or neglect. This can include such adults who have capacity to make their own decision. Statutory adult safeguarding duties apply equally to those adults with care and support needs, regardless of whether those needs are being met, regardless of whether the adult lacks mental capacity or not and regardless of setting.

The threshold for safeguarding adults therefore must be significantly lower than that required for adult protection.

Eligibility criteria case examples

■ Case study 1

Frieda generally has good health and maintains an independent life. Frieda rarely has tonic-clonic seizures, but a couple of days ago she suffered a significant seizure. She was admitted to hospital, as it was taking some time for her to recover from her seizure. The nurses have been very busy and Frieda was left without food or drink for 48 hours. A new shift of nurses arrived and noted that Frieda was severely dehydrated.

Does Frieda meet eligibility criteria for safeguarding?

Yes, Frieda has needs for care and support, and as a result of her care and support needs she cannot protect herself from abuse or neglect.

Does the case meet eligibility criteria for adult protection?

Yes, initial enquiries need to be conducted to determine whether anyone else has been affected, why this occurred and why it was not picked up sooner. It may be appropriate for a clinically trained person to conduct the enquiry as long as they are independent from the services provided by the hospital or ward. Information regarding outcomes should be shared with the local authority.

Does Frieda meet eligibility criteria for social work?

There is limited information and the enquiries/social work assessment should determine whether Frieda meets social work eligibility criteria. On the surface, it sounds unlikely that Frieda requires social work intervention.

■ Case study 2

John lives independently within the community. John has no identified health or social care needs, but he was admitted to hospital following a fall at home. Housing identified that John had a severe hoarding problem, significant risk of fire had been identified by the fire service and this was not the first time that John had fallen causing items to fall on top of him.

Does John meet eligibility criteria for safeguarding?

There is reason to believe that John has care and support needs because of his hoarding behaviours causing risk to himself and others. The enquiry will establish whether John has capacity to make decisions with regard to tenancy, health and wellbeing and support. The enquiry will determine when and why John began hoarding. A multi-agency plan to prevent the deterioration in John's physical and mental wellbeing is required.

Does the case meet eligibility criteria for adult protection?

John potentially meets criteria for adult protection, but this may not be established until enquiries have been made. Housing services have developed a good rapport with John and gain access more often than other services. Housing services have been assigned to lead the enquiry process and chair multi-agency meetings to put a safeguarding plan in place. Information will be fed back to the local authority regarding John's wishes, expectations and desired outcomes and progress toward this. An occupational therapist has been visiting with the housing officer to put a rehabilitation plan in place. John is working on a weekly basis with the occupational therapist. If it transpires that John is self-neglecting as a result of trauma, loss, bereavement or neglect, then therapeutic psychological interventions may be required and, depending on the circumstances, the enquiry may transfer to being led by psychology.

Does John meet eligibility criteria for social work?

It is not evident whether John meets eligibility criteria for social work intervention; however, as enquiries are made and a greater understanding of why John hoards is gained, it is likely that an assessment of need will be required to consider the impact of his experiences on his physical and mental wellbeing and to ensure timely support is provided.

■ Case study 3

Sarah has lived with her husband for 11 years and over the past nine years since she became pregnant with her first child she has suffered domestic abuse. Sarah's husband is both physically and verbally abusive towards her and controls her money. She has not been able to cope with the prolonged abuse and has regularly visited her GP for anti-depressants and anti-anxiety medication. Sarah is now drinking heavily, has a poor sleep pattern and has a poor diet. Sarah's weight is very low and the dietician has said that her weight is under the recommended body mass index (BMI) for her height and age. The police have a history of intelligence relating to the domestic abuse, but Sarah has always said that she will be fine and appears to choose to stay in the relationship.

Does Sarah meet eligibility criteria for safeguarding?

Sarah has needs for care and support as a result of her drinking, depression and anxiety. Considering the wellbeing principle, Sarah will only become more unwell both physically and mentally if appropriate care and support are not provided. In an effort to prevent the deterioration of physical and mental wellbeing caused by domestic abuse and delay the need for services down the line when Sarah's mental and physical wellbeing have been significantly affected, a safeguarding response is required.

Does the case meet eligibility criteria for adult protection?

The response may not need to be an 'adult protection' response coordinated by the safeguarding team or local authority. The referral may be presented to the local authority single point of access, enquiries conducted and the most relevant response determined. The enquiries should determine the level of risk, and a DASH Risk Assessment (Dashriskchecklist.co.uk 2018) may need to be completed to determine whether a referral to the MARAC (multi-agency risk assessment conference) is required. The risks to the children will need to be considered as well as the risks to Sarah, and a whole-family approach needs to be explored. If Sarah is looking to involve the police then the enquiry will be a police-led enquiry; if not then domestic abuse services may be best placed to coordinate the safeguarding response. They are more familiar with available services, can refer to an independent domestic violence advocate and relevant services, can enable access to refuges and counselling and can develop safeguarding plans with Sarah. The local authority may have oversight of the issues and provide guidance with regard to care and support services available, such as signposting to substance misuse services and local community support groups.

Does Sarah meet eligibility criteria for social work?

It is highly unlikely, given the current description, that Sarah will meet eligibility criteria for social work unless her drinking, depression and anxiety have a significant effect on her daily independence skills.

■ Case study 4

Joseph is a 27-year-old man who has a history of criminal offences, largely burglary and arms offences. Joseph has a maintenance prescription for methadone but he regularly injects heroin on top of his prescribed dose, claiming that he becomes paranoid, anxious and hallucinates because his prescription is too low. Substance misuse services are becoming increasingly concerned about Joseph's erratic behaviour and his health as a result of his injecting behaviours (he has recently been diagnosed with Hepatitis C), and a referral has been made to mental health services for assessment.

An allegation has been made from Jimmy, who attends the substance misuse clinic, that Joseph was in his house and stole his grandmother's diazepam from the medicine cabinet. The police were called after a fight broke out between the two men at the property and the older lady suffered a heart attack while trying to stop the fight. The lady was taken to hospital and a safeguarding referral was made alleging assault and theft. The police took Joseph into custody and sought medical attention for him due to the extent of his injuries. Police intelligence shows that Jimmy has a history of domestic abuse when in relationships with women and this is exacerbated when he uses a cocktail of drugs and alcohol in addition to his prescribed medication.

Who, if anyone, requires safeguarding?

Under the *No Secrets* guidance, as a safeguarding lead I would most probably have said that this is not a safeguarding case for Joseph, but a matter to be dealt with via the police, probation and substance misuse services. We may have considered the older lady's need for safeguarding; however, that would only have been if she met eligibility criteria for social work services and then we would consider Joseph's needs as a potential perpetrator. What has changed since the Care Act 2014 to make me consider this case a safeguarding matter and would my response be any different?

Does the older lady meet eligibility criteria for safeguarding?

The older lady has needs for care and support, as she is frail and has an existing heart condition. As a result of her heart condition she was not able to protect herself from abuse, therefore she meets the three-stage eligibility criteria. A multi-agency response to coordinate services would be beneficial. Health services have largely been involved in the older lady's care and therefore they are asked to convene a safeguarding meeting to coordinate the multi-agency response. The local authority provides oversight and guidance and is particularly interested in why the older lady was not identified as being in a vulnerable position caring for someone who has complex needs, while trying to manage her own ill-health (preventative safeguarding agenda), and a referral made for a carer's assessment.

Does Joseph meet eligibility criteria for safeguarding?

Joseph could be seen as both the perpetrator and the victim within this scenario, but safeguarding considerations mean that we would explore all of his needs. Considering the three-part eligibility criteria, Joseph has needs for care and support because he has substance misuse problems, but he is as capable as any other member of the public of protecting himself from abuse and neglect. In fact, Joseph has a history of aggression, and his care and support needs do not deter his aggressive behaviours or his ability to provide for himself. The three-part test may not be met and Joseph may not meet safeguarding criteria. I would, however, seriously consider a safeguarding response initially to coordinate and provide oversight and guidance within the process. Safeguarding covers victim and perpetrator support needs.

The care and support are provided by the substance misuse service, probation services are involved to monitor Joseph's rehabilitation and the police are considering further criminal charges. While Joseph may require an appropriate adult to support him through any police interviews, there are no further care and support needs to consider that are not currently being met through the appropriate services.

If Joseph becomes an imminent and serious risk to the public, then a referral for multi-agency public protection arrangements (MAPPA) should be made. If Joseph's mental health is deteriorating and he is becoming a risk to himself and the public, a statutory Mental Health Act assessment may be required.

Does the older lady meet eligibility criteria for adult protection?

The older lady lives with her substance misusing grandson, leaving her vulnerable to attack and exploitation. Further enquiries are required to consider the extent of risk, her capacity to make decisions and whether there is any domestic abuse considered within the home environment. Risks and capacity assessments will be collated from a variety of agencies, including health, GP, community police, foundation trust, ambulance service and the local authority. Perpetrator risk will also be considered.

Does Joseph meet eligibility criteria for adult protection?

Joseph is not eligible for safeguarding; however, he may be regarded as a potential perpetrator of abuse, pending enquiries. Enquiries are police led and may include criminal charges. Joseph's care and support plans will be provided initially by the police medical examiner and then as a result of information supplied by the substance misuse team.

Does the older lady meet eligibility criteria for social work?
The older lady does not meet eligibility criteria for social work as she is largely supported by health care provision and has little social care need. The safeguarding initial enquiries raise concern that she may be vulnerable as a result of letting her grandson stay with her and this is causing additional distress and increasing health problems. Short-term social work intervention is identified on the health care plan to address housing needs and to re-engage the older lady with people within her community. The police inform community safety officers of their concerns for the older lady and they agree to call in on her once she has returned from hospital.

Does Joseph meet eligibility criteria for social work?
Joseph was already identified as a person requiring social work services due to his substance misuse and mental health issues. The substance misuse team, probation services and, in the future, mental health services will provide this support.

What about Jimmy?
Jimmy requires a full assessment to gather further information about his care and support needs, his history of domestic abuse, his current living arrangements and his relationship with his grandmother. A risk assessment is required to determine risks posed by him, to himself and to his grandmother. Housing services may have further information about the use of the property and tenancy arrangements; police, health and substance misuse services will be key in providing further detailed information. This requires a full multi-agency enquiry into the potential for domestic abuse involving his grandmother and the impact of the arrangements and abuse on her health.

Case example conclusions

The case examples demonstrate that after dealing with the initial risks there are different considerations in relation to the safeguarding response:

- Does the person meet each aspect of the three-part safeguarding eligibility criteria? Often the part that considers whether the person can 'As a result of their care and support needs protect themselves from the risk of, or experience of, abuse or neglect' is the element that is the most difficult to determine.

- Is the person eligible for 'adult protection' or, in other words, does the local authority need to coordinate the response, is it best placed to coordinate the response, or should it just ensure oversight and guidance? This is relevant to the type of abuse and the form of care and support required by the person.

- Is the person eligible for social work intervention? This means that they may meet social work eligibility criteria or it is necessary to conduct an assessment of need. An assessment of need or a review of care provision may be required due to the safeguarding incident and the lack of preventative strategies in place to stop abuse or neglect from occurring.

- Has everyone else in the situation been considered and the risks identified?

- The sharing of information with the local authority for safeguarding purposes does not mean that the local authority is automatically expected to respond. It also means that the enquiry process must consider capacity consent and the potential of the person to make capacitated decisions that are deemed unwise but autonomous. An autonomous decision requires that the person is free from intimidating or coercive behaviours. If a person is deemed to be so mentally unwell that they require an assessment under the Mental Health Act for detention, then they cannot be automatically regarded as making autonomous decisions – this must be assessed.

Responsibility for safeguarding adults, application of eligibility criteria, risk assessment and response to enquiries

Under the *No Secrets* guidance, a referral made to the local authority that was determined to meet local authority eligibility criteria was managed by the local authority. This meant that, once the referral was made, the local authority took over the investigation and identified all care and support needs and support required. Under the Care Act 2014, a person requiring safeguarding may not be eligible for care and support under the local authority eligibility criteria, but still meet eligibility criteria for safeguarding. The types of referrals and the variety of responses are infinite in relation to the situation and needs of individuals. This means that once a referral is made to the local authority, partner agencies' duties and responsibilities remain and now safeguarding really is everyone's business throughout the process, to ensure true multi-agency coordination and response. While the person requiring safeguarding may not meet eligibility criteria for the local authority, the risks may determine that a social work assessment is required to prevent abuse or neglect, and the local authority may request an assessment and care and support plan to form part of the enquiry process.

To be at 'risk of abuse or neglect and unable to protect oneself from the risk of abuse or neglect' refers to the preventative agenda established under the Care Act 2014. All care and support provided meets this element of the criteria, and therefore just about everything that is done to provide care, treatment and support to a person is deemed to prevent the risk of abuse or neglect. The remit of safeguarding has become all-encompassing and expansive.

No longer can one small team within the local authority deal with everything that meets safeguarding eligibility criteria. This poses many difficulties during times of austerity and resource reduction within local authorities. When the former *No Secrets* guidance stated that safeguarding was everyone's business, largely this was interpreted as everyone must recognise abuse and neglect and make a referral to the local authority, after which the local authority would coordinate a response, often via multi-agency safeguarding arrangements. Under the Care Act 2014, safeguarding arrangements are part of a continuum of care and support around the person. The local authority is required to conduct enquiries (or cause enquiries to be made) to ensure that the care and support provided both prevents abuse and neglect and protects the person from abuse and neglect.

Local authorities should resist creating further thresholds or eligibility criteria for a safeguarding referral. The referral criteria are deliberately broad, and as a result of this many local authorities have created a triage system at the single point of access. Using this methodology, low-level concerns requiring advice, guidance or signposting can be directed to appropriate resources and advice given. Other referrals may require a social work assessment or review to meet needs and prevent abuse or neglect occurring. Others may require a more complex multi-agency response. The response to the referral will be established through the enquiries made, which can be anything from a telephone conversation to a full police investigation.

The use of language within adult safeguarding can be confusing, as the same word is used to describe many different things. As we have explored previously, the word 'safeguarding' within the *No Secrets* definition is related to those people who had or may have need for community care. This meant that local authority eligibility criteria were applied in the form of 'Fair Access to Care' criteria. These criteria varied from one local authority to another, with the threshold for some being low and for others moderate, substantial or critical need. Under the Care Act 2014, 'needs for care and support' do not refer to local authority eligibility criteria, but to any needs for care and support, and it is explicit that local authority eligibility criteria for services do not apply. Previously all referrals coming into the local authority would be eligible for local authority services and now many referrals would not meet local authority criteria for services.

The oversight and guidance element of safeguarding should not lay an over-burdensome task solely on the shoulders of the local authority to conduct safeguarding responses. There are many types of referrals for safeguarding: these may be 'alerts', concern reporting, vulnerable adult concern reports from the police or ambulance service among issues raised in daily practice, care home or hospital inspections and commissioning reviews. Considering the three-part eligibility test, some of these reports will require a safeguarding enquiry, some will require care management, some will require advice and guidance, and some are for information-sharing purposes only. Many will not be eligible for services under social work eligibility criteria, but will require other agencies to provide an appropriate response.

While the person requiring safeguarding may not meet eligibility criteria for the local authority, the risks may determine that a social work assessment is required to prevent abuse or neglect, and the local authority may request an assessment and care and support plan to form part of the enquiry process. This may be to prevent the deterioration of wellbeing and delay the need for services in the future, it may be to ensure that resources are directed to preventing further abuse from occurring, or to prevent the impact of abuse having a significant detrimental effect on the person's mental and physical wellbeing.

To be at 'risk of abuse or neglect and unable to protect oneself from the risk of abuse or neglect' refers to the preventative agenda established under the Care Act 2014. All care and support provided meets this element of the criteria, and therefore just about everything that is done to provide care, treatment and support to a person is deemed to prevent the risk of abuse or neglect. The remit of safeguarding has become all-encompassing and expansive. No longer can one small team within the local authority deal with everything that meets safeguarding eligibility criteria. This poses many difficulties during times of austerity and resource reduction within local authorities. When the former *No Secrets* guidance stated that safeguarding was everyone's business, largely this was interpreted as everyone must recognise abuse and neglect and make a referral to the local authority, after which the local authority would coordinate a response, often via multi-agency safeguarding arrangements. Under the Care Act 2014, safeguarding arrangements are part of a continuum of care and support around the person. The local authority is required to conduct enquiries (or cause enquiries to be made) to ensure that the care and support provided both prevents abuse and neglect and protects the person from abuse and neglect.

This requires some form of triaging process to assess the risks, identify the gaps in knowledge and determine what is required to fill those gaps. In cases where there is low-level or short-term care and support needs/low-level abuse or neglect, the safeguarding team may provide advice, guidance and signposting for the person concerned. Where there are moderate concerns/moderate care and support needs, the local authority may conduct an assessment of need and ensure care and support is provided, or ask a number of agencies to undertake actions, share information and make changes to care and support arrangements. The local authority may cause others to make enquiries and conduct multi-agency meetings where appropriate, with oversight and guidance from the local authority. In high-risk, high-vulnerability cases, it is likely that the local authority will provide coordination, delegation of responsibilities and oversight to safeguarding procedures. While all responses are safeguarding responses, the latter response I shall refer to as invoking 'adult protection procedures'.

Figure 5.2 illustrates the safeguarding adults risk assessment.

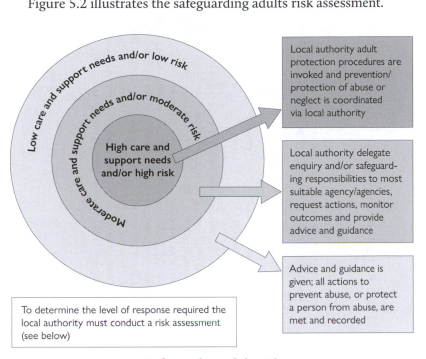

Figure 5.2: Safeguarding adults risk assessment

Table 5.1 and 5.2 are useful tools here.

Table 5.1: Risk Assessment Tool for Defensible Decision Making

NINE FACTORS					
1. Forms of abuse/ neglect/concern	Low risk	Moderate	High	Critical	Guidance (Defensible Decision Making – please record a rationale against all nine factors)
Physical					Refer to the table following risk assessment – Types of abuse and seriousness. Look at the relevant categories of abuse and use your knowledge of the case and your professional judgement to gauge the seriousness of concern. For low-level incidents (column 1), agencies are expected to take action to safeguard individuals involved. You may seek advice and guidance from the local authority and must record a rationale against this risk assessment and action taken to safeguard. Some cases falling within the low to moderate range may be reported to the local authority as an alert. Advice and guidance will be offered and safeguarding action requests monitored. Some cases will result in a Section 42 enquiry, others could be dealt with via staff training/supervision, care management and/or complaints procedures. Professional abuse can occur in relation to any of the categories listed left. **All cases of female genital mutilation, honour-based crime, sexual exploitation, forced marriage and grooming for terrorist activities should be reported to the police and adult safeguarding immediately. See specific tool for self-neglect (Table 5.2). Domestic abuse should also be considered in relation to safeguarding adults. This tool does not replace professional judgement or aim to set a rigid threshold for intervention. Note that professional decision making reflects the fact that the type and seriousness of abuse may fall within the low-risk category – other factors may make the issue more serious and therefore warrant progression via safeguarding procedures. All nine factors are to be considered and recorded against.**
Sexual/Exploitation					
Psychological					
Financial					
Neglect					
Self-neglect	See specific threshold tool				
Organisational					
Discriminatory (hate/mate crime)					
Modern slavery					
Domestic abuse					
Terrorist activity					

2. The vulnerability of the victim	Less vulnerable	More vulnerable			Can the adult protect themselves, and do they have the communication skills to raise an alert? • Does the person lack the mental capacity to make specific decisions relevant to the safeguarding issue? • Is the person dependent on the alleged perpetrator?
3. Patterns of abuse	Isolated incident	Recent abuse		Repeated abuse	Determine if the abuse is/was: • a recent incident in an ongoing relationship • an isolated incident or repeated abuse that has gone on for a length of time
4. Impact of abuse on victims	Low impact			Seriously affected	Impact of abuse does not necessarily correspond to the extent of the abuse. Sometimes serious acts can be withstood by an individual who has plenty of support, whereas even minor abuse can be devastating if perpetrated by someone who the person trusts or is the only source of support
5. Impact on others	No one else affected	Others indirectly affected		Others directly affected	Other people may be affected by the abuse of another adult. Determine if: • no one else is involved or witnessing the abuse • relatives or other residents/service users are distressed or affected by the abuse • other people are intimidated and/or their environment is affected
6. Intent of alleged perpetrator	Not intended			Deliberate/ targeted	Determine if the abuse is/was: • unintentional or ill informed • violent/serious unprofessional response to difficulties in caring • planned and deliberately malicious The act/omission doesn't have to be intentional to meet safeguarding criteria
7. Illegality of actions	Bad practice but not illegal	Criminal act		Serious criminal act	Seek advice if you are unsure if a crime has been committed. Try to determine if: • it is poor or bad practice (but not illegal) • it may be against the law or if it is clearly a crime
8. Risk of repeated abuse on victim	Unlikely to recur	Possible to recur	Likely to recur		Is the abuse: • unlikely to happen again or less likely with significant changes, e.g. training, supervision, respite, support? • very likely even if changes are made and/or more support provided?
9. Risk of repeated abuse on others	Others not at risk	Possibly at risk	Others at risk	Others at serious risk	Are others (adults and/or children) at risk of being abused? • Very unlikely • Less likely if significant changes are made

cont.

Types of abuse and seriousness	Examples of concerns that may not require formal safeguarding procedures. The individuals involved can be safeguarded by other systems, e.g. complaints, care/risk management, disciplinary, single-agency response. Use professional judgement		The examples below are likely to indicate the need for a referral for formal procedures. If there is any immediate danger to an individual evident, call 999 straightaway	
Level of risk	Minimal risk	Low risk	Moderate	High	Critical
Physical	• Staff error causing no/little harm, e.g. friction mark on skin due to ill-fitting hoist sling • Minor events that still meet criteria for 'incident reporting' accidents **Medication** • Adult does not receive prescribed medication (missed/wrong dose) on one occasion – no harm occurs	• Isolated incident involving service on service user • Inexplicable marking found on one occasion • Minor event where users lack capacity **Medication** • Recurring missed medication or administration errors that cause no harm	• Inexplicable marking or lesions, cuts or grip marks on a number of occasions • Accumulations of minor incidents **Medication** • Recurring missed medication or errors that affect more than one adult and/or result in harm • Potential serious consequences	• Inappropriate restraint • Withholding of food, drinks or aids to independence • Inexplicable fractures/injuries • Assault **Medication** • Deliberate maladministration of medications • Covert administration without proper medical authorisation	• Grievous bodily harm/assault with a weapon leading to irreversible damage or death **Medication** • Pattern of recurring errors or an incident of deliberate maladministration that results in ill-health or death
Sexual/Exploitation	• Isolated incident of teasing or low-level unwanted sexualised attention (verbal or touching) directed at one adult by another whether or not capacity exists	• Minimal verbal sexualised teasing or banter	• Recurring sexualised touching or isolated/recurring masturbation without valid consent • Voyeurism without consent • Being subject to indecent exposure	• Attempted penetration by any means (whether or not it occurs within a relationship) without valid consent • Being made to look at pornographic material against will/where valid consent cannot be given	• Sex in a relationship characterised by authority inequality or exploitation, e.g. staff and service user • Sex without valid consent (rape)

Psychological	• Isolated incident where adult is spoken to in a rude or other inappropriate way – respect is undetermined but no or little distress caused	• Occasional taunts or verbal outburst • Withholding of information to disempower	• Treatment that undermines dignity and esteem • Denying or failing to recognise adult's choice or opinion • Frequent verbal outbursts or harassment	• Humiliation • Emotional blackmail, e.g. threats or abandonment/harm • Frequent and frightening verbal outbursts	• Denial of basic human rights/civil liberties, over-riding advance directive, forced marriage • Prolonged intimidation • Vicious/personalised verbal attacks
Financial	• Staff personally benefit from user's funds, e.g. accrue 'reward' points on their own store loyalty cards when shopping • Money not recorded safely and properly • Non-payment of care fees	• Adult not routinely involved in decisions about how their money is spent or kept safe – capacity in this respect is not properly considered	• Adult's monies kept in a joint bank account – unclear arrangements for equitable sharing of interest • Adult denied access to his/her own funds or possessions	• Misuse/misappropriation of property or possessions of benefits by a person in a position of trust or control • Personal finance removed from adult's control	• Fraud/exploitation relating to benefits, income, property or will • Theft
Neglect	• Isolated missed home care visit where no harm occurs • Adult is not assisted with a meal/drink on one occasion and no harm occurs • Adult not bathed as often as would like – possible complaint	• Inadequacies in care provision that lead to discomfort or inconvenience – no significant harm occurs, e.g. being left wet occasionally • Not having access to aids to independence	• Recurrent missed home care visits where risk of harm escalates, or one missed where harm occurs • Hospital discharge without adequate planning and harm occurs	• Ongoing lack of care to the extent that health and wellbeing deteriorate significantly, e.g. pressure wounds, dehydration, malnutrition, loss of independence/confidence	• Failure to arrange access to lifesaving services or medical care • Failure to intervene in dangerous situations where the adult lacks the capacity to assess risk

cont.

Level of risk	Minimal risk	Low risk	Moderate	High	Critical
Organisational (any one or combination of the other forms of abuse)	• Lack of stimulation/ opportunities for people to engage in social and leisure activities • Service users not given sufficient voice or involved in the running of the service	• Denial of individuality and opportunities for service user to make informed choice and take responsible risks • Care planning documentation not person centred	• Rigid/inflexible routines • Service user's dignity is undetermined, e.g. lack of privacy during support with intimate care needs; sharing under-clothing	• Bad practice not being reported and going unchecked • Unsafe and unhygienic living environments	• Staff misusing their position of power over service users • Over-medication and/or inappropriate restraint used to manage behaviour • Widespread consistent ill-treatment
Discriminatory (including hate/ mate crime)	• Isolated incident of teasing motivated by prejudicial attitudes towards an adult's individual differences	• Isolated incident of care planning that fails to address an adult's specific diversity-associated needs for a short period • Occasional taunts	• Inequitable access to service provision as a result of a diversity issue • Recurring failure to meet specific care/support needs associated with diversity	• Being refused access to essential services • Denial of civil liberties, e.g. voting, making a complaint • Humiliation or threats on a regular basis • Recurring taunts	• Hate crime resulting in injury/emergency medical treatment/fear for life • Hate crime or honour-based violence
Modern slavery	• All concerns of modern slavery or human trafficking are deemed to be of significant critical level		• Limited freedom of movement • Being forced to work with little or no payment • Limited or no access to medical/dental care	• Limited access to food or shelter • Regularly moved to avoid detection • No access or no passport or ID documentation	• Sexual exploitation/ prostitution • Starvation • Organ harvesting • Imprisonment or unlawful detention • Forced marriage

Domestic abuse (please use the SafeLives DASH Risk Checklist to determine level of risk)	• Isolated one-off incident consistent with other above categories (minimal risk) within a family or with a current or past partner	• Occasional incidents (low risk) within a family or with a current or past partner	• Controlling behaviour • Limited access to medical and dental care • Limited access to funds • Power and control issues within relationship	• Accumulations of minor incidents, marks, bruising or lesions • Frequent verbal/physical outbursts • No access/control over finances • Stalking • Relationship characterised by imbalance of power • Threatening or harming animals	• Pregnancy increases threat • Sex without consent • Forced marriage • Female genital mutilation • Honour-based violence • Attempts to strangle, choke or suffocate
Terrorist activity	• All concerns of grooming/activities for any form of extremist group should be reported immediately to the police and adult safeguarding. This could include extreme right-wing activities, extreme animal rights activists or grooming for religious or cultural reasons		• Changes in types of friends • Online activities that cause concern that person is changing views • Changes in mood or behaviour that may indicate change of perspective about religious or political ideology towards an extremist group	• Engaging with extremist demonstrations • Radicalisation • Advocating violence, threat of violence or use of force to achieve goals on behalf of suspected terrorist organisation • Providing financial or material support to suspected terrorist organisation • Attempting to recruit people on behalf of suspected terrorist organisation	• Family ties or other close associations to known or suspected terrorist organisations • Statements that laws or perspectives of the country are destroying or suppressing people • Browsing or publicising on internet extremist perspectives • Statements or threats to kill or harm on behalf of potential terrorist organisations

If there are children within the household or present at the time of the incident, please consider contacting the local authority children's services regarding your concerns

Table 5.2: Self-Neglect and Hoarding Risk Assessment Tool

Factors	Guidance			
1. The vulnerability of the person	• Does the person have capacity to make decisions with regard to care provision/housing, etc.? • Does the person have a diagnosed mental illness? • Does the person have support from family or friends? • Does the person accept care and treatment? • Does the person have insight into the problems they face?	**Less vulnerable**	**More vulnerable**	
2. Types of seriousness of hoarding	• Refer to the table that follows – Types and seriousness of hoarding and self-neglect. Look at the relevant categories of hoarding and self-neglect and use your knowledge of the case and your professional judgement to gauge the seriousness of concern • Incidents that might fall outside invoked adult protection procedures (low risk) could potentially be addressed via preventative safeguarding measures such as engaging with the person, developing a rapport, supporting the person to address concerns, getting the person to engage with community activities and develop/repair relationships, access to health care and counselling, or a single-agency response. The aim is to effectively safeguard the person • If a social worker or nurse is involved in the care, report concerns to them as part of preventative measures This tool does not replace professional judgement and does not aim to set a rigid threshold for intervention. Note that professional decision making reflects the fact that the type and seriousness of hoarding and self-neglect may fall within the low-risk threshold – other factors may make the issue more serious and therefore warrant progression via safeguarding procedures	**Low risk**	**Moderate**	**High/ Critical**
Hoarding – property				
Hoarding – household functions				
Hoarding – health and safety				
Hoarding – safeguarding				
Self-neglect				
3. Level of self-neglect/hoarding (see Clutter Rating Scale for hoarding)	Determine if the hoarding/self-neglect is: • a fire risk • impacting on the person's wellbeing (Care Act 2014 definition) • preventing access to emergency services • affecting the person's ability to cook, clean and the general hygiene • creating limited access to main areas of the house • creating an increased risk of falls	**Low risk**	**Moderate risk**	**High risk**

4. Background to hoarding/self-neglect	Low impact		Seriously affected	• Does the person have a disability that means that they cannot care for themselves? • Does the person have mental health issues, and to what extent? • Has this been a long-standing problem? • Does the person engage with services, support and guidance offered? • Are there social isolation issues?
5. Impact on others	No one else affected	Others indirectly affected	Others directly affected	Others may be affected by the self-neglect or hoarding. Determine if: • there are other vulnerable people (children or adults) within the house affected by the person's hoarding/self-neglect • the hoarding/self-neglect prevents the person from seeing family and friends • there are animals within the property that are not being appropriately cared for
6. Reasonable suspicion of abuse	No suspicion	Indicators present	Reasonable suspicion	Determine if there is reason to suspect that: • the hoarding/self-neglect is an indicator that the person may be being abused • the person may be targeted for abuse from local people • a crime may be taking place • the person is being neglected by someone else • safeguarding is required **See the Risk Assessment Tool for Defensible Decision Making (Table 5.1)**
7. Legal frameworks	No current legal issues	Some minor legal issues not currently impacting	Serious legal issues	Try to determine if: • the person is at risk of eviction, fines, non-payment issues • there is an environmental risk that requires action (public health issues) • there are safeguarding and animal welfare issues • there are fire risks that are a danger to others

cont.

The examples below are likely to indicate the need for a referral for formal procedures. If there is any immediate danger of a crime or abuse to an individual evident, call 999 straightaway and make a safeguarding referral. Please see self-neglect hoarding journey to determine intervention process

Types and seriousness of hoarding and self-neglect	Minimal risk	Moderate	High/Critical
Level of risk			
Hoarding property	• All entrances and exits, stairways, roof space and windows accessible • Smoke alarms fitted and functional or referrals made to fire brigade to visit and install • All services functional and maintained in good working order • Garden accessible, tidy and maintained	• Only major exit blocked • Only one of the services not fully functional • Concern that services are not well maintained • Smoke alarms not installed or not functioning • Garden not accessible due to clutter, or not maintained • Evidence of light structural damage including damp • Interior doors missing or blocked open	• Limited access to the property due to extreme clutter • Evidence may be seen of extreme clutter seen at windows • Evidence may be seen of extreme clutter outside the property • Garden not accessible and is extensively overgrown • Services not connected or not functioning properly • Smoke alarms not fitted or not functioning • Property lacks ventilation due to clutter • Evidence of structural damage or outstanding repairs including damp • Interior doors missing or blocked open • Evidence of indoor items stored outside
Hoarding – household functions	• No excessive clutter – all rooms can be safely used for their intended purpose • All rooms rated 0–3 on the Clutter Rating Scale • No additional unused household appliances appear in unusual locations around the property • Property maintained within terms of any lease or tenancy agreements where appropriate • Property not at risk of action by Environmental Health	• Clutter causing congestion in the living spaces and impacting on the use of the rooms for their intended purpose • Clutter causing congestion between the rooms and entrances • Room(s) score 4–5 on the Clutter Rating Scale • Inconsistent levels of housekeeping throughout the property • Some household appliances not functioning properly and there may be additional units in unusual places • Property not maintained within terms of lease or tenancy agreement, where applicable • Evidence of outdoor items being stored inside	• Clutter obstructing the living spaces and preventing the use of the rooms for their intended purpose • Room(s) score 7–9 on the Clutter Rating Scale and not used for intended purpose • Beds inaccessible or unusable due to clutter or infestation • Entrances, hallways and stairs blocked or difficult to pass • Toilets, sinks not functioning or not in use • Resident at risk due to the living environment • Household appliances not functioning or inaccessible and there is no safe cooking environment • Resident is using candles • Evidence of outdoor clutter being stored indoors • No evidence of housekeeping being undertaken • Broken household items not discarded, e.g. broken glass or plates • Concern for declining mental health • Property not maintained within terms of lease or tenancy agreement where applicable and the person is at risk of notice being served by Environmental Health

Hoarding – health and safety	• Property clean with no odours (pet or other) • No rotting food • No concerning use of candles • No concern over flies • Resident managing personal care • No writing on the walls • Quantities of medication within appropriate limits, in date and stored appropriately • Personal protective equipment not required	• Kitchen and bathroom not kept clean • Offensive odour in the property • Resident not maintaining a safe cooking environment • Some concern with the quantity of medication, or its storage or expiry dates • No rotting food • No concerning use of candles • Resident trying to manage personal care but struggling • No writing on the walls • Light insect infestation (bed bugs, lice, fleas, cockroaches, ants, etc.) • Latex gloves, boots or needle stick safe shoes, face mask, hand sanitiser, insect repellent required • Personal protective equipment required	• Human urine and/or excrement may be present • Excessive odour in the property and may also be evident from the outside • Rotting food may be present • Evidence may be seen of unclean, unused and/or buried plates and dishes • Broken household items not discarded, e.g. broken glass or plates • Inappropriate quantities or storage of medication • Pungent odour can be smelt inside the property and possibly from outside • Concern with the integrity of the electrics • Inappropriate use of electrical extension cords or evidence of unqualified work to the electrics • Concern for declining mental health • Heavy insect infestation (bed bugs, lice, fleas, cockroaches, ants, silverfish, etc.) • Visible rodent infestation
Hoarding – safeguarding of children, family members and animals	• No concerns for household members	• Hoarding on Clutter Rating Scale 4–7 doesn't automatically constitute a safeguarding alert • Note all additional concerns for householders • Properties with children or vulnerable residents with additional support needs may trigger a safeguarding alert	• Hoarding on Clutter Rating Scale 7–9 constitutes a safeguarding alert • Note all additional concerns for householders

cont.

Level of risk	Minimal risk	Moderate	High/Critical
Self-neglect	• Person accepting support and services • Health care being addressed • Person not losing weight • Person accessing services to improve wellbeing • No carer issues • Person has access to social and community activities • Person able to contribute to daily living activities • Personal hygiene good	• Access to support services limited • Health care and attendance at appointments sporadic • Person is of low weight • Person's wellbeing partially affected • Person has limited social interaction • Carers not present • Person has limited access to social or community activities • Person's ability to contribute toward daily living activities affected • Personal hygiene becoming an issue	• Person refuses to engage with necessary services • Health care poor and there is deterioration in health • Weight reducing • Wellbeing affected on a daily basis • Person isolated from family and friends • Care prevented or refused • Person does not engage with social or community activities • Person does not manage daily living activities • Hygiene poor and causing skin problems • Aids and adaptations refused or not accessed
Responsibility	All workers to engage with the person, develop a rapport, supporting the person to address concerns, getting the person to engage with community activities and develop/repair relationships, access to health care and counselling, improve wellbeing – preventative measures	Workers to use resources in the toolkit. Consult with local authority for advice and guidance. Inform social worker or nurse if involved with person	Use resources in the toolkit

The tools above may be used as a guide or checklist to determine the appropriate safeguarding response, facilitate discussions regarding risk and record decisions in a defensible manner. These tools can be used during the referral process, in discussion with partner agencies and throughout the safeguarding process. You will need to consider escalating risks or the accumulation of risks and concerns as more information is revealed, and use the tools regularly.

In looking at the factors of abuse, begin at the 'Critical' column in Table 5.1 and work backwards. This will ensure that you are considering the level of investigation required and preserving any evidence for a potential police investigation.

If you are going to make a referral, record the situation against the Risk Assessment Tool for Defensible Decision Making to provide a rationale. Any disagreement can be settled by a conversation about where professionals feel risk fits within the factors of the tool. If you are not going to make a referral, record against the tool your rationale for this and identify the safeguarding actions taken to prevent the risk of abuse/neglect and protect the person from abuse/neglect. Do not forget that safety is about what the person feels safe with and not an imposed safety standard. You can still contact the local authority for advice, guidance and information regarding safeguarding matters, even if risks fall on the low side of the assessment tool. The important thing is that we respond to the needs, wishes and outcomes expressed by the person to determine their perception of safety to maintain their wellbeing.

It is also important to record whether the person consents or not to any safeguarding actions and whether they have capacity to consent. If a person does not consent, a referral can still be made where there is reasonable suspicion of a potential crime, risks to others, coercion or harassment of the person, or when it is in the public interest to do so. If a person lacks capacity to consent, a capacity assessment must be completed by the most relevant person and a best interests decision made regarding the referral. You do not need consent to make the referral, as the Section 42 enquiry duties require the local authority to:

- get a picture of the abuse/neglect/self-neglect

- make sure that the person is safe

- consider capacity assessments required and by whom

- rule out additional or historical abuse/neglect

- explore potential crime

- identify any coercive or controlling behaviours

- explore any mental health and substance misuse concerns

- consider risks to others (including children)

- determine the care and support needs of the individual and perpetrator

- consider advocacy and methods of communication

- determine whether a multi-agency response is required.

Do not forget to keep checking information gathered against the risk assessment throughout the process.

KEY POINTS

Eligibility criteria for safeguarding purposes are set at a much lower level than those for social services. The three-part eligibility test is the only threshold for safeguarding adults – other thresholds should not be added. Statutory duties apply in safeguarding where the eligibility criteria are met; however, responses can be as simple as a telephone conversation, or as complex as a full police enquiry. Local authorities will need to triage referrals for safeguarding and determine what response is required, or whether the agency has safeguarded the person and others, without the need for support and guidance.

CHAPTER 6

How Do We Respond to Increasing Safeguarding Demands?

During training sessions, I ask participants to forget about their current roles and consider that they worked in a call centre for an electricity company. The call centre deals with severe electrical problems that have resulted in harm and they also deal with complaints. There are many other facets to the business and different services deal with the different aspects of electricity supply, delivery, goods and maintenance. The electricity investigation and complaints service has explored the detail of the business and holds solutions to many of the daily difficulties experienced by all the other services. One day a law comes in that says that the complaints service must have oversight and guidance on all aspects of the work of electricity companies. There are one hundred investigation and complaints people as opposed to thousands of other workers dealing with other aspects of the business. You are the senior manager within the investigation and complaints service – what are you going to do?

Figure 6.1 shows how training participants respond to this question.

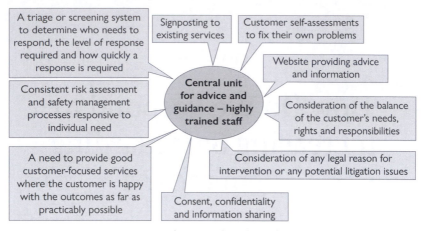

Figure 6.1: Front-door single point of access services

The answers in response to this question are obvious – a clear central unit which all calls come into must be created, or a single point of contact. This single point of contact is situated within the main investigation and complaints unit to ensure that the knowledge and expertise are utilised. The most highly trained staff will effectively and efficiently triage all calls and determine the level of response required. This may be low-level intervention such as signposting to the appropriate service, or asking for completion of a self-assessment, or providing fast solutions such as advice and guidance. It may be moderate risk situations where a person requires the situation to be assessed and a referral is made to the assessment team or where another service or services have the necessary skills to respond appropriately to the presenting difficulties and this is coordinated by an allocated person. Or it may be severe enough that it constitutes a severe risk or major complaint and the unit coordinates the response itself.

The analogy equates to that of the local authority's role within safeguarding. Within health and social care, strategies change with the changing social, technical, economic and political climate. The introduction of the Care Act 2014 has seen the remit of safeguarding adults expand rapidly, and with an influx of safeguarding cases, local authorities are struggling to manage using the traditional structures and methods of adult protection. To support the practitioners, a bottom-up and top-down approach needs to be used. Safeguarding adults board strategies need to be considered to assist practitioners across agencies. The structure of the service provision and screening of access to services are key in making sure that people who require safeguarding have equitable access to services and tailored advice, guidance and support, as well as access to statutory services.

The Care Act 2014 identifies the need for a single point of contact to ensure that effective triaging occurs. The single point of contact enables us to consider community options, signposting people and giving advice and guidance. It asks us to consider how we can prevent deterioration and delay the need for services by using the person and their own support networks as a resource. Low-level occupational therapy responses and low-level interventions may be determined during the initial enquiries. Existing community support needs to be explored along with the potential of assistive technology.

The health model to maintain wellbeing within the community is better understood and recognised than the social care model; however, the process is the same to maintain wellbeing within the community as long as possible and to triage, risk assess and evaluate the necessary, proportionate and appropriate intervention to meet need (see Figure 6.2).

The model identifies how health services are structured. General citizen wellbeing is maintained within the community using community health resources. When these health resources are no longer sufficient to keep the person well, either a referral is made or the person accesses a triage system to determine the level of care required. This may be via the 111 system or similar. If the person requires some help, short-term interventions are considered; where there are concerns for the person's physical health then they receive outpatient hospital services, and where serious concerns are identified then hospital admission is considered.

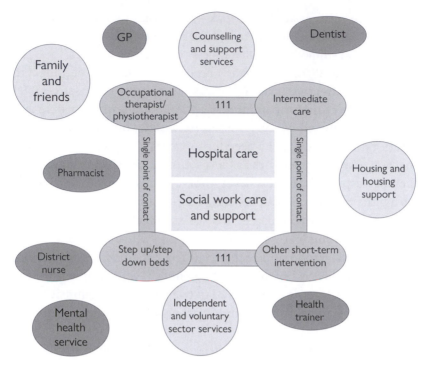

*Figure 6.2: Preventative community measures to maintain
health and delay or prevent the need for services*

The triage system is to determine the level of care and support required by the person and direct them to the most appropriate sources of support. The amount of time and the variety of professional support needed are determined by the nature of the ailment, injury or illness. The response reflects the health need. Where a person can be redirected to appropriate community resources, this is achieved via the triage system. If the person requires short-term interventions to get them back to community care, this is provided, and only those who need specialist or emergency care are admitted to outpatients, with hospital care being for the few.

Can you imagine a world where everyone was able to access any aspect of health care and the time given to patients did not reflect the need? In some local authorities, the access to safeguarding services reflects this, with everyone who meets eligibility criteria under the three-part test being referred to the safeguarding team and receiving the same level of response. This is unmanageable, and local authorities then want to create additional thresholds themselves.

This creates risk when someone falls between legislative thresholds for safeguarding and the additional threshold imposed by the local authority.

In response to the referral, low-level cases may be signposted to community services, and moderate care/risk cases may be addressed through multi-agency meetings and safeguarding plans chaired by a relevant involved agency such as mental health, housing or health. To achieve this in a realistic manner, safeguarding adults boards must ensure that all agencies are equipped to deal with safeguarding people and are accountable for their actions. It is no longer the case that an agency can identify and report abuse or neglect and expect someone in the local authority to manage all aspects of care, treatment, support and services. This is not a safe multi-agency response and would not consider the necessary relevant legislation requirements from all agencies' perspectives, the requirement for a variety of agencies to conduct capacity assessments, the effective communication and coordination of risks/risk management, the appropriate liaison with the person and their family to ensure that they are central to safeguarding and that the outcomes for the person, wherever possible, are positive.

In relation to the three-part test, some local authorities try to equate the first part of the test (has needs for care and support) to eligibility criteria for local authority involvement. This is an incorrect interpretation, as care and support needs are not the same as eligibility criteria for social work assessment or intervention. Care and support needs are deliberately a much broader concept.

The Care Act 2014 developed a system for social care that reflected the health care process in order that the two areas can work together to prevent deterioration of mental and physical wellbeing, delay the need for services and maintain people within their own local communities as long as possible. The local authority has a duty to ensure that community resources are sufficient to meet the needs of the community and that people have a choice in services. This is to assist in sustaining people within their own communities as long as possible. Where community services do not sufficiently support the person, the local authority is asked to establish a single point of contact for people making enquiries. The local authority's role is to signpost people towards suitable resources, or to triage and determine the appropriate response. To use an analogy, if someone were to contact the health 111 line with a bad cold, they would be redirected towards their pharmacy. If the person contacting the local authority has low-level needs, the local authority will ensure that those needs are met by directing them to community resources. If the community resources no longer sustain a person, then short-term interventions are considered, including assistive technology. Where these interventions no longer support the person, or are ruled out, then occupational therapy, intermediate care, physiotherapy, therapeutic interventions and rehabilitation are considered. When these interventions no longer sustain the person, then intensive social work intervention is required. In cases where people referred to the local authority do not appear eligible for local authority services, then the 'journey of support' that the person triaging must consider is the following.

Journey of support – not eligible for local authority services

1. Person contacts the local authority.

2. Single point of contact (SPC) determines eligibility for local authority and for safeguarding.

3. SPC staff determine whether the person requires an advocate to support them.

4. If not eligible for local authority services, the SPC determines whether there are any safeguarding issues, including self-neglect (meeting the three-part eligibility criteria for safeguarding). Immediate risks are discussed and addressed.

5. The contact person determines the safeguarding risks and the relevant course of action required by the person affected by the risks: signposting, information/advice, assessment, actions and outcomes for a number of involved providers, adult protection, or a combination of the above.

6. The contact person does not have enough information and therefore considers an enquiry to determine whether there are:

   • risks to others

- requirements for a carer's assessment (carer capacity, risks, ability, stress)

- potential criminal issues

- public interest issues

- issues of domestic abuse/coercive and controlling behaviour

- issues regarding mental ill-health requiring assessment under the Mental Health Act

- requirements for a capacity assessment

- legal issues affecting the person and their wellbeing, or conflicting legal issues

- communications that indicate a potential need for advocacy

- a number of agencies involved or that should be involved.

7. The contact person determines whether needs have been met and the person can be signposted to community support. Despite the person not being eligible for local authority services, their wellbeing may deteriorate as a result of abuse and neglect and therefore the local authority can conduct an assessment of need (with the consent of the person) to prevent wellbeing from deteriorating.

Having access to this form of triage requires a skilled worker at the single point of contact who is able to rapidly assess the situation and steer safeguarding issues in the appropriate direction. Triaging requires the person to undertake delegatory responsibilities, have confidence to manage risk effectively and give advice about managing situations where emergency services may require coordination with care and support. The person triaging also needs to recognise that a person's wellbeing is central to care provision, and if this deteriorates then costs and services are required, so early intervention to prevent deterioration is both person centred and cost effective for the local authority. This is particularly pertinent in cases of self-neglect, where there is often pressure to redirect cases back to single-agency support. Key enquiry topics are overlooked, because (often) the person is capacitated and states that they do not want a referral. It is clear that, without guidance, support and some intervention, the person's wellbeing will deteriorate.

The single point of contact will need to be skilled enough to make these autonomous decisions. Operational and strategic management will need to support decisions made by the workers at the single point of contact.

In some local authorities, safeguarding cases are not filtered through single point of contact but elsewhere such as duty social workers. This can place a burden on social workers in a busy duty system, or in completing rapidly increasing low-level assessments that detract from the complex targeted work that is required from our skilled workforce. Some local authorities have a multi-agency safeguarding hub (MASH) which undertakes the responsibilities instead of, or alongside, the single point of contact, by sharing resources, knowledge and skills. Whether the triage is conducted through a multi-agency, multi-skilled single point of contact or a MASH amounts to much the same thing with a change of wording – it is the commitment of the team in working together to support knowledge that is required. In cases where the single point of contact or MASH determines that the person meets eligibility for safeguarding and for social work, the assessment must consider that journey of support.

Journey of support – eligible for local authority services

All the previous journey of support issues will be considered and an assessment of need undertaken. In addition, the following steps are considered in order to meet needs:

1. informal support (family/friends willing and assessed as able to provide care identified on the care and support plan and to meet specified needs)

2. assistive technology, aids and adaptations

3. other agencies such as nurses, occupational therapists, tissue viability, falls assessors, physiotherapists and housing – these are identified on the care and support plan where they meet individual needs

4. community resources

5. therapeutic interventions

6. short-term interventions

7. low-level direct payments

8. creative solutions to commissioning care provision.

Each step should be considered and, if ruled out, records should justify why a less intrusive intervention has been ruled out in favour of a more intrusive one. If information is going to a panel then the panel will want to be reassured that the intervention proposed is the least intrusive, most proportionate intervention with consideration to value for money in the creation of care and support packages.

Social work intervention models

Community social work

In safeguarding situations, like many other cases since the Care Act 2014 was introduced, practitioners try to seek a ready-made service. In training, I regularly hear people say, 'We do not have time', 'We do not have services' or 'We do not have resources'.

The duty placed on local authorities to ensure that there is a sustainable market is failing in times of austerity (Carter 2015). Health community care provision is also groaning under the numbers of people wishing to access health care. Some creative solutions may be required by practitioners.

I try to understand service austerity by considering times when I have been less affluent. In times where I have more money I shop at the high-end shops, with easy prepared meals and good quality products. This saves time in preparation and shopping about for food. When I am less well off, the pick and mix of supermarkets come into play. I gladly accept vegetables from my friend's allotments, go to the market for the main things, then consider the cheap supermarkets and then middle-range ones, and if I cannot get a product anywhere else I go to the high-end supermarket. Meals are produced from scratch, are time consuming and shopping takes longer, but I get good food and great value for money. Services in times of austerity are doing the same:

- Can a family member or friend help support the person to engage with local community services? What are the 'circles of support' around the person?

- Could we find services in the community that the person may be interested in and support the person to engage with these services?

- Is there existing support from, for example, housing services that could be used to deliver part of the care plan?

- Could I create a detailed care and support plan and therapeutic interventions that could be delivered by someone whom the person trusts?

- Could assistive technology help the person?

- Are there therapeutic services that the person can access?

- Could a direct debit be used to employ someone to follow a devised care and support plan?

- How can I think outside the box and solve the resource dilemma?

Get out into the communities and be creative about your responses.

We are in a phase of transformation within services today, and social work in particular is at a time when reflection and learning from moments of historical austerity is required. I am old enough to recall social work during the time of Margaret Thatcher and the severe austerity measures imposed. I enjoyed the challenges and the creativity that developed in workers. In those days I was a community social worker, connecting people within a designated community. Today you may hear talk of asset-based social work. One of the most valuable things that we can do when working with socially isolated people is re-engage them with their interests, social contacts and meaningful activity within their own communities. People in the community, family and genuine friendships are of prime importance. The Care Act 2014 sought to develop community-level services, where the whole community is considered for change rather than the community support of individual families or people. The key aim is community capacity building, rather than individual intervention (Barnes *et al.* 2006). Community-based services and community social work seek to link individuals and families with other people and services within the community, developing community-strength resilience and support. The aspects of community practice are illustrated in Figure 6.3.

Figure 6.3: Aspects of community practice
(adapted from Banks et al. 2003)

Developing community work not only benefits those who may require safeguarding, but all sorts of people within the community. Links are created between local residents and community police, community centres and local businesses. People get to know each other and look out for one another. Community social work helps to link people and resources within communities from a strength-focused perspective and aims to prevent the need for statutory intervention. The ideal is that the community is developed to be largely self-sustaining and supportive of its own citizens.

Working within a small community area, the social worker gets to know every person in the area and helps to make connections with services and people. There is always someone there to recognise if a person has not been seen for a day or two, or if rubbish is building up, or if someone is isolated. Community social work sews communities back together, making them supportive and transformative.

Where people within communities have complex needs, then other aspects of social work may be required.

The structure of social worker teams could incorporate asset-based or community-based social work intervention as a community preventative measure, ensuring that ongoing community support is available to enable a person to feel safe within their own community and have easy access to support networks.

■ A case study: George

In 1976, George's father (Fred) died of a heart attack; George was 15 years old at the time. Fred was a keen gardener – he regularly wrote gardening articles for a number of magazines and he was an avid book collector. George loved his father and had also developed a keen interest in gardening. Following his father's death, George's mother became involved with a new man who was sexually, physically and verbally abusive towards George. The new man had no interest in gardening and tried to rid the house of the gardening books. George won the fight to preserve his father's books and articles at a huge cost. George was bribed to do sexual favours for the man in order to keep his father's belongings.

As an adult George became more and more socially isolated; he collected all gardening-related things, such as books, magazines, tools, newspaper articles and wire, and anything that could possibly be of use such as used yoghurt pots, glass jars and bits of piping. The house was so full of objects that George could no longer get to his bathroom or bedroom. George could not cook, clean or look after himself within his home environment. He used buckets from an outside tap to wash. George no longer worked or engaged in any social activities.

The community social worker had supported a young person (Ben) who had a learning disability to get involved in the local allotment scheme, but they appeared to be struggling because they had a lack of knowledge about plants and planting. The other allotment members did not offer much time to this young person. The social worker asked George if he would go along to the allotment and talk to Ben, providing guidance on gardening. Eventually, George was persuaded to go to the allotment, and before long Ben's garden was flourishing. People stopped by to seek advice and guidance from George and he became involved in the allotment meetings and was given his own plot. George eventually confessed that his own garden was run down and people donated plants and seeds. Some of the allotment owners came to help George do a makeover of his garden.

A young builder (Joe) from the allotment befriended George and asked if he could help out and mend some things in the house for him. George agreed to show the builder his home. They began by organising things, so that the bathroom could be accessed. While sorting out the objects the two men talked about George's feelings and how attached he was to the objects, how important his father's things were to him and eventually he told Joe how much he had suffered to keep them. Joe was upset for George and listened to his story, eventually asking him, 'Where are your father's things in among all this then George? Can I see them?'

It had been many years since George had seen any of his father's belongings; they were somewhere at the bottom of the piles of stuff. When George told Joe this, he realised that the rest of the stuff was nowhere near as important to him as his father's belongings. The link to his father was why he had begun collecting. Joe said that the link would always be there because he had the knowledge that his father gave him. Joe pointed out how much happier George was now that he had a garden and he could be so much happier if he had a house. Together they began clearing the property, sorting goods for the allotment and goods for the garage, as well as items that could go. George and Joe eventually got to the items belonging to George's father. Joe went out and bought frames for the articles and a shelving unit for the books.

Joe confessed to George that he had been off work sick with depression following the death of his mother and told George that the social worker had suggested he could help George out. Joe said that working with George had made him feel so much better.

George had a reasonably clear house, had friends at the allotment, regularly helped Ben out and for the first time in years could bath, watch television and cook while looking at the pictures of his father. Joe, Ben and George were brought together through their strengths and assets to help each other in the least intrusive manner possible. Intervention from services was minimal and the community became stronger as a result. Community members were looking out for each other and would continue to do so.

Individual social work

This is traditional care management-type social work, focused on the person themselves and their needs and outcomes. The task is to undertake an assessment and care plan to meet the needs and maintain wellbeing. This type of social work is very person centred. We safeguard the person from abuse and neglect. The down side to only having this type of social work is that there are never enough hours to assess the person, within the family and within the community. Family strengths and resources, or community strengths and resources, may go unidentified. This is a costly service that largely involves the commissioning of resources to meet needs. The opportunities for creativity may go unnoticed due to time pressures and processes. Therapeutic social work assessment and approaches are not used.

Therapeutic social work

Therapeutic social work uses forms of therapeutic assessment and intervention designed and delivered by the social worker, or developed for someone else to deliver. Psychological approaches are used as tools to both assist the person in ongoing change and development and determine a clearer picture of the person and their goals. In cases where abuse and neglect has occurred or serious trauma, it is advisable that a psychologist leads interventions. In the absence of access to psychology services, the social worker may be able to seek psychology supervision while undertaking assessment and therapeutic intervention with someone who has suffered abuse or neglect.

Family social work

In safeguarding adults, the Care Act 2014 identifies a 'whole family approach' which means that we must consider everyone actively involved in the person's life. This may be a person providing care and support, or a family member who is struggling to cope and neglecting themselves as a result of providing care and support. The dynamics of the family will need to be explored – how the family interacts, communicates and supports each other. Barriers, obstacles and ability to provide care and support require assessment. This approach sees the person as part of a family and aims to support the family to function well. Considerations of vulnerability, children and other safeguarding matters are explored in the context of family. Any concerns regarding domestic abuse will be highlighted within the safeguarding forum and coercive and controlling behaviours identified to enable appropriate support to be given to the person suffering domestic abuse. The importance of family and family support is recognised within this model.

Key elements of the social work process in working to safeguard people are to:

- empower and enable those seeking support to resolve difficulties

- break down barriers of oppression and discrimination
- increase life skills and support behaviour change to increase options
- promote independence and autonomy
- consider conflicts
- reduce or delay the need for services, and maintain wellbeing
- support the person to move through a process of change towards their goals
- develop new skills or build on existing abilities
- support a person to address loss, bereavement and trauma
- balance needs, rights and responsibilities
- consider moral and ethical conflicts
- facilitate access to family and community
- maintain human rights.

To achieve this during times of austerity, an increased older population, increased safeguarding referrals and increased pressure on services requires creative strategies that utilise all existing resources available. Change must take place in the structure of services if we are to meet the outcomes and expectations of people who use our services, enable access to therapeutic interventions, and practise in an ethical manner that is justified within law, models, methods, theories and research.

Observation, assessment, hypothesis development and exploration of potential interventions to achieve the person's desired outcomes may need to be considered and applied within a variety of social work contexts: individual/family, community and therapeutic social work. In addition to this, the impact of any abuse or neglect would require community mental health responses to prevent the escalation of mental illness and to maintain mental wellbeing.

Deprivation of Liberty Safeguards (DOLS) exists to safeguard individuals when a deprivation of liberty is an unavoidable part of a best interests care plan. This is a legal process which is scrutinised and monitored. As a reform of the DOLS procedure, Liberty Protection Safeguards (LPS) began as a proposal from the Law Commission about how the changes to current legislation might look in relation to people who are deprived of their liberty. This process is still under consideration. A consideration to free up social work staff for safeguarding purposes may be to better utilise the review of DOLS or LPS assessments. If the care provision is being considered properly and in its entirety to determine least restrictive options and the impact on care and support for the person, then it may be possible to utilise this as a social work review instead of repeating this task all over again. The DOLS reviews must be conducted at least once a year and the LPS initially once a year, and then potentially after a couple of years, they will be conducted every three years. Thousands of people each year require a review to ensure that the deprivation of their liberty is an appropriate need and is proportionate. This is a complex reviewing process, and it would not take too much additional effort to utilise this as the yearly social work review if conducted in enough detail. This would free up vast amounts of social work time to focus on safeguarding tasks.

KEY POINTS

We respond to increasing demands by:

- triaging

- prioritising

- utilising assistive technology

- not being risk averse

- creating new preventative measures

- considering the structure of social work and whether it is possible to meet the duties and responsibilities identified within the Care Act 2014 with current structures

- considering how we support the mental wellbeing as well as the physical wellbeing of people.

This is a major change in service provision that would require a refocus on preventative measures. In addition to the physical and physiological aspects of care and support, the mental and emotional impact of disability would be further explored, with the person receiving targeted and timely support. In cases of abuse or neglect, we not only have to restructure social work and social care responses to be more sustainable for the future and prevent the increase in mental and physical illness, but we must also work in conjunction with health and mental health services to achieve this.

CHAPTER 7

Making Safeguarding Personal

While the language used to describe the disempowered is harsh, it is the fact that often the disempowered are regarded as the 'rejects in society' that maintains the oppression and prevents them from taking control. Empowering people within safeguarding is about giving the power back to the person that has been stolen from them as a result of oppression and discrimination, rather than rescuing them from abuse and neglect and maintaining the power and control ourselves. If we always rescue and rarely do that extra work to give the power back to the person, we are maintaining their dependency on us. Doing something for someone is the easy option, but helping them to understand enough to do it for themselves is the right option. We should have to justify why we have chosen the former rather than the latter option.

Brandl and Horan (2002), in trying to understand the power and control dynamics in later life, identify that, in many cases of abuse and neglect, power and control over the victim is the cause. Consider other forms of abuse such as sexual exploitation, modern-day slavery, human trafficking, financial abuse, female genital mutilation, hate and mate crime, psychological abuse, being groomed for terrorism – they are all issues where someone is asserting power and control over someone, and in safeguarding cases, as a result of their care and support needs, they are unable to protect themselves from that abuse or neglect. The very definition of the eligibility criteria for safeguarding tells us that the person is suffering oppression/discrimination, because someone else is using their power against the frailties of the person with care and support needs. The real task therefore is to give as much of that power and control back to the person and only use protective measures where it is lawful and ethical to do so, or, better still, where the person is in control of those protective measures themselves.

> Safeguarding must respect the autonomy and independence of individuals as well as their right to family life. The fundamental point is that public authority decision making must engage appropriately and meaningfully both with the person, as well as their partner, relatives and carers. Those affected must be allowed to participate effectively in the decision-making process. It is simply unacceptable – and an actionable breach of Article 8 Human Rights – for adult social care to decide, without reference to the person and their carers, what is to be done and then merely to tell them – to 'share' with them – the decision. (Munby 2010)

Making safeguarding personal means that people and organisations work together not only to break down barriers of oppression and discrimination and embed equitable access to services and support, but also to place the person in the centre of their own decision making, to maintain their wellbeing and regain their own freedom, power and control. It is also about supporting them to relocate back to a supportive family and community life where tokenistic gestures to remove risk are replaced with structures that support safety, choice and wellbeing.

Equitable access to services, equitable treatment and reasonable adjustments

It is good practice to ensure that safeguarding policies and procedures enable all parties who require safeguarding to have equitable access to all safeguarding preventative and protective measures. This requires a review of these services to ensure that they are accessible to people who have disabilities and to make reasonable adjustments to ensure access. Services are required to make sure that they are not treating people who have disabilities less favourably than others. If the treatment of the person who has a disability places them at a clear disadvantage compared with other service users, then this would be classed as less favourable treatment (Equality Act 2010). If the quality of the service or the manner in which it is offered is comparatively poor, this *could* amount to less favourable treatment, as in the example that follows.

■ Jane is self-neglecting, and she suffers from agoraphobia, anxiety and depression. Jane is someone who hoards, and the environment in which she lives has become increasingly dangerous and unstable. There are concerns about the amount of goods piled in most places above head height, and the potential for rats, vermin and fly infestations. She has suffered a number of recent falls, resulting in goods falling on top of her, causing injury and hospital admission. A letter has been sent to Jane by the mental health team inviting her to attend an appointment at the clinic. If the mental health team are aware of Jane's anxiety and agoraphobia in addition to her potential hoarding disorder, they should be aware that she may not even open the letter sent to her by nature of her hoarding disorder and anxiety, and even if she does open the correspondence, her agoraphobia would prevent her from accessing the service. Jane is entitled to equitable access to services, and reasonable adjustments must be made to ensure that she can attend an appointment. Jane is also entitled to a complete assessment of her mental and physical health conditions and any existing co-morbidities in line with others who attend the service.

Housing services are threatening to evict Jane, but there is reason to believe that she does not understand the tenancy agreement and her capacity to understand that agreement has not been reviewed, or assessed at the point of concern, or since. Reasonable adjustments have not been made to accommodate her disabilities, including potential hoarding disorder.

Consider whether this scenario has empowered Jane, and whether she has been treated equitably under the Equality Act 2010. Are her human rights being met? Under the Care Act 2014, consider whether Jane has a right to assessment, and under the Equality Act 2010, consider whether reasonable adjustments have been made. Are we preventing or delaying the need for future services and maintaining Jane's physical and mental wellbeing? Lastly, consider whether this is an ethical course of action, or an effort to prevent those 'difficult cases' from affecting already stretched services.

■ James has autism and has been subject to financial abuse. Due to his diagnosis, the police deem him to lack credibility as a witness and end their investigation. Diagnosis is not the same as credibility as a witness, and the police are preventing equitable access.

■ The local authority produces information about safeguarding arrangements, but in order to save time and money it does not produce leaflets in accessible formats. A person with autism and speech and language disabilities has difficulty reading the leaflets and makes a complaint. The man feels that he is at a disadvantage as he does not have the same information about keeping himself safe and access to safeguarding services as people who have a physical disability would have. The local authority has not made reasonable adjustments.

Under the Equality Act 2010, this raises the question about whether responses are proportionate and have legitimate aims rather than, for example, the sole aim of discrimination being a cost reduction. Legitimate aims include:

- ensuring that services and benefits are targeted at those who most need them

- the fair exercise of powers

- ensuring the health and safety of those using the service provider's service or others, as long as risks are clearly specified

- preventing fraud or other forms of abuse or inappropriate use of services provided by the service provider

- ensuring the wellbeing or dignity of those using the service.

And...the aim must be proportionate.

■ Jonathan is homeless; he suffered childhood abuse and had a number of foster carers, but after a particularly difficult foster placement he left and disengaged from services. Jonathan did not trust people or relationships and therefore spent a lot of time alone, his mental health deteriorated significantly and he became physically very frail. He stopped looking after himself, stopped feeding himself and on cold nights he sometimes urinated next to his sleeping area, leaving him smelly and unkempt. Jonathan drank alcohol to 'drown his sorrows'. Recently Jonathan has been taunted by local youths who kick at him during the night, follow him when he tries to get away and throw his belongings in the bin if he leaves them for even a brief period of time. On occasions, Jonathan has asked for assistance from the police, and while some are supportive, nothing changes and the police often just tell him to use his energy to find somewhere to stay. A homeless charity has become involved and it has made a safeguarding referral stating that he is a homeless man, is suffering physical and emotional abuse and is very vulnerable. The charity is concerned that Jonathan might be critically unwell. The local authority policies and procedures state that they have a zero-tolerance approach to abuse and neglect. Here is a man both abused and neglected and yet the referral for safeguarding is rejected. The person triaging the case states that 'homelessness' is not a care and support need and therefore does not meet safeguarding criteria.

If the referral in this case had said that the man has mental health problems, substance misuse problems, self-neglects and although undiagnosed there are symptoms of trauma associated with childhood abuse and neglect, then he *might* be accepted for safeguarding. Why would we not want to support him to keep himself safe? Could it be that people are making ill-informed judgements about deserving and undeserving recipients of care and support? In Jonathan's case, his mental health will not improve, his physical health will also deteriorate, his mistrust of services will grow and he will at some point either present to services and require intensive support and intervention, or he may die. What happened to the wellbeing principle? What happened to preventing or delaying the need for services? What happened to empowering someone to take control and address oppression and discrimination? Does it all boil down to a financial and resource implication that creates a situation where services are pressured into choosing between those they deem accepting and therefore deserving of services?

In her article 'The language of shirkers and scroungers?', Kayleigh Garthwaite (2011) challenges welfare reform to stop focusing on the 'deserving' and 'undeserving'. She challenges us to stop observing the appearance, living conditions and the lack of work life of a person and focus on the life experiences. What they say about their life and how the person feels as a result of their experiences are of prime importance in the safeguarding assessment. 'By listening to the narratives of people who are labelled in this way, perhaps then the vilifying discourse surrounding them can be erased or at least challenged by giving a voice to people who are not "other" but could be any of us' (Garthwaite 2011, p.372).

To empower people and achieve equitable access to services, treatment and reasonable adjustments, we must be consciously aware of the potential for further oppression and discrimination. We must consider how we empower people (see Figure 7.1).

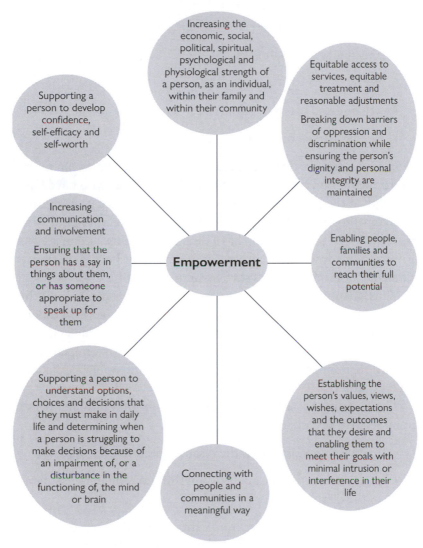

Figure 7.1: The sociological process of empowerment

To achieve empowerment, we must ensure that people are treated with dignity, respect and not discriminated against on grounds of:

- age
- disability
- gender reassignment
- pregnancy and maternity
- race
- religion and belief
- sex and sexual orientation.

People who have a disability are protected from harassment and discrimination under the Equality Act 2010. People who have had a disability in the past are also protected under the Act. Non-disabled people are protected where they are perceived to have a disability or are associated with someone who has a disability. In some circumstances, a non-disabled person is protected where they have experienced harassment or unlawful acts such as victimisation.

The Equality Act 2010 deems a person to have a disability if they have a physical or mental impairment which has a substantial and long-term effect on their ability to carry out day-to-day activities. Impairments can include but are not exclusive to sensory impairments, severe disfigurement, mental illness, mental health problems, diabetes, epilepsy, cancer, HIV infection and multiple sclerosis.

The Equality Act 2010 says that treatment of a disabled person amounts to discrimination where:

- a service provider treats the disabled person unfavourably
- the treatment is because of something arising in consequence of the disabled person's disability
- the service provider cannot show that this treatment is a proportionate means of achieving a legitimate aim.

These apply unless the service provider does not know, and could not reasonably be expected to know, that the person has the disability.

Increasing communication and involvement

We have already established that one of the most important aspects of safeguarding is listening to the story that the person tells of their life. Their wishes, values and expectations for life are important in establishing a rapport and gaining an understanding of the person, and writing this narrative in the first person 'I' statements within your assessment humanises the assessment from the beginning, ensuring that the person is central to their own story. If the assessment process puts into place preventative safeguarding measures in this manner, then the safeguarding interventions (if these preventative measures fail) should continue to explore the person's narrative to establish what they think went wrong and how they would like to address it. 'Narrative analysis enhances listening and responses to people's stories, the ability to identify common themes from experience, and aids understanding of why some interventions are not working' (Garthwaite 2011, p.372). In recording a person's narrative, practitioners must be aware of their own judgements and deconstruct any assumptions. Table 7.1 provides some examples.

Table 7.1: Practitioners' observations and judgements

Recorded observation	Challenging this perception	Preferred recording
Tannish is not engaging	Ask why Tannish is not engaging. It may be for health reasons, mental health reasons, lack of funds, anxiety around service intervention, misconceptions about intrusive services, bad experiences of service interventions, value-based, cultural or religious beliefs	Tannish was brought up in residential care services following severe neglect as a child. When asked about rejecting current services Tannish said, 'I don't trust them, they let me down as a child, and I became homeless. I learned that the only way to survive is to look out for number one, yourself.' When asked 'How does that make you feel?', Tannish replied, 'I feel alone and upset. Why does it feel like no one cares?'
Mary is both verbally and physically aggressive	Ask why Mary is verbally and physically aggressive. It may be that she is afraid, stressed, distressed, coping with trauma, dealing with change, managing complex or difficult situations or is not coping with the nature of the intervention	When asked what was upsetting her and making her feel angry, Mary replied, 'I was sexually abused three months ago. I didn't make a statement to the police and I feel angry with myself for not fighting back, not being strong enough to say something and stop the person. Everything reminds me of my inability to cope. I have nightmares, don't sleep and get even more upset and irritable. People come here and ask me to do everyday tasks, trivial things that I feel that I cannot achieve'

cont.

Recorded observation	Challenging this perception	Preferred recording
John's self-neglect is a 'lifestyle choice'	Ask why a person might self-neglect to this extent and why they may be worried about any service intervention	When asked about his life John said, 'I was seven when my mother died. I loved her so much, I can still remember feeling her hair against my face as a child. My father remarried within six months of my mother dying, and it was obvious even as a child that he was close to this woman before my mother died. Afterwards they went on holiday and left me at home; she didn't care about me and he was bowled over by her. I was 11 when they both died in a car accident. I went to live with my gran who was too old to be bothered by me and didn't care about me. After my mother died, no one cared, no one taught me how to care for myself and people told me that I was ungrateful when I talked about how unhappy I was with my gran. They said that people like me never change, we are always scroungers and ungrateful for the kindness given by others. I feel unworthy of love, no one wanted me, and everyone rejected me, no one really wanted to help me, even as a child. I just get by here – my newspapers and books don't reject me. They come to the door and I am embarrassed, not worthy of their time and energy. I know that they are busy people. I just tell them that I am fine, that this is the way that I am, you can't change me anyway'

In some cases, the person may have difficulty speaking up for themselves, or making decisions, and might require an advocate. Boylan and Dalrymple (2011) identify the benefits of advocacy as offering the person:

- a voice in services or actions

- support to achieve active citizenship

- support to challenge inequality

- the opportunity to challenge social injustice, inequality and unfairness.

The Care Act 2014 places a duty on the local authority to ensure that independent advocacy is available for those who need support and where a family member would not be a suitable advocate. Family members may not be suitable advocates when:

- they have a vested interest in a certain outcome or outcomes
- they are involved in any safeguarding allegations
- there is suspicion of coercive or controlling behaviour
- an independent person would be more beneficial in the given circumstances
- the person would prefer someone independent from the family.

There are different kinds of advocacy:

- self-advocacy
- peer advocacy.

There are also professional advocates such as:

- independent mental capacity advocates
- independent domestic violence advocates
- independent sexual violence advocates
- independent mental health advocates.

It is important to discuss with the person the benefits of each type of advocacy and help them to understand who might be the most appropriate advocate for their situation. A person may already have an advocate they wish to stay with as they have built a relationship with them; however, if this is not the case, you will need to consider the circumstances of the abuse/neglect and who might be best placed to advocate for the person in these circumstances:

- A person may lack capacity to make a few decisions, but the main issue is the impact of domestic abuse on the person – it may be better to consider an independent domestic violence advocate.

- A person may have suffered domestic abuse, but the matter that impacted on them the most was the sexual violence – it may be better to consider an independent mental capacity advocate.

- A person may have suffered domestic abuse and sexual abuse, but they lack capacity to make a number of decisions, including big decisions such as change of residence. It is likely that an independent mental capacity advocate is best placed to support the person.

- A person should be an active participant rather than a passive recipient of safeguarding services. This will require you to engage with the person, gather information about their values, wishes, expectations and desired outcomes and gain an understanding about why the outcomes they have chosen are important to them. This is not a one-off interaction followed by professionals conducting the safeguarding business – active participation means that the person and/or the family (with their agreement or consent) should be involved by all professionals throughout the process. Part of the safeguarding action plan should be to agree with the person and family the communication methods that they would find most helpful, such as meetings, letters, confidential emails or telephone contact. Establish the frequency of direct involvement, or pertinent times when they would appreciate discussion. The frequency of meetings, attendance at meetings and timeliness of feedback should be discussed with a view to the person controlling the personal safeguarding outcomes, rather than professionals dictating safeguarding actions. It may be that there are additional safeguarding concerns that have come to light not pertaining to the person themselves; for example, a perpetrator may have abused or neglected more than one person and there may be a risk to others, in which case the safeguarding meeting would be staged in two parts, the second part to accommodate those matters not directly relevant to the safeguarding of the individual.

The *Making Safeguarding Personal* guide (Lawdon, Lewis and Williams 2014) identifies 'outcomes' as the need to find out the following:

- What do people want our involvement to achieve – how can we help to make a difference?

- How can we help them to express what they want through social work?

- How can we work out what people who lack capacity want through engaging with them, and with their representatives, independent mental capacity advocates or using a best interests assessment?

- How can we develop and support practice that does this effectively?

- How do people experience the support they receive?

- What is best practice in terms of working with people to achieve effective outcomes?

'Making safeguarding personal' throughout the process

In 1996, I moved to work in learning disability services and I was told that I would become a point of contact for staff to report concerns about abuse. It was the early days of safeguarding and there was little national guidance, so it was only the very serious cases that were brought to my attention. I remember asking my senior manager what my role was, about what I could add to the police investigation in these cases. The answer was simple:

> Deb, we provide health and social care services around the person to lessen the impact of abuse and neglect. We question why it happened and how we can stop it happening again to anyone. You make sure that the access to support is equitable and that the person's mental and physical health does not deteriorate after experiencing abuse. We need to do something so that people recognise that it is not alright for people who have disabilities to be targeted for abuse.

Over two decades later, after all the changes in safeguarding, I still reflect on this advice every day. I consider whether I have achieved this to the best of my ability. The two key additions to the advice above that I have learned in the last couple of decades are that, first, adult protection enquiries require a multi-agency response, and second, we are not safeguarding the person unless it is about their own definition of safety. My opinion is that we are safeguarding ourselves, what we errantly think would keep us safe from challenge when the process moves away from the person's own narratives of safety.

Some local authorities have safeguarding referral forms to complete in order to identify a safeguarding matter for them. When local authorities have received such a form, rather than having the initial telephone conversation with the person who has care and support needs or their family member or advocate, there are a number of things that they may need to be aware of. People completing forms will all need to be well versed in achieving best evidence and how to gather information, preserve evidence, be person centred in their approach, but consider all risks to others. They will have to manage the initial aspects of information gathering and confidentiality and recognise potential crime to report appropriately to the police. They will also need to understand what evidence to preserve and how. In trying to triage through the referral form process, we are placing a lot of onus on individuals within agencies to understand a lot about safeguarding, and local authorities are running the risk of not having sufficient oversight and guidance in the early aspects of intervention. The benefit of this method is that cases can be prioritised and responded to in relation to risks presented.

The use of forms can create more process-driven safeguarding, with the practitioner being directed to ask questions about risk, advocacy, capacity, perpetrator and location of abuse, but often doing little to address the person's needs, or what the person's perception of safety might be. The description of safeguarding, and the methods used to help a person understand what can and cannot be done to help them achieve the outcomes that they want, are not always identified on these forms and therefore the issues relating to informed consent are not as evident as they should be. The other worry that I have about this methodology is that people become concerned about whether they have provided enough information. They ask questions and investigate further, and this may well affect evidence in a potential criminal investigation, with the outcome being that credible evidence is destroyed. Leading questions, or questions asked that invoke particular responses in the person, can mean that future criminal investigations are tainted by the early methods of enquiry used.

Defining a Section 42 enquiry and the level of personalised support

The Care Act 2014 statutory guidance and guidance on the Social Care Institute for Excellence website suggest that an enquiry can be anything from a telephone conversation with the referrer to a full-scale police investigation. This poses difficulty because the initial triage is part of a safeguarding enquiry, so, for example, a care worker has reported that medication has been missed for Mrs Jones. The local authority speaks with the care worker, who says that they have checked with the GP and there are no adverse effects, there have been no other medication errors, the person administering the medication has identified a clear reason why the medication was missed and this has been recorded in their supervision records. Relevant parties have been informed. In other words, this is a one-off, isolated incident with little risk of it being repeated and no risk to others. The impact of the incident was minimal to nothing, and all appropriate action has been taken. A Section 42 enquiry has been conducted; however, the safeguarding matters are all concluded and the person has been safeguarded by staff at the care home. Some local authorities will record this as a Section 42 enquiry response and others will not. Some local authorities only record contact as a Section 42 enquiry response when the case has been escalated for further safeguarding action, making the statistics for enquiries as complex and diverse as the statistics for previous alerts or concern reporting.

I am going to define the difference between the two enquiry responses for the purpose of clarity in this book, but not as a definitive answer to the language of safeguarding – this must be determined within each agency's processes.

Safeguarding enquiry response:

- Low-level cases of prevention or protection where, following risk assessment, we might consider the need to provide oversight and guidance, or minimal intervention that can address initial concerns, or occasions where agencies need direction, or clarification during triage.

- Those who require a social care/health needs assessment and care and support plan that would entirely meet the needs and address the concerns.

Adult protection enquiry response:

- Where a person's physical or mental health is deteriorating as a result of abuse, neglect or self-neglect (impact of abuse).

- Where a number of agencies are involved in the care provision of this person and we are either not preventing the risk of abuse or neglect, or not protecting the person from abuse or neglect (prevalence).

- Where there is a high-risk perpetrator involved.

- Where there is potential crime.

- Where the person is very dependent on the perpetrator.

- Where there is a risk of further abuse to the person or others.

- Where there may be coercive or intimidating behaviours or grooming.

- Where a risk assessment identifies that the concerns are escalating.

I am calling the low-level risk cases a safeguarding enquiry response and those enquiries that necessitate a more detailed enquiry an adult protection response. I am therefore making a definition between low-level responses and more complex multi-agency interventions. I feel the need to define the issues in this way because I currently see many safeguarding referrals that require a full multi-agency, considered and coordinated response being given to a social worker or care manager and a single-agency response is delivered that in no way addresses the complexities of the case. The only potential outcome is a stressed worker, feeling isolated and alone with a complex case and no solutions. No single person or single agency has all the answers.

Single-agency measures are not a sufficient response when multiple agencies are, or should be, involved in the care and support of the person. This is what leads to a lack of coordinated risk assessments and capacity assessments, a lack of agencies being held accountable for their provision of information and capacity assessments, a lack of information sharing and a lack of consideration for legislation used by each of the agencies and how this fits with the person's human rights. This approach can become very process driven, with what the person wants being overtaken by the worker following instruction about perceived safety from the agency's perspective. The appropriate agency to lead the enquiry is almost never identified within this model of practice, meaning that credibility of evidence for court can also come into question. For example, a person is returned to a care home with severe pressure sores after a stay in hospital. The safeguarding allegation is one of negligence. The person concerned has had a significant procedure requiring anaesthetics and surgery over a prolonged period of time, they have diabetes and they are very frail. The social worker sent to make enquiries does not know enough about tissue viability; the nurse may know slightly more, but the tissue viability nurse would provide credible evidence and may be the best-placed person to lead the enquiry. The tissue viability nurse would be the best-placed person to help the individual understand what has happened to them and involve them in decision making as much as possible.

Once the initial risks are addressed, the starting point for any enquiry is: 'What are the gaps in my knowledge and who can help fill in the gaps?'

The first gap in my knowledge is: 'What does safe look like for the person concerned?'

What does being safe look like to the person?

The first person to contact is the person who has care and support needs and is suffering or at risk of abuse and neglect. The person leading the safeguarding enquiries will be the coordinator and delegator and will not always have the time to conduct the enquiries themselves, so clear instruction supported by explicit training in personalised safeguarding is required for all agencies potentially involved in enquiries. The most appropriate person to ask the initial questions will be someone who has been working with the person, developed a rapport with them and is independent of any allegations or affiliations. Support or advocacy should be sought for the person where they would want support, or where they might have difficulty being involved in the safeguarding process. Where the person is not able to communicate their needs themselves, then information may need to be sought from carers.

During initial discussion, the person may be wary about talking with someone, fearful that control of events may be taken away from them. It is important that the person knows about what can and cannot be shared (see Chapter 4), and this is done in a sensitive manner. You need to make it very clear that in relation to them as an individual, if they are able to make an informed choice or decision, no one can change that.

The next thing to establish is what does safe look like for that person. This is in addition to the outcomes that a person wants to achieve and is part of an ongoing and changing process. Below in this section, a social worker is grappling with the reality of making safeguarding personal and the preventative agenda. I shall describe the discussion with the case study in question.

■ Mrs Barnes is an 80-year-old woman who lives in rented accommodation near to her daughter and grandson in X Local Authority. Money has been going missing from Mrs Barnes' bank account and there is some evidence to suggest that the grandson has been taking significant amounts of money from Mrs Barnes on a regular basis. Mrs Barnes does not believe that it is her grandson who has been taking her money and agrees to contact the police. Initially, Mrs Barnes says that she wants to find out who has been taking her money.

The police identify that all Mrs Barnes' money has been taken over a two-year period, amounting to just over £10,000. Police have evidence that it is her grandson who has been taking the money. Mrs Barnes is devastated and wants some support to speak with her daughter, but is worried about this. An advocate supports Mrs Barnes to talk through her concerns with her daughter, but her daughter refuses to listen, or have anything to do with Mrs Barnes' concerns. Mrs Barnes feels isolated, lonely and abandoned by her family. Mrs Barnes loves her daughter and grandson, but they have both deeply hurt her. She feels that she has been a terrible parent/grandparent to raise people who could treat her this way and describes how she feels guilty and blames herself. Mrs Barnes now feels unable to manage her own daily needs, she has become low in mood, does not go out of the house and is not addressing any of her financial affairs. Mrs Barnes has stopped eating and is not taking her medication.

When asked what *outcomes* she wants from a safeguarding intervention, she says that she does not want any outcome, that she cannot prosecute her family, she just wants the pain in her heart to go away. The advocate supports Mrs Barnes to speak with some people in domestic abuse services who can help her understand these feelings. Mrs Barnes attends the local women's domestic abuse service for six weeks. When asked what would make her *feel safe*, she says that she no longer feels as if she belongs with her family in X Local Authority, she doesn't feel loved, secure and safe with them. The answer to the question about *outcomes* described by Mrs Barnes directly relates to the specific incident itself; however, a person's understanding of *safety* relates to their life's experiences and a personal perspective on what they would need to feel safe. People who use our services do not always recognise the options or choices on offer, or the level of support that can be provided; asking what would make them feel safe allows a narrative to open up about the wider aspects of safeguarding.

Mrs Barnes has a daughter who lives in York (Jane) and she says that she would feel safer living nearer to Jane. Jane has agreed to get a joint account with Mrs Barnes and to have regular oversight of her finances and transactions, at Mrs Barnes' request. Mrs Barnes has been assessed as having capacity to make decisions about finance, but is in the early stages of dementia and has agreed to establish a lasting power of attorney for Jane to make financial decisions on her behalf once she loses capacity to make these decisions for herself. Mrs Barnes says that she feels safe in the knowledge that there will be no opportunity for financial abuse in the future and has established her own way of preventing abuse from occurring. This has helped her feel safer; however, her feelings about herself, her self-confidence and her self-esteem have been severely affected after being a victim of domestic abuse.

The social worker assesses Mrs Barnes' needs and puts a plan in place to support the transfer of her care to York. Suitable accommodation is identified and care and support packages provided. The Age UK services are nearby, and Mrs Barnes is encouraged to get involved in the activities from the beginning. A bereavement counsellor attends the centre regularly and staff ask Mrs Barnes to speak with the counsellor. The counsellor identifies that it is like a huge loss causing bereavement, grief and trauma. The impact on Mrs Barnes of finding that her family could perpetrate abuse against her, not support her when she raised concerns and her doubts about their love, alongside her own feelings of guilt, are affecting both her mental and physical wellbeing. Mrs Barnes agrees to see the counsellor at Age UK on a weekly basis. Assessment after three months identifies that Mrs Barnes is more involved in family life with Jane, she has established friends within her local community through Age UK and says that she has a wonderful social life. Mrs Barnes says that she is no longer rich in money, but is much richer in love. When asked if she is happy with the support that she has received, Mrs Barnes said that she was reluctant to speak with the counsellor but she identified that they were an important source of support. Mrs Barnes said, 'They not only helped me feel better after my money was taken, but they also helped me to feel more confident about a lot of things. I am very happy with the support I received.'

This scenario may be considered by some people to be fairly moderate abuse, but when we explore the impact of the abuse on the person, it is very substantial and could become critical in the future, and so the duty to prevent the need for future services is triggered. In this situation, the safeguarding lead, police, victim, support, social worker, advocate, domestic abuse services, housing, family (Jane), solicitor (lasting power of attorney), Age UK and counselling were the agencies involved in providing the appropriate support at the appropriate time.

When the social worker was asked about what traditionally would have happened in her local authority area, she said:

The referral would be received by the safeguarding team who would ask a social worker on duty to triage. Mrs Barnes had very low-level dementia and this did not usually affect her ability to cook, clean, dress or get out and about in the community. It is unlikely that she would be seen as meeting the social work eligibility criteria. Mrs Barnes initially consented to the police investigation and therefore we would have supported her to contact the police and may have considered her eligible for safeguarding, on a very low level. We would ask what outcomes she would want from safeguarding, and when she said that she did not want to prosecute, it is likely that the case would be closed without further action. We would have assumed Mrs Barnes to have capacity to make her own financial decisions and in this assumption might have missed the opportunity to give her advice and guidance about things like joint bank accounts and lasting power of attorney. Financial abuse would probably have been the route of the referral, so I am not sure whether we would have considered domestic abuse services for support. Because Mrs Barnes had capacity to make her own decisions, I don't think that we would have considered advocacy.

If I was honest, I thought asking people about what makes them feel safe was about street lighting and police presence, I have not thought about it in this context before.

The social worker was asked about how the duties to prevent abuse or neglect and provide personalised care and support would be justified in traditional safeguarding responses. The social worker replied:

We make enquiries, or cause police enquiries to take place, we ask what outcomes the person wants and determine whether they are able to make those decisions, we prevent abuse from occurring by addressing the abuse and stopping further financial abuse and we provide services to meet the needs of those people assessed as eligible for social work.

When the social worker was asked to consider the benefits of working with Mrs Barnes in the way that we did, she said, 'Well it wasn't really about safeguarding and protecting Mrs Barnes, was it? It was about Mrs Barnes taking control of her life again and managing things so that she didn't need us in the future.'

When asked to describe what services Mrs Barnes would have needed in the future after the traditional methods of safeguarding intervention and to estimate the cost and time that would be required, the social worker replied:

Mrs Barnes was not eating, socialising or taking medication after the financial abuse. I could see that on some occasions her dementia was more evident, identifying a significant deterioration in a short space of time. Mrs Barnes' physical and mental wellbeing would deteriorate quickly and it would not take long before she would be fully eligible for social services. Without the love and support of other family members, I am not sure what impact this might have had on Mrs Barnes, but I know that she felt guilty and blamed her own poor parenting for the incident occurring, and this guilt would not have left her without domestic abuse services and counselling services. I think that Mrs Barnes would have become quite socially isolated.

The cost would be that she would require regular social work, nursing and mental health intervention, perhaps future safeguarding, as she was beginning to neglect herself. Eventually we would need supported living, hospital care and potentially residential care provision if she continued to deteriorate. Perhaps she would remain capacitated and refuse all these services and then there would not be a cost.

When asked about the cost in terms of Mrs Barnes' quality of life and how we can delay the need for services, making safeguarding personal and our duties to ensure that needs are assessed and met to maintain physical and mental wellbeing, the answer was: 'We would love to do this work, we want to put the preventative aspects of safeguarding in place, but we do not have the time and so we have to strike a balance of what we can achieve and justify. We do not have the time to do all of this with all of the cases.' When asked whether it would be achievable if every agency were doing this and not just the social worker, she said, 'But they won't, will they? There is no coordination of safeguarding and so no one really holds agencies accountable – it's a vicious circle.'

The matter of agency cooperation and being held accountable at a strategic level is clear in the social worker's narrative, and the question of how much is enough is raised again. With a few hours' additional safeguarding work at this stage, we have someone who could manage quite independently for many years in the community. Without this personalised and preventative agenda we would have created dependency in the future, at not only huge cost financially, but also cost in terms of the amount of health and social services' time that would need to be dedicated to Mrs Barnes as her mental and physical health deteriorated. Hours and hours of services would be added to the care and support plan much sooner than would have been necessary, if the initial few hours' care and support had not been identified.

Ethically, I do not think that we can justify these low-level responses that do not consider the impact of the events on the person, or ask them what would make them feel safe. Pragmatically, the only answer to achieving this is if we were to hold every agency accountable for the outcomes. The whole safeguarding adults board needs to reassure itself that it has defined how much is enough and for each service. Have we demonstrated true consent, have we recorded the actions taken to help a person understand their options, and where there is reason to doubt a person's ability to provide consent, have we assessed that person's capacity to make that decision?

This debate begins with our definition of safety (see Figure 7.2) and continues in every safeguarding intervention or interaction. The truth is that asking a person if they want to be safeguarded, assuming that they are capacitated and accepting their refusal as a lack of consent is easy, but I would suggest it is too simplistic as well as being unethical.

Figure 7.2: The cogs that represent our definition of safety

To fully explore what being safe means to a person, we must explore a number of aspects that define safety. We cannot assume that a person would hold physical safety more important over emotional safety or vice versa. Past experiences and the impact of past experiences will inform our definition. For example, a person who has suffered domestic abuse and has been emotionally tortured and controlled may try to evoke a physical abuse response to end the emotional trauma, and therefore the feeling of safety is associated with their ability to make choices, freedom and the ability to relax and feel secure. A person who has suffered physical abuse and threats of physical abuse (e.g. gang fights) may define safety as somewhere where you don't have to be watchful, where there is no threat of violence, and a place that you can head towards if feeling threatened. We explored some of these concepts in the preface of this book. Our perception of safety can be explored more widely considering the impact of the media, culture and popular culture and religion on our perception of safety, and we can also add into these concepts the irrational fears such as phobias. Once we have established a clear picture of why a person feels a certain way, we can gain a clear pathway for supporting the person to feel safer and to be safe.

Increasing the economic, social, political, spiritual, psychological and physiological strength of a person, as an individual, within their family and within their community

The more a person is involved and actively engaged in family life, friendships and their community, the safer they will feel. To achieve this safety net, we must conduct holistic individual, family and community-based assessments to meet the identified needs of the individual, family and community. Care planning must enhance participation and remove or reduce presenting barriers.

One of the things that we can do is to help the person identify the strengths and interests that they have to facilitate active participation. Here are some questions you might ask (in a sensitive and timely manner):

- What has been important to you in your life?

- What is important to you now? Has that changed?

- Who do you like to contact when things go wrong or you need support?

- Who would you like to talk to when you need to talk about something important?

- Who helps you out when you need it?

- What do you like about the area that you live in?

- What about where you live feels safe?

- What about where you live feels pleasing?

- What makes your home a good place to be?

- What is of value to you?

- What makes you feel stronger?

- When do you feel the most well?

- What about your character is good?

- What things have you been good at throughout your life so far and what things are you good at now?

- How do you get around?

- When do you feel the strongest and why?

- What skills do you have that you are proud of?

- What do you care about?

- What strengths do others see in you?

- What do you see as a personal achievement?

- When do you have the best sleep?

- What have been your educational strengths?

- What are and were your career strengths?

- What strengths do you have when things go wrong?

- As a child, what were you good at?

- What do you do to feel safe?

- What makes you feel proud?

- What would you describe your best qualities to be?

- What is working well at the moment?

- How could things be improved for you at the moment?

- What would take at least some if not all the risks away?

- Could things be done in a different way?

These questions form part of any assessment process – in some cases safety plans may be required.

Example of a person-centred safety plan

Here is an example of questions that you might ask in cases of domestic abuse to ensure that the plan is centred around the person:

Adult safety

- How safe do you feel?

- Is it safe to talk now?

- Do you have a safe contact number?

- What do you do to make sure that you and others around you are safe?

- Think about your own actions to help keep things safe – what has worked in the past?

- What about the actions of others?

Child safety

- What are the things that make your child safe? When is your child not safe?

- What is dangerous for your child?

- What are you concerned about in relation to your child? Think about the area you live in, home, streets, the food they eat, drugs and drink, safety from partner/others.

Risk management

- What are the risks at the moment and have you managed these risks in the past?

- What new risks might there be?

- Have you left before? How did you manage this and what would you do differently this time?

Strong relationships

- Who makes you feel happy?

- Who would you go to talk to when you needed to talk about something important?

- Do you have strong religious and/or cultural beliefs?

- What are your concerns?

- Who helps you out when you need it?

Short-term planning

- What would make you feel safe?

- How might you achieve this?
- What do you need to plan now?
- Who would you tell and who would you not tell?
- What contact numbers do you need?

Children's schooling

- What do you like about your children's school?
- Think about activities, people, attendance, transport, friends – is school a safe place?
- What do you need to plan for your child's schooling?
- Have you informed the school or are they aware?

Enough money

- What do you do well to handle your money?
- Can you put aside money to prepare for leaving? Do you have enough money for necessary things? For extra things?
- Who is around that can help you out or help you to get more money when you need it?
- What ways have you tried to earn more money?

Good health

- Is your family healthy? Does anyone have any specific mental or physical health needs?
- What do you need?
- What is good about your family's health care?
- How far away is your GP?
- How do you get there and are there any other health services that you use?
- Are you sleeping?
- Do you take regularly prescribed medication?

- How might you get this if you leave?

- Might you be pregnant?

Transport

- How do you get around?

- What transport is there to help you to do this?

- Are there other transport resources that you can use if you need them?

Drugs and alcohol

- Is anyone drinking a lot of alcohol or using a lot of drugs at the moment?

- How do you and your family stay away from drugs that you feel are not helpful?

- What are the drugs that your family members are choosing to stay away from?

- What drugs are you choosing to use that are helpful?

- Is your GP aware?

Planning to leave

- Do you have key documents such as passport, bank cards, national insurance number, bus pass, payment information, medical information and contact numbers easily available?

- Do you have cash to get you to where you need to be?

- Do you require a refuge? Where will the children go?

- Do you have medication ready?

- Do you have a mobile phone that is not tracked?

- Are you able to access the internet without being tracked?

What else is important to you?

Maintaining human rights, including the right to private life (autonomy)

There is a balance between keeping a person safe and a person's autonomous decision making. There may be occasions where a capacitated person is making what appears to be an unwise decision. If that decision does not affect others in an adverse manner, then they are entitled to make their own decisions, even if the decision results in significant personal risk. The person must realise the consequences of their actions. Safeguarding is therefore not about keeping people safe but is more about maintaining a person's human rights.

The Human Rights Act 1998 sets out the rights and freedoms that everyone within the UK is entitled to. The Act ensures that the rights established by the European Convention on Human Rights are set out in domestic British law. Public bodies like the courts, the police, local authorities and hospitals are required to carry out their functions to respect and protect human rights. It is a foundation act, which means that Parliament will nearly always try to ensure that new laws are compatible with the rights set out in the European Convention on Human Rights. In multi-agency practice, where laws may sometimes appear to be in conflict with each other, the multi-agency forum can scrutinise decision making through the Human Rights Act. In safeguarding, all aspects of the Human Rights Act will be considered:

- Article 2: Right to life
- Article 3: Freedom from torture and inhuman or degrading treatment
- Article 4: Freedom from slavery and forced labour
- Article 5: Right to liberty and security
- Article 6: Right to a fair trial
- Article 7: No punishment without law
- Article 8: Respect for your private and family life, home and correspondence
- Article 9: Freedom of thought, belief and religion
- Article 10: Freedom of expression
- Article 11: Freedom of assembly and association

- Article 12: Right to marry and start a family

- Article 14: Protection from discrimination in respect of these rights and freedoms

- Protocol 1, Article 1: Right to peaceful enjoyment of your property

- Protocol 1, Article 2: Right to education

- Protocol 1, Article 3: Right to participate in free elections

- Protocol 13, Article 1: Abolition of the death penalty.

Article 2 of the Human Rights Act 1998 states that 'The state must do everything possible to preserve life', and is important in safeguarding. Lessons learned from safeguarding adults reviews can highlight where things are going wrong in safeguarding and things that should have been considered along the way. It is often useful to work back from lessons learned and implement these in relation to the application of law and methods of practice into daily safeguarding work.

Article 2 of the Human Rights Act 1998 requires us to determine the level of risk and whether risk is potentially life threatening. We must ask whether we have done everything possible to prevent a person's death. Article 2 also identifies that there should be an official investigation into deaths where the state has failed to protect life. Section 44 of the Care Act 2014 provides further detail and guidance on this matter for the purpose of safeguarding adults reviews:

Section 44, Care Act 2014, Safeguarding adults reviews

(1) A Safeguarding Adults Board must arrange for there to be a review of a case involving an adult in its area with needs for care and support (whether or not the local authority has been meeting any of those needs) if:

(a) there is reasonable cause for concern about how the Safeguarding Adults Board, members of it or other persons with relevant functions worked together to safeguard the adult, and (b) condition 1 or 2 is met.

(2) Condition 1 is met if:

(a) the adult has died, and

(b) the Safeguarding Adults Board knows or suspects that the death resulted from abuse or neglect (whether or not it knew about or suspected the abuse or neglect before the adult died).

(3) Condition 2 is met if:

(a) the adult is still alive, and

(b) the Safeguarding Adults Board knows or suspects that the adult has experienced serious abuse or neglect.

(4) A Safeguarding Adults Board may arrange for there to be a review of any other case involving an adult in its area with needs for care and support (whether or not the local authority has been meeting any of those needs).

Following the case of *Osman v UK* (Lawteacher.net 2018), public bodies can be held to be negligent if they have not prevented death as there is a positive requirement to ensure preventative measures. The issue of negligence arises in relation to determining whether agencies could have worked more effectively to protect the adult. Bryden and Storey (2011), writing about medical negligence, considered the duty of care first established in 1932. During the case *Donoghue v Stevenson* (1932), Lord Aitkin established that there was a general duty to take reasonable care to avoid foreseeable injury to a neighbour. Bryden and Storey (2011) identifies a three-part test to determine whether:

- a person is owed a duty of care

- there is a breach if that duty of care is established

- as a direct result of that breach, legally recognised harm has been caused.

Negligence is a failure to exercise the appropriate and/or ethically ruled care expected to be exercised in the given circumstances – the need for public bodies to exercise reasonable care in their actions, by taking account of the potential harm that they might foreseeably cause to people or property. In other words, on the balance of probabilities, is the person owed a duty of care that has been breached by failing to meet the standard of care required and as a result the person has suffered loss or damage which is not too remote? The ethical concept of non-maleficence – non-harming or causing the least harm to reach a beneficial outcome – is therefore a consideration in whether public bodies have acted negligently.

For example, in cases of self-neglect, the local authority might recognise that the person is self-neglecting to the point that there is a serious and imminent risk of death. Under Article 2, how do we demonstrate that we have not acted negligently? In considering Tort Law, we can reasonably foresee the likelihood of death and we are in a position (proximity) with the person to recognise this. Do we then need to consider whether it is fair, just and reasonable to impose a duty of care? We need to determine capacity in relation to autonomous decision making and Article 8, Right to private life, and accept occasions where a person may be making an autonomous decision to end their life. This therefore would need to be explicitly assessed and determined to rule out all other options:

- Have we considered whether a person's mental health may be impacting on their decision making?

- Are we sure that trauma is not affecting decision making?

- Have we tried and exhausted all appropriate therapeutic interventions?

- Have we recorded all capacity assessment outcomes?

- Have we engaged all relevant agencies and involved them in the decision-making process?

- Do all agencies agree, or have we resolved any potential conflicts?

Sometimes a person may have very good reasons why they do not wish to address these things. For example, consider the case of a person abused at the age of nine years old who has suffered with the impact of abuse all their life. At the age of 90 it is discovered that they are self-neglecting. They are clear that they do not wish to drag up all the trauma and spend time, energy and effort addressing this. They would like to live out their final years without this intrusion of services in their life. It is clear that the person knows what they want and why they feel they do not wish to address the issues, but they must also recognise the potential consequences of this course of action.

The person has a right to choose to die in a particular manner as long as there is no one else adversely affected. This may feel particularly uncomfortable, and legal support will be required regarding decision making. The court might also need to be involved in this type of decision making. Ethically, non-maleficence may need to be considered; is the current intervention becoming an intrusion into a person's life where they have a right to private life (Article 8)?

Coming to this decision in cases of self-neglect can be particularly challenging. Under Tort Law, there is no general duty to act positively for the benefit of others, but if the duty is assumed then obligations may be imposed. So, if needs have been assessed and identified and duty of care to meet those needs is assumed, then there is a positive obligation to meet those needs. Section 9 of the Care Act 2014 corroborates this, identifying the duty to assess and plan to meet needs. Sections 11a and 11b identify that if a person refuses an assessment we must still continue with the assessment if:

- they are deemed to lack capacity to make this decision and it is determined that an assessment is in their best interests, or

- where there is reasonable suspicion of abuse or neglect.

Safeguarding therefore involves our duty of care, meaning that we must not act negligently and must demonstrate all steps taken to maintain the human rights of those with whom we work.

In these cases where there is limited access to the person for assessment purposes, the balance between a person's right to private life and our duty of care must be identified and a clear rationale provided for a course of action chosen. Consider ethical decision making and the impact of intervention on the person versus the risks.

Tort Law identifies two elements for consideration:

- *Subjective* – that the person is knowingly exposed to substantial risk.

- *Objective* – that a reasonable person would have realised the risk.

This means that the practitioner must be explicit in identifying and discussing the risks with the person concerned. In safeguarding situations where a person is making the choice to remain in a dangerous situation, the practitioner needs to try and communicate the risks to the person concerned and record communication methodology.

If the person does not appear to be understanding the risks, then a capacity assessment must be conducted to determine whether they have the capacity to make decisions about the dangers that they are placing themselves in. If the person lacks capacity, a best interests decision is required. If the person has capacity, then the practitioner will have to return to the matter of whether all reasonable steps have been taken to preserve life and all considerations explored via the multi-agency meeting. Where the risks are so great that a person appears to be making decisions that could potentially end their life, the failure to warn of risks and determine whether a person has capacity or not to make this decision may mean that the actions of the public body could be construed as negligent. The explicit capacity assessment regarding whether a person is able to make an autonomous decision to end their life, or that they were unaware that actions could result in this risk, therefore must be an aspect of our duty of care.

In conducting capacity assessments that are so significant, we must consult with family, friends and professionals involved with the person and any advocate for the person. All lawful options for intervention must be considered, including the issues relating to potential for undiagnosed trauma impacting on decision making. It must be demonstrated that it would be a disproportionate interference from public sector bodies and why it was not lawful to act.

Where public sector workers have not prevented death, or where serious abuse or neglect have occurred, a safeguarding adults review may be considered. Under Article 2 of the Human Rights Act 1998 the investigation must be effective, independent and prompt. The duty to investigate is even stronger where the death has occurred while a person was detained by the state. The leading authority on this is *Salman v Turkey* (2000). The judgement states that:

> Where the events in issue lie wholly, or in large part, within the exclusive knowledge of the authorities, as in the case of persons within their control in custody, strong presumptions of fact will arise in respect of injuries and death occurring during such detention. Indeed, the burden of proof may be regarded as resting on the authorities to provide a satisfactory and convincing explanation.

So in safeguarding cases where a death has occurred within a residential care home or hospital setting and the person is deprived of their liberty, there is the question of whether this is defined in the

Human Rights Act as a death while under detention, or whether the coroner's definition of state detention within the Police and Crime Act 2017 applies:

Coroners' investigations into deaths: meaning of 'state detention'

(1) Section 48 of the Coroners and Justice Act 2009 (interpretation of Part 1: general) is amended as follows.

(2) In subsection (1), in the definition of 'state detention', after 'subsection (2)' insert '(read with subsection (2A))'.

(3) In subsection (2), at the beginning insert 'Subject to subsection (2A)'.

(4) After subsection (2) insert:

(2A) But a person is not in state detention at any time when he or she is deprived of liberty under section 4A(3) or (5) or 4B of the Mental Capacity Act 2005.

In considering whether to conduct a safeguarding adults review, the definition of a deprivation of liberty and 'state detention' will be a significant consideration. The *Salman v Turkey* (2000) judgement would suggest that we had full knowledge of the person detained and control of the care provision and therefore the burden of proof lies with the local authority, meaning that a safeguarding adults review will be required where the criteria for the review are met. The impact of the deprivation of liberty on the person's wellbeing will form part of the enquiry. The recent Care Quality Commission research into deaths of people who have learning disabilities and/or mental health problems highlighted some of these issues, stating that the duty of candour in the Care Act 2014 means that services should be transparent and held accountable for their actions (Richards, Lelliot and Baker 2016).

In daily safeguarding practice, ongoing capacity assessments are required, along with scrutiny of restrictions and restraints, consideration of the risks and the ongoing communication about risks with the person concerned. Those who need safeguarding help are often older and frail, living on their own in the community, or in care homes. They may be people who have physical or learning disabilities and people who have mental ill-health or other care and support needs. They are people at risk of suffering harm both in institutions and in the community.

Safeguarding means protecting an adult's right to live in safety, free from abuse and neglect. It is about people and organisations working together to prevent and stop both the risks and experience of abuse or neglect, while at the same time making sure that the adult's wellbeing is promoted, including, where appropriate, having regard to their views, wishes, feelings and beliefs in deciding on any action. We must recognise that adults sometimes have complex interpersonal relationships and may have mixed, contradictory, unclear or unrealistic feelings about their personal circumstances.

All organisations should work to promote the adult's wellbeing in their safeguarding arrangements. People's lives are a complicated mixture of feeling safe and taking personal risks. Without the risk taking, part of a person's identity is missing. Being safe is only part of this complex picture. Professionals should work with the adult to establish what being safe means to them and how that can be best achieved. Local authorities must cooperate with each of their relevant partners, as described in the Care Act 2014, and those partners must also cooperate with the local authority in the exercise of their functions relevant to care and support, including safeguarding functions and those to protect adults.

There is a duty to share information for safeguarding purposes. When abuse or neglect is reported to a local authority, it has a duty to make enquiries and determine the response required to prevent abuse or neglect, or to protect from abuse or neglect. Many people who have care and support needs can experience difficulty maintaining physical and mental wellbeing following abuse or neglect, and the safeguarding process should support the person to maintain wellbeing and gain equitable access to criminal justice.

Equitable access to criminal justice

Imagine that you are a criminal and you make money by unscrupulous means. The last thing that you want to do is get caught for your crimes. You search the obituaries hoping to find a widow. You call her and tell her that her husband left behind thousands of pounds in unpaid debt and that this will cause huge embarrassment and potentially property repossession or eviction if the debt is not paid immediately. In distress and not in a position to make reasoned, rational decisions, the widow pays you the debt. Nothing is recorded, the distress has caused confusion and she is too frail and upset to face being a witness.

The following year you decide to look for older people who are alone living in private homes. You watch certain areas to identify those who have no family visiting and then you call round, a friendly face offering to tidy the garden, dig the snow from the path or do some shopping. You make friends and visit for an hour every week. You have identified 20 other people who are in a similar situation and groom them to believe that you are their only friend and heir. Within a year or two you have made significant amounts of money, and within ten years you are very wealthy. They love you, they are your friends and they want you to have their money.

Older people are not the only ones targeted for criminal activity. We have people groomed for terrorism, to be sexually exploited, targeted for hate and mate crime and abused in domestic abuse situations. To ensure that your family member with a disability, your older mother, your grandmother or your friend who has poor mental health all have the same access to criminal justice and can protect themselves from abuse or neglect, there is a lot of work to be done. So why is it when I ask within service user feedback why a case was not referred to the police, a vast majority of cases state that the person did not wish to contact the police? We all contact the police when a crime is committed against us, we teach our children to contact the police, so what is going wrong to make people who have care and support needs believe that it is not a good thing to get police support?

The Crown Prosecution Service guidance (2017b) identifies that:

> Many older people, people who have mental ill health, learning disability or impairment who are victims of, or witnesses, to criminal offences are reluctant to report the crime, because they fear the consequences of reporting. They may think that they will be deemed to be unreliable witnesses; that they will not be taken seriously; that they may be victimised, lose their independence or be placed into an institution or care home as a result of giving evidence. They may also be embarrassed or ashamed. Fear, power and loyalty are factors that can prevent abuse being reported.

In cases where the person is dependent on a family member for care and support and they are subject to abuse by that family member, the abuse can be particularly difficult, distressing and confusing for the person. Consideration should be given as to whether the situation constitutes domestic abuse and the use of coercive and controlling behaviours (Section 76, Serious Crime Act 2015) and therefore affects the person's ability to autonomously choose a course of action, or whether there is sufficient evidence for the police to consider evidence-led prosecution (see Chapter 2 of the Criminal Justice Act 2003).

In relation to other fears such as loss of independence or autonomy, the Care Act 2014 identifies that we must do everything that we can to support the person in understanding the decisions that they are making and the actual outcomes from those decisions. The Care Act 2014 identifies that a person is able to make autonomous decisions, and the Mental Capacity Act 2005 is explicit in that if a person has capacity to make a decision then they can choose to make that decision even if it is an unwise decision. Public bodies should take all possible steps to inform the person of the potential outcomes of decisions made. If a person were informed that the outcomes of an investigation would not impact on their autonomy or self-determination in other areas, then they may be more likely to consider taking action. For example, it is impossible for any public body to make a decision to remove a person from their own home without informed consent, merely because they have reported a crime.

Part of the enquiry process should be to consider whether we have sufficiently supported the person in understanding the real consequences of reporting to the police or not. Through the way in which we handle the case, we must try to ensure that the person has the confidence, knowledge and support to enable the necessary action to be taken to prevent further offences and to hold the offender accountable.

It may be important (e.g. as a future preventative measure) to assess a person's capacity to make a certain decision. For example, in the case of theft, a social worker may assess whether the person has capacity to manage their own finances in order to decide whether they need to provide aids or adaptations or seek family or court-appointed support for the person's finances. The person would be entitled to an independent advocate to speak up on their behalf if they lacked capacity, and the social worker would have to ensure that the outcome was the least restrictive, least intrusive intervention and proportionate to the financial risks, balanced alongside the person's wishes and feelings. In this example, the social worker would need to consider the capacity assessment; however, the outcome of whether the person is capacitated or not to make decisions about their finances should not be seen by the police as an indicator of whether the person might be a credible witness in court. If faced with a potential crime, in this example theft, the police should not be asking the practitioner whether the person has capacity, but rather, would they know the difference between right and wrong, could they describe in some way, shape or form what happened to them and could they with all available support answer questions posed to them? In other words, would they be a reliable and credible witness?

Anyone can conduct a capacity assessment if they require consent, agreement or understanding for a course of action, but if that capacity assessment is going to be used in court then the Crown Prosecution Service guidance (2017b) identifies that, under the Mental Capacity Act 2005, the people who decide whether or not a person has capacity to take a particular decision are called assessors. Anyone can be an assessor – for example, a family member, a care worker, a nurse or a social worker. However, health and social care practitioners, or other relevant professionals and experts, must be involved when an assessment and/or decision has significant consequences. These include when the person's capacity may be challenged by someone; when reporting abuse or a crime; or where the decision has legal complications or consequences.

Prosecutors and the police should discuss, at an early stage, whether the witness is likely to be accepted as a competent witness by the courts, taking into account information provided by others, for example a doctor, family members or a social worker.

The Youth Justice and Criminal Evidence Act 1999 sets out the general rule that people are competent to act as witnesses unless they cannot understand questions asked of them at court and answer them in a manner which can be understood (with, if necessary, the assistance of special measures).

KEY POINTS

- Do your local authority policies and procedures support personalised safeguarding?

- Are your processes supporting system-led safeguarding?

- Are practitioners sufficiently trained to understand how to support the person, gain their understanding of safety and desired outcomes and work with other agencies prior to the referral being received by the local authority?

- Have you considered equitable access to civil and criminal justice?

- Have you provided enough information for informed consent?

- How much do we expect a person to know and manage in safeguarding situations before we provide the advice and guidance?

- Are we being risk averse?

- Are we really being person centred?

CHAPTER 8

Working with the Police
Reasonable Suspicion, Reporting Crime and Preserving Evidence

The law in relation to reasonable suspicion of abuse and neglect and the immediate preservation of any evidence when abuse or neglect is reported is very important. Contemporaneous evidence, or evidence that has been gathered as soon as possible after an event, is the most credible evidence. In order to understand what evidence is relevant and what is not, we must understand a little about how the police gather evidence where there is reason to suspect a crime. This is not to make us into police officers or mini-detectives, but to recognise our limitations in asking questions and extracting evidence and to seek the appropriate information from investigating police officers.

Within this chapter, we shall begin to explore the concept of working alongside the police and within legislative frameworks. This chapter introduces us to reasonable suspicion, or 'reasonable cause to suspect' that abuse or neglect is occurring. It is useful to consider from the very beginning of the intervention what questions to ask, how to ask them and when not to ask questions. The question of reasonable suspicion provides us with this answer. Reasonable suspicion requires a greater level of fact than reasonable belief. A belief is a hunch or a gut instinct, whereas suspicion is backed up by some evidence such as witness evidence, CCTV and corroborative evidence.

The Police and Criminal Evidence Act 1984 codes of practice, the Criminal Justice Act 1994 (Section 60) and the Terrorism Act 2000 (Section 44), among other Acts, identify that police officers can stop and search where there is reasonable suspicion of a crime. The Equality Act 2010 makes it unlawful for police officers to discriminate against, harass or victimise any person on the grounds of the 'protected characteristics' of age, disability, gender reassignment, race, religion or belief, sex and sexual orientation, marriage and civil partnership, pregnancy and maternity when using their powers. There is also a duty to eliminate unlawful discrimination, harassment and victimisation. Under Section 24 of the Police and Criminal Evidence Act 1984, as amended by the Serious Organised Crime Act 2005, powers of arrest without warrant are available to the police.

Police powers of arrest

Safeguarding processes follow police powers of arrest, as any form of abuse or neglect must be considered as a potential crime, and at the point the practitioner determines reasonable suspicion of a crime, the enquiry becomes a police-led enquiry. A practitioner can and should ask direct questions leading up to disclosure of abuse, neglect or a crime, or reasonable suspicion of any of these; however, at the point of reasonable suspicion, the practitioner should ensure the person's safety, stop making enquiries, preserve evidence, contact the police and share relevant information. To understand reasonable suspicion and the relationship with safeguarding, we can explore police powers of arrest, which state that a constable may arrest, without a warrant:

- anyone who is about to commit an offence

■ Mrs Smith contacts the police and says that her husband Billy is on his way to see her mother (Isabelle) who has dementia and lives nearby. Mrs Smith says that Isabelle is unable to make decisions about finance due to her dementia and therefore lacks capacity to make financial decisions. Billy has all the documents downloaded from the internet for a lasting power of attorney to be completed and is taking it over for her mother to sign, in order that he can get access to her funds to spend on himself. Mrs Smith said that they had a huge row about this as she would not support him to get the lasting power of attorney. Billy has got a family friend to complete the witness and capacity aspects of the form, claiming them to be independent. The person assisting Billy knows that Isabelle lacks capacity to make financial decisions. Billy is about to commit an offence, and he can be arrested and evidence can be gathered to determine the facts.

- anyone who is in the act of committing an offence

■ The social worker goes out to visit Jenny who has a physical disability and lives with her partner Sue. Sue has been getting increasingly angry with Jenny and has been saying that she can no longer cope with providing care and support. Arriving at the property, the social worker hears Jenny screaming and crying, Sue is shouting at her and there is a lot of crashing and banging. The social worker contacts the police, who knock on the door. Jenny manages to open the door but Sue drags her away and continues to hit her. The police arrest Sue and the social worker ensures that Jenny is medically checked by her GP and is safe. Sue is in the act of committing an offence and can be arrested. The enquiry identifies people and evidence to fill the gaps in knowledge.

- anyone whom they have reasonable grounds for suspecting to be about to commit an offence

■ James and John are two brothers who regularly visit their mother Ada in a residential care home. Ada has a diagnosis of Alzheimer's disease, diabetes, severe arthritis and Raynaud's disease. Raynaud's disease means that her fingers and toes feel numb in response to cold temperatures. The blood supply to these areas is limited and therefore she feels the cold more than most would.

Care staff have reported concerns about James and John on a number of occasions. Incidents include:

- regularly opening windows in their mother's room and removing layers of clothing, resulting in Ada shivering and becoming unwell, later requiring the GP's attendance

- pushing their mother around the home in a wheelchair and spinning her fast, saying that she likes it when she screams. On a few occasions there was no lap belt attached, and on one occasion the wheelchair caught another resident

- drag lifting their mother from her wheelchair to seats or the bed rather than seeking care staff support to use the appropriate hoisting equipment

- bringing chocolate in for their mother and feeding it to her.

Safeguarding measures have been put into place to provide medical information to the brothers to identify why this is inappropriate behaviour. The occupational therapist has explained to the brothers how important it is to ensure that Ada is moved using care and with the appropriate moving and handling equipment by the appropriately trained people, and the safeguarding lead has asked the brothers to a meeting to discuss their behaviours and identify concerns that the consequences of their actions may cause their mother serious harm and could potentially be a crime. The brothers are challenging and flippant, and disregard the concerns of others.

The brothers arrive at the care home, remove their mother's clothing, drag lift her into her wheelchair, without any seat belt or safety mechanism, and say that they are taking her out for the day. It is raining and cold outside and care home staff are so concerned for Ada's safety that they contact the police. The police try the least restrictive intervention and ask the brothers to comply with the care plan provided for their mother; however, if the brothers continue to demonstrate actions to take Ada out into the cold inappropriately dressed and leave her at risk of falling out of her wheelchair, alongside statements from them saying that they are taking her for tea and cake, which would be quite dangerous for Ada due to her diabetes, then the police officers may arrest the brothers.

The police officers have reasonable grounds for suspecting that the brothers are about to commit an offence.

- anyone whom they have reasonable grounds for suspecting to be committing an offence

■ Nurse A contacts the police officer stating that she has seen the senior care worker and qualified nurse (B) giving Mrs Jones oramorph in excess of her prescribed dose. The senior care worker has been identified in Mrs Jones' will as the executor to her estate and the nurse believes that if Mrs Jones continues to receive this level of medication it could kill her. The senior care worker is due to administer Mrs Jones her next dose of oramorph in two hours' time.

The police have reasonable grounds for suspecting nurse B to be committing an offence.

- anyone whom they have reasonable grounds to suspect of being guilty of committing an offence (if they have reasonable grounds for suspecting that an offence has been committed)

■ Sally is the daughter of Mrs Bell, an 80-year-old woman who lacks capacity to make decisions about finances. Mrs Bell's son John has had a look at a bank statement and has identified that over the past two weeks £300 per day has been taken out of her account from a cashpoint machine withdrawal. As far as John is aware, it is only his sister Sally who has access to the cashpoint card. John knows that his mother does not require that amount of cash for her daily needs. There is reasonable grounds to suspect that an offence has been committed and that Sally is guilty of the offence.

On reasonable suspicion of a crime a police officer will:

- try to stop the clock and maintain safety

- preserve evidence, including verbal or written statements

- identify the gaps in their knowledge

- identify those who might be able to fill the gaps in their knowledge

- provide appropriate support to the victim and witnesses to provide evidence

- determine what the potential victim wants to happen

- consider a hypothesis or a number of hypotheses and make enquiries to determine or rule out whether a crime has taken place.

In order to ensure that we are working effectively with the police, maintaining credible evidence and effectively conducting safeguarding enquiries, we must work with the same type of definition of 'reasonable suspicion' of abuse or neglect. This ensures that information can be shared with the police at the point where enquiries demonstrate the reasonable suspicion of a crime. We should not be conducting enquiries after the point of reasonable suspicion of a crime without the prior guidance of the police.

Once reasonable suspicion is established, the enquiry becomes a police-led enquiry. If subsequently it is determined that there is a lack of evidence for criminal prosecution, safeguarding measures may still be required and the most appropriate person to lead the enquiry will need to be identified. A lack of evidence does not necessarily mean that the person is or is not guilty, it simply means that the police cannot prove guilt. For the Crown Prosecution Service to take a case to court, it must be in the public interest to do so. There must be significant evidence to justify the use of public funds on court processes. Safeguarding is not just about criminal prosecution, it is also about identifying the impact of abuse on the person and supporting them to maintain physical and mental wellbeing. There will be care and support issues to consider, risks to be managed, care and support plans to be evaluated, and the consideration of civil redress may also be possible.

Points to prove and safeguarding support in preserving evidence

For each crime, there are 'points to prove'. The police must provide evidence of each point to present to the Crown Prosecution Service as evidence. If you ask the police about the points to prove and evidence that would be useful, this opens up a greater discussion about how we can support them in their duties. Using the points to prove for theft, I shall demonstrate this by asking you what you consider theft to be.

Most people respond by saying 'taking something without consent'. This is not what theft is to the police; it is: 'dishonestly appropriating property belonging to another with the intention of permanently depriving the other of it' (Theft Act (1968, Section 1 (1))). The law does not say what is honest; however, it does say what is not honest or what an average man in the street would consider dishonest (*R v Ghosh* (1982)).

There is no statutory definition of dishonesty, although Section 2 of the Theft Act 1968 gives three instances of when a person is not to be regarded as dishonest:

- If he appropriates the property in the belief that he has in law the right to deprive the other of it, on behalf of himself or of a third person.

  In other words, it is not dishonest if the person has an honest belief that they have the right to that property in law.

■ In 2012, an older mother borrowed £2000 from her son to enable her to go on a cruise. At the time, the mother had no impairment of brain function or mind. Shortly after the cruise she suffered a stroke and required residential care provision. She is unable to manage her finances, so her son has control of her money. The care home informs the safeguarding team that the mother has no money to pay for her toiletries, trips or clothing and the son is claiming that he is unable to pay. The police investigate and discover that the son has removed £2000 from his mother's bank account; however, he produces statements and an IOU note from his mother to say that she borrowed £2000 from him. There is no apparent evidence that the mother paid her son back this money.

At the moment, it appears that the son has an honest belief that he has the right to the property in law. If you know evidence or arrangements to the contrary, this would be important information and evidence for the police. For example, it may be that the mother has said that her son could live in the property rent free, or that she will pay for all his food for the next two years in order to pay him back. This could mean the difference between proving or disproving dishonesty.

(Please see the section on capacity and credibility later in this chapter to explore how this might affect criminal enquiries.)

- If he appropriates the property in the belief that he would have the other's consent if the other knew of the appropriation and the circumstances of it.

  In other words, if the person believes that the owner would have consented to the taking of the property if they had known the circumstances.

■ A mother has always provided her son with everything that he wanted or needed. Throughout her life, she has regularly gone without to ensure that his needs were met before her own. If her son was hungry, she would go without food; if her son could not pay his bills, she would pay them for him.

Her son has got into terrible debt and mains services are threatening to cut his supplies. His mother now has dementia and her son has control of her finances. He takes £2000 out of the account to pay his bills. His mother is unable to go on a trip with the local day service and they grow concerned about her lack of financial resources. A safeguarding referral is made and the police become involved in enquiries. The son tells the police that his mother would always have helped him in this way if she knew how desperate he was. The daughter has evidence that her mother has always paid off the son's debt and gets quite upset that she was not afforded the same support from her mother. The son has an honest belief that his mother would have consented to the taking of the property had she known the circumstances.

If you know that things have changed in the mother and son relationship, they have fallen out or the mother has stopped giving to the son at a certain point, making him responsible for his own mistakes, and you can provide some evidence of this, then this is important information for the police enquiry.

- If he appropriates the property in the belief that the person to whom the property belongs cannot be discovered by taking reasonable steps.

In other words, if you have had possession of the property, the owner is not known and you have taken all reasonable steps to find out who the owner is.

■ If a domiciliary care provider finds some money lying on the pathway of a house which belongs to someone that they are caring for, they should take reasonable steps to find out who the owner is. This might include asking the person and any relevant representatives of that person whether any money has gone missing, and depending on the amount, they may wish to report having found the money. They would also have to check that there was nothing to identify who the money belonged to, for example if it was in a wallet with identification.

While it may be helpful for inter-agency working, all practitioners do not need to know about the specific points that the police are trying to prove. All practitioners do need to have sufficient awareness of the existence of points to prove, in order that they can support the police in gathering credible evidence.

Social workers and health and care staff are highly skilled in asking questions in a manner that a person may be better able to understand and provide a response. The police should seek the assistance and support of staff to gain adequate responses to questions, rather than dismissing a person who is diagnosed with an impairment of the mind as lacking credibility as a witness. An intermediary, witness supporter or social worker may be able to identify the way that information is presented to the witness within the interview or court process as part of special measures, or additional measures. A profile of the witness and their support needs may be developed prior to attendance in court. The profile may need to consider things such as the background information about the person, any special measures that may be required, any additional measures required, medical or medication needs, general functional skills, comprehension, concentration, communication, vocabulary and advice to counsel.

The Crown Prosecution Service guidance provides advice regarding some of these matters within court and offers an example about medication:

> Medication issues may be relevant when considering the timing of giving evidence and the need for maximum lucidity. This factor may be equally relevant to any witness taking medication, whether mental capacity is an issue or not. (Crown Prosecution Service 2017b)

Evidence-led prosecution

The College of Policing: Authorised Professional Practice (www. app.college.police.uk) identifies that, when investigating incidents of domestic abuse, police officers should not only be searching for evidence of a crime but also indicators that abuse may be occurring. This is part of a risk-assessment process and ensures that safety measures can be put in place to prevent escalation. The guidance suggests proactive policing aimed at building an evidence-led case that does not rely on the support of the victim. In safeguarding situations, there are many reasons why someone may not want to prosecute a perpetrator – they may be too afraid, they may be concerned about who will look after them or they may think that people will judge them. Sometimes it is difficult to get care and support in to help the person as the perpetrator is a threat to staff or they refuse admission. Table 8.1 is from the College of Policing website and describes evidence-led cases that have resulted in guilty pleas or the person was found guilty.

Table 8.1: Evidence-led cases resulting in guilty pleas or guilty verdicts

Evidence	Result
Partial admissions, injury photos and bad character evidence of the accused	Guilty plea
Initial account given on body-worn video, denied but no account given by the defendant, and injury photos	Guilty plea
999 call, injuries captured on body-worn video and hearsay evidence from the victim recorded in the responding officer's statement	Found guilty after trial
Victim's 999 call as res gestae and officer's description of injuries	Found guilty after trial
Victim's account on body-worn video as hearsay (witness unable to give evidence through fear)	Found guilty after trial
Victim's account recorded in officer's pocket notebook entry as hearsay (witness unable to give evidence through fear) and injury photos	Found guilty after trial
Victim's account recorded in section 9 statement as hearsay (witness cannot be found), injury photos and independent eyewitness testimony	Found guilty after trial
Circumstantial evidence from a neighbour who hears an argument between the victim and perpetrator and notes injury to the victim in the immediate aftermath	Found guilty after trial
Victim's original written account supported by other key evidence including evidence of injury preferred by court over hostile victim's contradictory live evidence at trial	Found guilty after trial

© College of Policing Ltd – Reproduced with permission under licence number SF00186

In cases of severe domestic abuse cases, the police may consider evidence-led prosecution. In some situations, it may be worth having a conversation with the police about this possibility, for example if the person is too afraid of the perpetrator to make a statement.

Competence, giving evidence and special measures

An example of the court's consideration of competence, giving evidence and special measures was identified in the case *DPP v R* (2007) concerning an 81-year-old person who had Alzheimer's disease:

> The court held that it was correct, when determining whether a witness was competent, to consider competence at the time of the interview and at the time when the witness was called on to give evidence, where the evidence-in-chief was given via a video recording under the provisions of section 19 of the Youth and Criminal Evidence Act 1999. The fact that a witness now had no independent recollection of the facts, such that he/she was unable to give intelligible answers, did not mean that he/she was no longer competent.
>
> The court also held that where a video interview was already in evidence it could not be retrospectively 'unadmitted' and that where it had been admitted pursuant to a perfectly proper special measures application under section 27 of the 1999 Act, it did not need consideration as hearsay evidence. The video interview was admissible independently of any question of hearsay under the quite separate provisions for special measures.
>
> In the case of supervening loss of memory, as distinct from supervening loss of competence, the court found that sections 139 and 120 of the Criminal Justice Act 2003 would also apply, and the video interview would be admissible as evidence of its contents as a means of refreshing the memory of the witness who had forgotten. The court did not determine whether sections 139 and 120 had any application in the event of supervening incompetence.
>
> Where the video-recorded interview was admissible for all those various reasons, and independently of section 114, it did not mean that the video had to be accepted at face value. On the contrary, the assessment of it was a matter for the trial court.

The use of contemporaneous recording is extremely important in cases where a person may later be unable to recall significant events. This means that understanding of reasonable suspicion of abuse/neglect and reasonable suspicion of a crime is paramount during any safeguarding enquiries. The statement of the person as soon as possible after the event and supported by appropriate professionals will aid prosecution. Even if the person is unable to recall the events later due to cognitive impairment or the effects of trauma, the original recording is still admissible evidence in court.

Capacity and credibility

The Crown Prosecution Service provides guidance regarding the difference between witness credibility and the capacity of the person to understand and make a decision. Before a case goes to court, the Crown Prosecution Service has to decide whether there is sufficient credible evidence provided by credible sources and credible witnesses for it to have a significant chance of success. Questions about credibility and reliability go to the weight of the evidence and not the capacity of the witness to understand the crime. This was clearly described by the judge in the case of X.

In May 2009, a man was convicted of anally raping a child barely three years old at the time of the alleged rapes. The case was appealed, and the question before the appeal court was whether the conviction could be deemed unsafe because a child so young could not be deemed competent. Child X was four years old when the case went to court. Counsel for the defendant criticised the interview techniques used to elicit evidence from X and suggested that because X was so young at the time of the alleged rapes and some time had passed since then, the evidence was not credible. The question raised before the court was whether a conviction based on the truthfulness and accuracy of a very young child could be safe. The court concluded that the ultimate decision as to the competency of a child witness rested on the jury and that in finding the appellant guilty of the offence there was no basis for quashing the appellant's conviction. In other words, the jury decides whether the weight of evidence is sufficient.

The judge for the X case ruled:

> The purpose of the trial process is to identify the evidence which is reliable and that which is not, whether it comes from an adult or a child. If competent, as defined by the statutory criteria, in the context of credibility in the forensic process, the child witness starts off on the basis of equality with every other witness. (R v B (2010))

The issue of credibility is determined in the courts; however, the police must satisfy the Crown Prosecution Service that it is in the public interest to take the case to court. In making this decision, the Crown Prosecution Service should consider this judgement.

The Crown Prosecution Service guidance goes on to say:

> Police and prosecutors should also recognise that the competence of a witness is a separate issue to that of the mental capacity of a witness. Further information can be found in 'Guidance on prosecuting crimes against older people and in Victims and Witnesses who have mental health issues and/or learning disabilities – prosecution guidance'. (Crown Prosecution Service 2017a)

This guidance is very important guidance for the police to understand, because so often the police ask whether a person has capacity in cases where what they are really seeking is whether the person can be a credible witness. The police are not really asking for a specific and timely capacity assessment, they are errantly asking about the competency of the witness; however, given the above guidance, as long as the witness can provide credible evidence, the person may be deemed a competent and credible witness.

An example from my practice involved a young woman who had a learning disability – we shall call her Sue. Sue lived alone in rented accommodation; she didn't have very much money and so she rarely went out. Sue enjoyed watching the dramas and soaps on the television – she even watched the omnibus editions and repeats. Sue was quite frugal with her money and even in very cold weather she would refrain from putting the heating on. Shopping was at the local cheap supermarket which she ventured out to on a number of occasions a week. It was during these trips that the hate crime began, but soon the perpetrator was following her back to her house. On one occasion, she opened the door and the person who had been targeting her for abuse physically assaulted her, causing severe bruising and a leg fracture. Even when the fracture was healed and the bruising subsided, Sue was afraid to leave the house. Sue lost weight, as she was shopping at more expensive supermarkets so that she could order her food without leaving the house, but she could not afford as much food.

The police went out to interview her and requested a capacity assessment from the social worker. The social worker was a bit confused but assessed the woman's capacity to understand the safeguarding/police referral and stated that Sue lacked capacity to understand this.

The police went out to see Sue and asked when the assault took place, but she was unable to state the specific time. The police asked what time of year she thought that the assault took place, but Sue was unable to respond. The police determined that Sue was not a credible witness.

The safeguarding lead raised concerns in the safeguarding meeting that this man might target other vulnerable people, that the impact on the victim had been severe and that she was sure that an independent social worker could support the woman to answer any police questions. The police agreed to give it a try.

The social worker went out to see Sue and asked what was on the television at the time of the attack. Sue said that she had been upset because a really good episode of *Coronation Street* had been interrupted. The social worker asked Sue if she usually had a cup of tea or coffee during the programme and Sue said that she always had a cup of tea during the break. 'Was the attack before or after your cup of tea?' asked the social worker. Sue told her that it was before her cup of tea and described what was happening on the screen. To ensure that the episode was not a repeat, the social worker asked what Sue was wearing when she answered the door. Sue said that she had put her pyjamas on, a pair of comfortable shorts and a vest top. 'Was it light or dark when you answered the door?' asked the social worker. Sue informed her that it was dark, and when the social worker asked whether she was cold when she answered the door she said that she was warm. The specific date and time of the event had been determined in less than five minutes of conversation. This enabled the case to be taken to court.

Sue was unable to understand the complexities of the safeguarding referral or process and did not fully understand what the criminal justice process entailed, but she could provide full evidence when asked the correct questions in the appropriate way and with support. Sue could understand enough to know that she must tell the truth and that to lie about things had consequences, and she understood that her information could result in the person who assaulted her going to prison.

Because the independent social worker was privy to information about the case, the social work manager allocated the work to another social worker to develop a profile of the person for the court to understand how best to communicate with her. The local authority IT system was reviewed to include an allocation process for court work. The profile is part of planning and preparing a person for court.

Witness support, preparation and profiling (based on the Liverpool model)

To plan and prepare support for a person who has care and support needs can ensure that they have more equitable access to criminal justice. The Liverpool model of Witness Support, Preparation and Profiling (WSPP 2017) is reflected within the following suggestions. If services have WSPP then this is the most superior model, but in the absence of a specific service supporting victims of crime who have care and support needs, then practitioners such as social workers, occupational therapists or speech and language therapists may be able to support the person and create a profile of that person's support needs to keep them safe and make them feel comfortable enough to give credible evidence in court. The police often seek support from professionals about how to best support a person throughout the criminal justice process. Any relevant person can provide this information, but must not be implicated, or involve themselves in anything that relates to the criminal proceedings, including the safeguarding strategy meetings. Some models use an extended version of victim support services to support the witness. This is a separate piece of work that will need to be conducted.

Why provide specific support?

Support and preparation help vulnerable and intimidated witnesses to produce better evidence as well as reduce the trauma and distress from participating in the criminal justice process. Children, rape victims, people who have been subject to domestic abuse, witnesses with learning difficulties and people who have mental ill-health have been identified as especially prone to finding the criminal justice processes stressful and, on occasions, traumatic. High stress reduces the witness's ability to participate and respond to questioning, or effectively recall events in order to assist the fact-finding process of the criminal justice system. In addition, vulnerable and intimidated witnesses may also be coming to terms with severe personal difficulties and trauma. This process of healing and recovery can be delayed or even set back by being involved in a court case. In terms of equitable access to criminal justice, the Crown Prosecution Service may be more likely to allow a case to go to court where appropriate support and preparation to give evidence have been available.

Learning disabled children and adults may have problems with memory, vocabulary, level of understanding and suggestibility to leading questions. Some learning disabled people are acquiescent or compliant to the demands of those impositions of power and authority. In addition to these difficulties, such witnesses may lack knowledge or understanding of the criminal justice system, so the support process aims to create a safety network around the person to provide a sense of security.

Adults or children who have been victimised may have special difficulties as witnesses in criminal proceedings. They may need help to overcome the feeling that it is they, rather than the accused, who are on trial. The context and process of the trial itself may also bring back old memories and patterns of reaction and response within the vulnerable witness. They may be especially sensitive to feelings of their own guilt or feelings of responsibility for the alleged actions of the accused. People with mental health problems can find the criminal justice system especially stressful. Those with post-traumatic anxiety disorders can have special problems prior to and during the trial, particularly if their problem is related to the alleged offence.

Preparation and support are necessary for enabling witnesses to give their best evidence as well as to safeguard their welfare. The profile provides guidance to those supporting all young, vulnerable and intimidated witnesses and preparing them to give evidence, and to those planning and coordinating the attendance of such witnesses at court.

The roles and responsibilities of witness supporters

All witnesses, including those who may be vulnerable or intimidated, require support before the trial. Witnesses, whether giving evidence for the prosecution or defence, are entitled to an explanation of their role at court and assistance to ensure that they can give their best evidence. There are two distinct kinds of supporter: those who offer support prior to trial ('pre-trial supporters'), and those who offer support at trial ('court witness supporters'). The court witness supporter must meet the witness before the trial, but have no interest, knowledge or involvement in the specifics of the case. Similar restrictions do not apply to the pre-trial supporter.

The Youth Justice and Criminal Evidence Act 1999 enables many such witnesses to have access to special measures to help them give evidence in the best way and with the minimum of stress and trauma. Children, for instance, may be examined and cross-examined via video-recorded interview at an earlier stage in the investigation. Vulnerable adult witnesses, too, may take advantage of a range of special measures, at the discretion of the court, on individual application by the defence or prosecution.

The first task is identification of those adults and children who are vulnerable and therefore may need to have special considerations during their involvement with the criminal justice process. It is usually the police who first identify witnesses' vulnerability, though sometimes this task may fall to others. Once a witness has been identified as either intimidated or vulnerable, there is potentially a long period before the court hearing takes place. During this time, preparation and support need to focus on arrangements surrounding any interviews with the witness, pre-trial arrangements and preparation for any court hearing. If the case goes ahead, support will also be required during the court hearing and in the immediate aftermath. These activities will probably occur over many months in the average criminal case.

There is a range of possible activities which can be undertaken with vulnerable witnesses by pre-trial and court witness supporters. Here are some examples of what supporters can do:

- Provide emotional support.

- Give information and education.

- Understand the witness's views, wishes and concerns and any particular vulnerabilities that might affect them during the criminal process.

- Familiarise the witness with the court and its procedures.

- Support the witness through interviews and court hearings.

- Undertake court preparation and provide information about the forthcoming trial.

- Accompany the witness on a pre-trial visit to court.

- Accompany the witness when memory is refreshed.

- Liaise with family members and friends of the witness.

- Liaise with legal, health, educational, social work and other professionals.

- Offer therapeutic and counselling services prior to a criminal trial.

- Arrange links with other professionals with special expertise in any specific vulnerabilities or difficulties which the witness has, such as language communication problems, learning disabilities, specific cultural or minority ethnic group concerns or religious priorities. They cannot under any circumstances discuss the evidence, which might lead to allegations of coaching the witness. It is clear from the range of tasks listed that in many cases more than one person will be involved in providing the assistance the witness requires.

The profile may be submitted by someone working with the individual; however, if the full witness support role identified above is to be offered by a local authority or victim support worker, then it is important to distinguish the WSPP role from the role of those involved in the enquiries. Prior to beginning the work, the police, in requesting the completion of a profile, should clarify who the appropriate person to complete the profile or to undertake work might be.

Agreement should be reached on a local basis on who is responsible for pre-trial preparation and also for ensuring that the necessary preparation has been or is being undertaken. *Regardless of which profession is identified as best placed to coordinate pre-trial preparation and support, it is vitally important that it begins as soon as the witness's vulnerability is identified and the police and/or the Crown Prosecution Service become aware that he or she may need to attend court.*

Different terms have been used over the years to describe the personnel who carry out these functions. Here are some examples:

- *Interview supporter* – providing support during investigative interviews. Can be a friend or relative provided they are not party to the proceedings. Might also be an appropriate adult, but not necessarily so.

- *Appropriate adult* – protects the interests of the perpetrator, assists communication with the witness and ensures that the interview can be carried out fairly.

- *Pre-trial supporter* – provides witness support, information and preparation for giving evidence.

- *Intermediary* – approved by the court to relay questions from advocates to a vulnerable witness, in order to assist the witness to give their best evidence at both pre-trial hearings and the trial itself.

- *Court witness supporter* – providing the necessary support during the court process and in a TV link room where necessary. It is likely this person would have met the witness before, but would not know the details of the case.

The skills involved in pre-trial preparation and support include:

- an ability to prepare the witness to give their evidence without coaching them in any way

- knowledge and understanding of court procedures, relevant legislation and policy

- knowledge about, and an aptitude for working with, vulnerable individuals

- an ability to liaise with other professionals and family members.

The police and the prosecutor require information about both the needs and the wishes of the witness for the purpose of pre-trial preparation, planning how the witness should give evidence and in making related applications to the court. The police should ask witnesses for details of any difficulties they might have in giving evidence, and explain how the special measures might assist them. Witnesses can then make an informed choice as to whether to apply for relevant measures. Offering choice and control can have a beneficial effect on the person concerned.

The police may also seek information about the needs of the witness from his or her court witness supporter, relatives, friends or carers (provided that they are not party to the crime under investigation), or other agencies. There is a form called the 'Witness Profile' in Chapter 9 that can be used by the police to request this information. In the case of defence witnesses, it is the responsibility of the defence lawyer to enquire about the witness's needs.

During the planning phase, information about the witness will have been gathered from contact with the witness directly, as well as those providing care, education or special services. For example, if a social worker is going to conduct preparation and profiling, they may need to gather information from other services such as health, psychiatry, speech and language therapists or occupational therapists, as well as any family or friends not involved in the safeguarding incident or potential crime. The profile is developed in a similar way to a care and support plan; however, all aspects are specific to the needs of the person within the court process rather than the everyday needs of the person. The detail required will be significant.

Considerations may include communication difficulties, but also differences connected with cultural and minority ethnic values and sometimes religious practices which are likely to have an influence on the investigative and pre-trial support and preparation phases. The police should consult with the witness and those who know the witness best in order to seek their advice on these matters, provided that they are not a party to the crime under investigation and can act without bias or prejudice. Appropriate advice and interpretation may be needed during the interview, when providing support, when providing information about the court process and when giving evidence at trial, in order to prevent the witness becoming confused and to enable them to give their best evidence. National guidelines covering the engagement of interpreters have been agreed by the Trials Issues Group and these guidelines should be adhered to.

At an early stage, the police will pass relevant information to the Crown Prosecution Service. However, as the time of the hearing approaches, witness support work should adopt the more specific focus of preparing the witness for giving evidence in court. In some cases, therapy prior to trial will be organised too.

The interval between the investigative interview and the final trial hearing can often be long. Over the months, the tasks range from initially assessing need, either by direct enquiry and observation by the police, or through gathering information from others. It is likely that a pre-trial support person would then be identified for vulnerable or intimidated witnesses. Their role would be to:

- seek the witness's views about giving their evidence and being at the court

- provide information about the criminal process

- liaise with others, as appropriate.

The police should always pass on their views on a witness's requirements for assistance in court to the Crown Prosecution Service. The police must establish the appropriate person to conduct the profile and describe the boundaries of the role; however, in doing so they may use the witness credibility questions found in Chapter 9 as a profile to support witness credibility.

Special and Additional Measures

Special and additional measures may be used and adapted to support a witness.

The Youth Justice and Criminal Evidence Act 1999 introduced a range of measures that can be used to facilitate the gathering and giving of evidence by vulnerable and intimidated witnesses. These measures help with the giving of evidence in court and are designed to alleviate some of the stress. The police usually have to ask the judge on behalf of the court whether special measures can be applied, as they are at the court's discretion. It can take a little while to organise special measures, and therefore an early request is preferable. To be eligible for special measures an adult must:

- be suffering from a mental disorder (as defined by the Mental Health Act 1983)

- have a significant impairment of intelligence or social functioning

- have a physical disability, or suffer from a physical disorder.

An intimidated witness for the purposes of special measures is described as someone whose quality of evidence is likely to be affected by fear or distress (including sexual offences and domestic abuse). The Youth Justice and Criminal Evidence Act 1999 lists a number of factors that the court must take into account in assessing whether the witness qualifies for special measures. These include:

- the nature and circumstances of the offence

- the age of the witness

- the social and cultural background and ethnic origins of the witness

- any religious or political opinions of the witness

- any behaviour towards the witness on the part of the accused, his or her family or associates, or any other witness or co-accused.

Those eligible for special measures under the criteria in the preceding paragraph may include a wide range of witnesses, including victims of sexual offences and of domestic violence, as well as victims of racially motivated offences and serious crime. Special measures include:

- the use of screens (to shield the witness from the defendant and, in some cases, the court)

- a live link (a televised link to the courtroom enabling the witness to give evidence either from within the court building or from another suitable location)

- the removal of wigs and gowns

- evidence given in private (exclusion from the courtroom of members of the public and the press)

- video-recorded interview (a video-recorded interview before the trial may be admitted as the witness's evidence unless this would not be in the interests of justice, or would not maximise the quality of the complainant's evidence)

- video-recorded cross-examination

- aids to communication

- an intermediary (someone skilled in supporting the person to give evidence – methods of communication will be assessed and presented to the court and the intermediary is allowed to explain questions and answers in so far as is necessary)

- other additional measures that may be considered as reasonable adjustments.

A witness under the age of 17 is always eligible for help. In the case of witnesses who are, or who claim to be, victims of sexual offences (complainants), there is a presumption that they are eligible for assistance unless they inform the court otherwise. In deciding eligibility, courts must consider witnesses' own views about their status.

The court has some limited inherent powers to make measures available to assist witnesses who do not qualify as eligible or who need measures for reasons other than age, incapacity, fear or distress. These powers pre-date the 1999 Act and are untouched by it. They extend, for example, to the provision of screens and aids to interpretation, the removal of wigs and gowns, and the provision of a foreign language interpreter.

Special measures can only be authorised where they are likely to improve the quality of a witness's evidence. 'Quality' encompasses coherence, completeness and accuracy. Coherence in this sense means that the witness is able to address the questions put and give answers which can be understood, both as separate answers and when taken together as a complete statement of the witness's evidence.

The circumstances in which special measures may be invoked may range from a case where the witness's evidence would otherwise be unintelligible (e.g. the provision of an intermediary to assist a very young child to communicate) to cases where the evidence, though intelligible, would otherwise be of a worse quality than it could be, because of the circumstances making the witness eligible for help. This might occur, for example, where the witness has poor long-term memory but pre-recorded evidence-in-chief and cross-examination can ensure that the court hears a more complete account. Special measures directions can be made at a pre-trial hearing, before the beginning of the trial or before a hearing to which witnesses are called to settle the factual basis on which sentence will be passed. When courts decide, on application from the prosecution or defence or of their own accord, whether special measures might be appropriate for a witness, they must consider:

- whether the witness is eligible

- whether special measures would improve the evidence of an eligible witness in the circumstances of the case (which include the witness's own views and the possibility that the measures might tend to inhibit the evidence being tested effectively)

- if special measures would improve the witness's evidence, which of the measures, alone or in combination, would be most likely to maximise the quality of the witness's evidence (again, the court has to bear in mind the views of the witness and the possibility that the measures might tend to inhibit the evidence being tested effectively)

- details of where, when and how the measures specified should be provided.

The court needs to be informed about the wishes of the witness in relation to special measures and should be updated as necessary. Special measures directions are binding until the end of the trial, although courts can alter or discharge a direction if it seems to be in the interests of justice to do so.

Either party can apply for the direction to be altered or discharged, but must show that there has been a significant change of circumstances since the court made the direction or since an application for it to be altered was last made. This provision is intended to create some certainty for witnesses, by encouraging the party calling the witness to make applications for special measures as early as possible and by preventing re-applications on grounds the court has already found unpersuasive. The court must record its reasons for giving, altering or discharging a direction or refusing an application so that it is clear to everyone involved in the case what decision has been made and why it was made. This is intended to include, for example, the court's reasons for deciding that a witness is ineligible for help. Applications for special measures are subject to the rules of court.

The use of screens

Screens may be authorised to shield the witness from seeing the defendant. The screens must not prevent the judge, magistrates or jury and at least one legal representative of each party to the case (i.e. the prosecution and each defendant) seeing the witness, and the witness seeing them. If an intermediary or an interpreter is appointed to assist the witness, they too must be able to see and be seen.

Live links

'Live link' usually means a closed-circuit television link, but also applies to any technology with the same effect. The essential element of a live link is that it enables the witness to be absent from the place where the proceedings are being held, but at the same time to see and hear, and be seen and heard by, the judge, the magistrates or jury, at least one legal representative of each party to the case, and any intermediary or an interpreter appointed to assist the witness. The judge, magistrates, court clerk or justice's clerk control the equipment and should be comfortable with it and familiar with any likely difficulties such as the distorted image which may appear on the witness's monitor if those in court lean too close to the camera. Judges and magistrates must also ensure that the witness understands what is happening.

There is a presumption that a witness who gives evidence by live link for a part of the proceedings will continue to give evidence by this means throughout. Where a party to the proceedings argues that the method of receiving the witness's evidence should change, the court can make a direction. If there are no live link facilities at the magistrates' court where the proceedings would normally be held, the proceedings may be transferred to another court where a live link is available. Alternatively, if the witness is an adult and screening them is considered to be equally likely to enable them to give their best evidence, then the court may choose to screen the witness instead. A young witness who is required by Section 21 or 22 of the Act to give all or part of their evidence by live link must do so, unless a live link is not available at all in the area where the proceedings are to take place.

The live link is available to vulnerable and intimidated witnesses whether or not their evidence-in-chief is presented in the form of a video recording, and there may be some witnesses for whom the live link provides the only special measure required to enable them to give their best evidence. Even in the case of a child witness who is subject to a presumption that a recording will be used as evidence-in-chief, it may be necessary to resort to the use of the live link alone if no recording is available, or an available recording has been ruled inadmissible.

Where the witness who is eligible for special measures is not a young witness to whom the special presumptions in Section 21 or 22 apply, the court making a special measures direction will be able to choose between a screen and a live link as a means of assisting a witness to give their best evidence. The live link has the advantage that the witness does not have to be physically present in the courtroom. It may also be more accessible for some physically disabled witnesses, including wheelchair users. However, the screen is not necessarily an inferior alternative to the live link in all cases. Screens are flexible, easy to use and permit the witness to stay in court. It is also easier for the jury or magistrates to gain an impression of some physical attributes of the witness where this is relevant, for example in a case where the issue is whether the accused used reasonable force to restrain the witness.

The views of the witness are likely to be of great importance in deciding which of the two very similar measures is most suitable. A witness who is greatly distressed at the prospect of being in the same room with the accused is likely to give better evidence if permitted to use the live link.

The principle of open justice normally requires that evidence is given in open court – in other words, in the presence of representatives of the press and of members of the public who wish to attend. Proceedings in the youth courts form a major exception to the rule, as these are conducted in private for the protection of the accused.

To dispense with the wearing of wigs and gowns

The courts have traditionally exercised a direction to dispense with the wearing of wigs and gowns by the judge and by advocates in cases where child witnesses are concerned. The inclusion of this power as a special measure in the 1999 Act makes it clear that the same dispensation can be made in the case of vulnerable adult witnesses. Not all witnesses want the court to depart from its traditional way of dressing – some feel more comfortable if the judge and barristers are dressed in the way which is most familiar to them, perhaps from watching television drama.

Video-recorded evidence-in-chief

A video-recorded interview can take the place of a witness's evidence-in-chief. Video recording can be considered in significant witness interviews, for example in murders, sexual assault and robberies with firearms. Vulnerable witnesses may also use this for interview purposes, with age, capacity, emotional health, language skills, the need for an intermediary and the potential for witness intimidation considered throughout the process. If the witness is a child, the presumptions mentioned above will apply, and the nature of the offence will be relevant to which measures are presumed to benefit the child. The fact that a witness may give evidence in this way does not necessarily mean that they will have taken part in a video-recorded interview early in the investigation of an alleged offence. The decision to record evidence-in-chief may be taken at a later stage, for example as a consequence of a plea and directions hearing in the Crown Court.

The video recording (as edited, where that is required) normally forms the whole of a witness's evidence-in-chief, and will be watched by the witness before cross-examination takes place. The witness will normally have had an opportunity to see the recording on a previous occasion too, in order to refresh their memory in preparation for the trial.

In some exceptional cases, the witness may be asked to give additional evidence to that recorded during the interview. This usually occurs when matters have not been covered adequately or in sufficient detail. To do this, it must be demonstrated that there has been a material change of circumstances since the direction to admit the video recording was made. Depending on the circumstances, a live link or screen may be used for the additional evidence. Where a witness who has recorded an interview subsequently attends an identification parade or a similar procedure under the Code of Practice for the Identification of Persons by Police Officers (Police and Criminal Evidence Act 1984, Code D), it may be necessary to supplement the witness's video-recorded evidence to include the outcome of the additional evidence.

Video-recorded cross-examination

The cross-examination is not recorded in the physical presence of the defendant, although they have to be able to see and hear the cross-examination and be able to communicate with their legal representative. Witnesses who have been cross-examined on video are not to be cross-examined again unless the court makes a direction permitting another video-recorded cross-examination. This might occur if additional information relevant to the trial becomes available. Video-recorded cross-examination both minimises the delay between examination in chief and cross-examination and helps to alleviate stress associated with court attendances.

The use of intermediaries

The Youth and Criminal Evidence Act 1999 sets out the primary role of an intermediary to advise police officers, judges, magistrates and lawyers on the communication requirements of the witness within the court process. Aids to communication may be used.

Witness profiling

The profile of a witness is classed as an additional measure under special measures. The profile is developed by a suitable person who has not been involved and does not have knowledge of the safeguarding or criminal issues. The person is impartial and gathers evidence about how the witness might act under stress, the care and support needs they may have during the trial, the communication needs they have, and any religious or cultural matters that might need consideration. The profile will be shared with all relevant parties within court – judge, jury members, barristers. The following is an example of a profile that might be developed to support a person to give credible evidence. This can be used by a victim support professional, a social worker or other relevant professional. A version of this document is available to download from www.jkp.com/voucher using the code COUCOMO.

WITNESS PROFILE

The person completing the witness profile should not ask any questions relating to the offence. This profile is to support individuals in court, and those who interact with the witness, to understand the best way to communicate to get the most accurate and credible evidence.

Name and date of birth of witness:

(The police should select the most relevant professional for the issues affecting the witness. This may be a social worker, a speech and language therapist, an occupational therapist or someone similar.)

Prepared by:

(name and occupation)

Introduction

The introduction should give an overview of the person and their background information. This should include their age, where they live, any work or education that they have been involved in and any relevant medical diagnosis. Identify any relevant issues regarding the person's personality, persona or appearance that the court may need to be aware of, be sensitive to, or take into consideration.

You can use relevant aspects of the assessment and care and support plan where there is lawful jurisdiction to do so, with the consent of the person concerned, or if it is deemed to be in the best interests of a person who lacks capacity to consent to the sharing of this information.

This section should also include the views, wishes and feelings of the witness.

Special measures (as detailed in Sections 23–30 of the Youth Justice and Criminal Evidence Act 1999)

- Have special measures been considered? Might the person benefit from special measures such as the removal of gowns and wigs, the use of screens and the use of intermediaries or advocates such as an independent domestic violence advocate (IDVA) or independent sexual violence advocate (ISVA)? Might the person be better giving evidence via video link or being cross-examined via video link? The witness does not have to watch their DVD interview at the same time as the jury, if there is a better time for their cross-examination, or if they require regular breaks.

- Special measures and additional measures are raised by the police with the judge for a 'ground rules hearing'. If you know of any measures that would assist the witness to provide clear and credible evidence, please complete the relevant sections of this form.

Additional measures to assist

Under Section 20 of the Equality Act 2010, courts are expected to make reasonable adjustments and remove barriers for people who have disabilities. They must take every reasonable step to facilitate participation and prepare the person for court. This document falls under 'additional measures'. You may consider other things such as:

- introducing the person to those who will be in court including the judge

- practising reading the oath/affirmation

- turning off the picture on the screen if this distracts the witness

- allowing the witness to write and draw to clarify answers

- permitting witnesses unable to give evidence due to distress to return the next day

- allocating a female judge

- allowing a witness supporter to assist with communication and relay answers

- being ACE (adverse childhood experiences) and trauma informed.

There are many more potential additional measures that can be considered.

Medical needs

Does this person have any medical conditions which could affect them during the court process, such as epilepsy, heart conditions, breathing problems or any other medical conditions?

Does this person have any hearing or sight problems?

Does the person need regular medication?

Is this medication taken at specific times?

Does the person need support to move around, or to use the toilet?

Is the person dependent on substances such as drugs or alcohol and what would need to be considered in relation to their dependency?

Does the person use breathing or other equipment on a regular basis?

Is the person able to sit for long periods of time?

Is the person able to stand for long periods of time?

Are there any other medical needs that may impact on the person's ability to be a witness in court?

General functional skills

How does this person manage stressful situations?

Would this person require support during the court process? If so, with what?

Is there anything that startles, confuses or upsets this person that may arise within a court setting?

Does this person have any sensory sensitivities such as light, sound and smell that may have an impact on them within a court setting?

Does this person like certain things to make them feel safe, for example a blanket, hat, material, toy or mascot?

Does this person have any allergies or phobias that may present themselves during the court process?

Does the person have dyspraxia, dyslexia or something similar that may affect their functioning in the court?

Can the person read and write?

Is there anything else about the person's functional skills that may affect them during the court process?

Comprehension

Does this person have difficulty understanding some things?

Is this person able to take instruction?

Can instruction for two or more things be given at the same time?

Is this person able to understand past tense and present tense – the difference between the past and the present?

Is this person able to put things into a chronology?

Is this person able to understand negatives, or is communication required within a certain context?

Does this person struggle with particular words, analogies or methods of dialogue?

Might emotive description affect the person's ability to understand?

Does the person need information broken down using short sentences or, in the case of making a choice, choosing from fewer options?

Does this person need an interpreter?

Does this person need glasses to read or a hearing aid or device to clearly hear?

Is there anything else about this person's ability to understand communication that the court would benefit from knowing?

Concentration

Is this person able to concentrate and process information for a prolonged period of time?

What type of things cause this person to become distracted?

How long might this person be able to concentrate and process information before needing a break?

Is there anything that affects this person's ability to concentrate?

Is there anything that supports this person's ability to concentrate?

Has there been a traumatic incident that affects concentration?

Communication

Does this person become upset, angry or distressed by certain non-verbal methods of communication, such as eye contact, proximity and personal space, touching things near them or touching parts of their body such as hands and arms?

Are there any forms of non-verbal communication that this person may find confusing or confrontational?

Might certain forms of communication be affected by trauma?

Does this person recognise and respond to facial expressions and body language?

Does this person struggle with any aspects of verbal communication?

Does this person use aids or adaptations to communication?

Are there certain environments in which this person feels more comfortable communicating within?

Is there anything that the court may need to know about this person's ability to communicate?

Vocabulary

Is there anything about this person's vocabulary, speech or use of words that the court might benefit from understanding?

Does the person have a large vocabulary or is it limited?

Does the person mimic words without understanding the meaning or context?

Are any of the words that the person avoids associated with trauma?

In relevant cases, it may be useful if the person uses certain words to describe particular body parts or the person may not like a particular word that describes a body part.

Advice to counsel

When asking x questions

When questions are answered

Conclusion – matters for court consideration

Name:

Signed:

Qualifications:

Work address:

Contact details:

Date:

The pre-trial supporter can provide the witness with information about the court process, or direct their carer or specialist service to the relevant sources. The witness is likely to benefit considerably from a pre-trial court visit. This will enable them to familiarise themselves with the layout of the court, in particular where court officials sit, the location of the witness box and the facilities available in the court. They will also have an opportunity to run through basic court procedure, dicuss any particular fears or concerns and gain an idea of the roles of different court personnel and what can be expected. They should also be given an outline of the services offered by the Crown Court Witness Service or Magistrates Court Witness Service, as appropriate, on the day of trial.

A pre-trial court visit will also make witnesses better informed about the choice of special measures to assist them to give evidence. It is a good idea to support the witness to practise reading the oath or affirmation within the court setting and to help them to understand what the oath or affirmation means.

Witnesses are entitled to see a copy of their statement before giving evidence. Where the investigative interview of the witness has been videotaped, the tape is often used to refresh the witness's memory before the trial – the equivalent of reading the statement beforehand. Viewing the video ahead of time in more informal surroundings helps some witnesses familiarise themselves with seeing their own image on the screen and makes it more likely that they will concentrate on the task of giving evidence. The Crown Prosecution Service recommends that the first viewing of the videotape should not be on the morning prior to trial, to avoid the person having to view the tape twice in one day.

It is Crown Prosecution Service policy that a videotaped interview may be shown to the witness before the trial for the purpose of refreshing memory unless the video has been ruled inadmissible. If such a ruling is made, the prosecution may identify an acceptable alternative method of refreshing the witness's evidence. Decisions about admissibility should be made in sufficient time to allow other steps to be taken. If the witness is to give live evidence-in-chief, the prosecutor should consider seeking a ruling on whether it is appropriate to allow the witness to see the video before evidence is given. Supporters should be informed promptly about any decisions on video admissibility and editing.

It is the responsibility of the police to arrange for prosecution witnesses to read their statements or view videotaped interviews. They should consult the prosecution about where this should take place, whether a record should be kept of anything said at the showing and who may be present.

The time interval between showing the video for the purpose of refreshment and actually giving evidence should take account of the witness's needs and concentration span. Minimising delay should be balanced against the difficulty experienced by some witnesses in concentrating through two viewings on the same day. If the witness loses concentration or becomes distressed during the viewing, a break will be necessary.

Witnesses need to receive appropriate explanations about the purpose of watching the video before the trial, and their views about this must be taken into account. Sometimes videos will be edited for legal reasons, for example if the video contains irrelevant material or inadmissible matters of fact or law. Witnesses need to be alerted to any editing so that they will not be surprised, suspicious or confused when the recording does not match precisely their recollection of the interview.

Supporting the witness involves assessing their needs both directly and by information from others. Where support will be provided and by whom will need to be considered. The liaison and communication needs, and a number of considerations to prepare the witness for trial, will need to be explored. The following bullet points can act as a reminder of these witness support, preparation and profiling considerations.

Witness support, preparation and profiling considerations

Assessing the needs of the witness

- directly
- obtaining information from others.

Support

Liaison and communication

- with the witness
- with other professionals in the legal case

- with the witness's family and friends
- with the witness's circle of professionals.

Therapy and counselling

Preparing for the trial

- information concerning courts
- options for giving evidence
- the victim's wishes
- pre-trial visits
- refreshing memory
- meeting the advocate.

Witnesses are likely to be anxious about the progress of the case and decisions about whether and how they will give evidence. Once a trial date has been arranged, the police and defence solicitor should provide their respective witnesses with as much notice as possible of the date and the time they are required to give evidence, at least within four working days of receipt of the list of witnesses to attend court. If it becomes apparent that the trial will not proceed, the witness should be told as soon as possible.

While continuing efforts are made to minimise delays in the criminal justice system, witnesses should be forewarned at an early stage that some cases take a long time to reach trial or may be discontinued pre-trial, and that some trials may be adjourned for unforeseen reasons. They should also be advised beforehand of the possibility of waiting to give evidence on the day of trial. It may be possible for witnesses to wait at locations at some distance from the court, and to be summoned by pager when their evidence is to be heard.

Witnesses should be told who is responsible for keeping them informed of significant developments in their case. Supporters must ensure that they are kept informed about key decisions, for example about how the witness is to give evidence.

In June 1998 the Home Office report *Speaking Up for Justice* was produced by an interdepartmental working group that considered the treatment of vulnerable or intimidated witnesses in the criminal justice system. Recommendation 28 of the report said, 'Vulnerable or intimidated witnesses should not be denied the emotional support and counselling they may need both before and after the trial.' Good practice guidance has subsequently been issued on the Crown Prosecution Service website (Bradley, Hartmen and Smith n.d.).

Victims, service provision professionals and forensic investigators have a mutual interest in ensuring, wherever possible, that those who receive therapy prior to a criminal trial are regarded as witnesses who are able to give reliable testimony. The concern that therapy could be considered as tainting evidence or that the prosecution may be lost is not a valid argument for preventing access. There is a need to ensure that witnesses are able to have immediate and effective treatment to both support them through the process and assist their recovery. Witnesses should not be denied access to any therapeutic help in a criminal trial, in particular if they have a mental illness.

Directions for special measures can be made at the pre-trial hearing as well as in other circumstances. The court has power under the Youth Justice and Criminal Evidence Act 1999 to make rules governing how confidential or sensitive information may be disclosed to other parties, and what may be withheld.

In addition to providing pre-trial and court witness support and preparation, the witness service has an essential role in coordination of arrangements at the court building in liaison with the court officials and the Crown Court liaison officer where appropriate. Issues to be covered may include:

- parking or drop-off arrangements

- the avoidance of confrontation between the witness, other parties and their supporters

- using a side entrance for the witness to enter and leave the building

- making arrangements for appropriate facilities for waiting

- the number of people required as escorts within the court building, if there is more than one vulnerable or intimidated witness, to avoid allegations of cross-contamination of evidence

- coordinating arrangements for witnesses during breaks, the lunch hour and on leaving court after giving evidence.

Courts should consider the order and timing of witness attendance, so as to minimise inconvenience. Such an approach will benefit vulnerable or intimidated witnesses, who may be able to request waiting in a different area of court, or getting into court prior to others or after others. It is possible to speak with court liaison officers to make pre-trial familiarisation visits, liaise with the judge, make practical arrangements and arrange separate waiting areas as required.

The Bar Code of Conduct allows advocates to introduce themselves to witnesses and assist with procedural questions, provided the evidence is not discussed. Supporters should ask witnesses whether they wish to meet the advocate prior to giving their evidence. An increasing number of judges, accompanied by the prosecution and defence advocates, meet young or vulnerable witnesses before they give evidence. Experience suggests that this can assist in demystifying the court process and that putting witnesses more at ease assists them to give their best evidence.

Though judges and lawyers should invite vulnerable witnesses to tell the court when they need a break, their ability to identify when this is necessary should not be relied on. The police and supporters should ensure that information is passed to the prosecution about the witness's attention span, bearing in mind that it is likely to be shorter in the stressful atmosphere of court. This will enable the judge and advocates to plan breaks in the witness's testimony. Scheduled breaks are also less likely to occur at a time that would favour one side over another.

Personal qualities of vulnerable adults may put them at particular disadvantage in relation to investigation and court proceedings. For example, some people with mental disorders can be particularly sensitive to perceived challenge or criticism, or fear recurrence of traumatic events. Similarly, learning disabled people may have a relative lack of adaptability. These and similar differences and vulnerabilities might lead such witnesses to require longer and more extensive support and preparation. Naturally, the precise type and amount will vary according to the alleged offence, the witness's character, the level of understanding, and life experience. It will also vary according to the purpose of the support; for example, whether it is designed to encourage the most reliable testimony or to reduce the trauma of proceedings on the witness, or both.

Delay within the criminal justice process can add disproportionately to the stress on witnesses who are vulnerable. For example, learning disabled people may have particular difficulty understanding the basis and reasons for a delay. For this reason, and because delay is likely to adversely affect the memory of a person with learning disability, decision makers should be reminded of the need to treat such cases as a priority.

Witnesses have been found to give better evidence when they have a choice about the way in which it is given. This especially applies to vulnerable witnesses, many of whom need preparation and support in order to be able to make an informed choice. Vulnerable witnesses should have an active role in choosing, to the extent possible, how to give their evidence. The most appropriate method of doing so depends not only on the individual's objective capacity but also on what they wish to do, taking into account the options that are available for them.

Issues of special importance for those planning support for vulnerable adult witnesses include:

- taking account of witnesses' choices and views

- amount of time needed

- best time of day

- designing appropriate breaks

- method of asking for a break

- witnesses' level of understanding concerning courts and any prejudices they may have, for example it is they, the witness, who is on trial

- familiarisation with the place of the hearings

- explanations regarding video and closed-circuit TV

- short attention spans while giving evidence (especially for the learning disabled)

- speech and communication aids

- planning approach to the oath and/or admonishing the witness.

In the period leading up to the trial, there are a number of precautions that officers can take when dealing with fearful and intimidated witnesses. Throughout the course of the case, the police should develop coping strategies to enable the witness to handle the threat of possible reprisals, and should give the witness appropriate information and advice. Some police forces issue a small booklet to all officers outlining measures for witness support. Others use a pre-printed tear-off sheet as part of the statement form, and this is handed to the witness.

The identification of suspects should make use of identification suites with screens, and face-to-face identification should be avoided. Video identification procedures can serve to reduce stress on the witness. Witnesses should be kept informed of the progress of their case, as lack of knowledge (concerning, for example, the offender's whereabouts) can add to feelings of fear and uncertainty.

Full and accurate information about special provision required to assist vulnerable and intimidated witnesses is needed to inform decision making and pre-trial planning. In the Crown Court, it is preferable for issues to be raised and resolved as far as possible at the plea and directions hearing (PDH). It will be at this hearing that initial decisions will be taken, or a date fixed for rulings to be made, about the special measures directions which are possible under the Youth Justice and Criminal Evidence Act 1999. It is important to achieve as much certainty as possible about how the witness will give evidence and arrangements for court attendance.

The needs and wishes of vulnerable and intimidated witnesses should have been identified as part of the pre-trial preparation. It is vital that *advocates* taking part in the PDH in the Crown Court are given full instructions prior to the hearing, including up-to-date information from and about the witness, so that the judge will be in a position to complete the judge's questionnaire. Issues addressed in the questionnaire include the mental or medical condition of the witness and staggered witness attendance. A copy of the judge's questionnaire is completed as far as possible with the agreement of both advocates, and is handed in to the court prior to the start of the PDH hearing. Judges may be expected to ask for information about witnesses if it is not provided.

Other matters raised by the questionnaire include applications for a live link, screens, pre-recorded evidence-in-chief and the use of videotape playback equipment at trial. Steps may be taken to provide support to the witness and refresh the witness's memory subject to the judge's decision in advance of the trial.

KEY POINTS

- Has a referral been made where the three-part eligibility criteria are met and there is reasonable suspicion of abuse or neglect, or the risk of abuse or neglect?

- Have points to prove been discussed in relation to preservation and presentation of evidence?

- Has the person been supported to access criminal or civil justice?

- Has the local authority/police considered witness support and preparation for court and profiling?

- Have special measures been considered?

CHAPTER 10

How Do I Manage Cases of Escalating Risk or Multiple Abuse?

When there is multiple abuse, or when an individual self-neglects, where there is domestic abuse of a vulnerable person, or a person has been trafficked, used as a slave, forced into marriage or sexually exploited, there are often barriers to achieving positive outcomes for the person. The risks may continue escalating, with the practitioner raising concerns over and over again, but repeating the same patterns or actions. This can lead to practitioner stress and anxiety over the potential negative outcomes of a case, such as substantial harm or death – a severe outcome for someone who was dependent on services for protection, and devastation for the family.

In many local authorities, there is little intervention when safeguarding procedures are failing. Serious harm occurs in cases already known to those whose position it is to safeguard adults, and safeguarding adults reviews have highlighted the risk. A stage of senior intervention when there is escalating concern that could lead to substantial harm or death of an individual, or when strategic direction is needed as a result of care home or hospital ward failings may be required. This stage requires a strategic coordinated meeting to consider the larger strategic barriers and issues affecting outcomes. Local authorities call these strategy meetings a variety of names relating to the escalating risk and the strategic nature of the meeting. I am going to call these meetings 'executive strategies'.

For those who work within safeguarding adults, the perception of the victim has a great impact on the elicited response of professionals. In cases of self-neglect, the person is often perceived as making a lifestyle choice. Research suggests that self-neglect impacting on physical and mental wellbeing is often a result of trauma, loss, bereavement or abuse and is a well-defended coping mechanism to maintain some personal control (Braye and Orr 2011).

Practitioners feel unable to respond to what appears to be capacitated decisions and do not explore when a person began making unwise decisions and why. A person may be suffering domestic abuse and may be coerced into making decisions, an intimidating perpetrator may be so threatening that the person is afraid to speak out, or the psychological impact of abuse, neglect or loss may be so severe that the person is unable to respond to their own needs. The person may be suffering mental ill-health and require a Mental Health Act assessment. These things need to be ruled out as part of the enquiries. Strategic barriers to safeguarding a person and appropriate care and support require strategic responses at a senior level.

Concerns are raised in relation to some aspects of safeguarding adults such as domestic abuse of a vulnerable person, or a person who has been trafficked, used as a slave, forced into marriage or sexually exploited. The person may not recognise the abuse themselves and they may appear to be making an informed consenting decision; however, they have been groomed or coerced over a long period of time. We may be concerned about the impact of abuse and how this affects the person's understanding and decision making, or there may be concerns about undiagnosed mental ill-health.

Organisational abuse or abuse affecting a number of people within a care home or hospital requires a strategic approach to matters as well as individual safeguarding responses. Mantell and Scragg (2009) identify the influence of organisational cultures as being of prime importance in safeguarding work, and with the local authority providing oversight and guidance, our culture impacts on all organisations subject to the policies and procedures of safeguarding adults. Johnson and Scholes (2002) introduce the concept of an organisational web of culture seen through rituals, routines, stories, structures and systems:

- *Rituals* – the way we do things around here.

- *Routines* – the way people behave toward each other and towards outside organisations.

- *Stories* – embed history and flag important events, highlighting mavericks who deviate from the norm.

- *Symbols* – logos, offices, titles, language, terminology.

- *Control* – measure and reward.

- *Power* – what is valued by the people with most power in safeguarding adults? Relates to assumptions, values and beliefs.

- *Structure* – formal and informal hierarchical power, defining important relationships, working practice, constraints and norms that exercise control over individuals.

In the reports of the Commission for Social Care Inspection and the Health Care Commission into Cornwall and Sutton and Merton learning disability services (Commission for Social Care Inspection and Healthcare Commission 2006; London Borough of Sutton 2007), there were issues highlighted that give insight into the culture of the services. Both services had poor leadership with a lack of strategic vision and inadequate management arrangements for safeguarding adults. Attitudes toward service users were paternalistic and failed to provide opportunities for the development of greater independence. Within executive strategies, it is imperative that the cultural web of empowering practice and strong leadership extends and impacts on all organisational cultures.

Planning excellence as an example to all requires strategies that consider verbal and non-verbal communication with the organisations involved. The minutes and actions from executive strategy meetings reflect organisational culture, intention, leadership and management – they also circulate the local authority's intent for safeguarding, identifying our rituals, routines, stories, symbols, control systems, power structures and organisational structure.

Stevenson (1996) provides us with a warning and alerts us to the dangers of over-proceduralisation occurring within safeguarding adults. It is important to highlight that procedures alone do not always immediately assist practitioners or managers as they tend to focus on procedural guidance and not on the professional skills required, such as legal and operational knowledge, practical experience, confidence to assertively question, enquire and challenge allied professionals, assumptions of care providers in relation to capacity, risk, malpractice, poor standards of care and aspects of discrimination. With pressure for clear and accurate recording reflecting the intentions of the local authority linked with a need for fluidity and open professional discussion, this poses difficulty in achieving accurate and concise minutes.

The aim of an executive strategy meeting is to engage at senior management level, partner agencies in a meeting to prevent escalating concerns and use an executive and strategic approach to address these concerns. Consideration for such a meeting may be given when:

- complex or serious organisational abuse is alleged or suspected

- multiple abuse is alleged or suspected and requires a strategic approach in addition to safeguarding individuals

- organised abuse is alleged or suspected

- there are escalating concerns regarding someone seriously self-neglecting or someone whose physical and mental wellbeing is deteriorating significantly and public sector services are not preventing deterioration

- the alleged perpetrator holds a senior position within a care setting or organisation

- there are large numbers of victims to be interviewed or supported

- cases may attract significant media attention.

This process may be used when there is a clear need, because of the severity or seriousness of the issues being addressed, to gather a multi-agency forum where attendees have a sufficient level of seniority and authority to act and direct resources on behalf of their organisation at a strategic level. This effectively coordinates strategic responses to safeguarding and prevents escalating concerns that may result in serious harm or death. It is intended to be utilised as a step between safeguarding responses and safeguarding adults reviews to ensure that senior managers are informed and have the opportunity to respond in a preventative manner. Learning from these meetings may be shared to prevent similar concerns escalating.

An executive strategy enables a strategic approach that is clear, directed and effective at breaking down barriers in access to services and coordinates the necessary strategic responses, informing all appropriate senior managers of matters of significant concern and enabling action to be taken. Coordination is more effective, as a number of people potentially affected by abuse or neglect are not being discussed within one large meeting. Individuals are considered for individual safeguarding responses, which maintains a person-centred focus and provides feedback of any strategic concerns to the executive strategy group.

Figure 10.1 identifies how a number of individual safeguarding responses are coordinated, leaving the executive strategy to focus on matters relevant to senior managers within individual organisations.

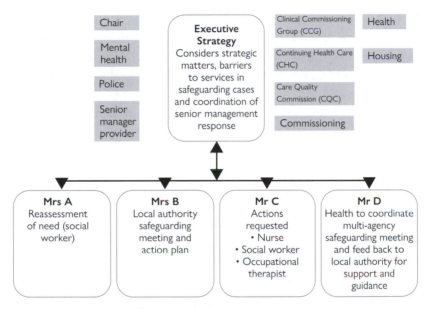

Figure 10.1: Executive strategy

In cases of self-neglect, or individual cases of significant concern, the focus may be more on the barriers to services, support and appropriate assessment. A human rights focus will be required to ensure that all duties and responsibilities are being met and a lead person is effectively navigating the legislative frameworks.

The executive strategy process

It may be apparent from the point of a safeguarding referral that an executive strategy meeting needs to be convened to fully and jointly address highlighted concerns and issues. This, however, is unusual, and large-scale or organised abuse, or significant neglect or self-neglect, usually comes to light in the course of already-established safeguarding enquiries, or where safeguarding responses have not been effective in preventing abuse, neglect or self-neglect.

Referrals may be made via the safeguarding operational manager who can discuss concerns with the safeguarding business manager or the independent chair when relevant. The appropriate senior manager will then take steps to ensure that an executive strategy meeting is convened. Senior representatives from each of the other necessary partner agencies may need to be invited to that strategic meeting to look at the overall issues regarding care and treatment. Both the police and the local authority legal department may be informed of any impending executive strategy meeting and will make an informed decision, based on the nature of the concerns, regarding whether they will need to attend.

A relevant commissioning manager will attend any strategy meetings concerning multiple organisational abuse. A regulation manager or regulatory inspector from the Care Quality Commission will play a key role in the executive strategy process and any subsequent safeguarding work regarding organisational failures. The senior manager may also need to inform the council's chief executive, depending on the severity of the allegation. An executive strategy chair will need to be appointed to coordinate the case from that point onwards, and will ensure that everyone who can assist the enquiry will be engaged and that a balanced enquiry will take place.

Outcomes in cases of organisational abuse may result in ongoing auditing and monitoring of those services and may even involve suspension of placements, regulatory action such as enforcement, cancellation of registration, or termination of contractual arrangements (decommissioning). Effective communication and collaboration between the partner agencies will therefore be essential. Additionally, in the event of any safeguarding referral which requires a response at executive strategy level and where any of the above factors are present, the police may take the decision to implement response protocols at senior level.

Safeguarding strategy arrangements made at this senior level must also be made within five working days of the executive strategy meeting being identified as necessary.

As with the safeguarding meeting processes, regular follow-up meetings may need to be conducted so that plans can be jointly reviewed and revised if necessary. Protocols for information sharing and recording will need to be implemented in the same way, and the minutes of strategy meetings and records of strategy discussions must only be circulated in accordance with the relevant guidance set out in these inter-agency procedures. Media management in such cases will also need to be coordinated at executive level.

Executive strategy meetings are not established to address all individual safeguarding concerns. These meetings are to look at key issues relating to a significant event, multiple safeguarding referrals, institutional abuse, abuse or neglect where public sector services are struggling to prevent individual deterioration resulting in potential death and/or senior staff members being involved in abuse. The chair will refer the case of each individual person who has been affected by abuse or neglect to safeguarding leads as per the policies and procedures for individual safeguarding responses. The information from each individual safeguarding response will be collated and summarised, and anything that affects the contracting, management, commissioning or standards of service from the provider will be reported to the executive strategy chair. The chair will decide the necessary attendees from the individual strategies.

The executive strategy meeting will address the provision of care, care assessment, care planning, provision of treatment, staffing issues, training issues and risk management within an establishment, but not concern regarding individuals in cases of multiple abuse. This will be addressed in separate meetings and fed back to the executive strategy chair.

In cases of self-neglect or significant concern regarding an individual whose health is rapidly deteriorating and public sector services are not preventing deterioration, the coordination of capacity assessments, the legal frameworks, communication with the person, legal matters and legislative frameworks, barriers to services and lack of cooperation from agencies may need to be considered at a strategic level. Once the strategic matters have been addressed, the case may be referred back to traditional safeguarding procedures.

Improper use of restraint may amount to the criminal offences of assault and/or false imprisonment and/or choking. It may also amount to a criminal offence of breach of Regulation 24 or 25 under the Care Standards Act 2000.

The Mental Capacity Act 2005 defines restraint as:

> the use or threat of force to help do an act which the person resists, or the restriction of the person's liberty of movement, whether or not they resist. Restraint may only be used where it is necessary to protect the person from harm and is proportionate to the risk of harm. (Section 6)

Where a person is in need of restraint on a regular basis, this may be classed as a deprivation of the person's liberty and only the court can determine whether it is appropriate, proportionate and in a person's best interests to deprive that person of their liberty. The local authority supervisory body currently acts on behalf of the court in cases within residential and hospital care or state-imposed services; however, the Law Commission is considering a revision to this, to enable health services to take on the supervisory role for health-related cases.

The Department of Health published statutory guidance describing good practice for restrictive physical interventions in 2002. When considering matters such as whether a criminal offence has been committed or whether the public interest requires a prosecution, prosecutors may find Deprivation of Liberty Safeguards guidance helpful in assessing whether the use of restraint was lawful, appropriate and proportionate (Crown Prosecution Service 2018).

KEY POINTS

We do not necessarily need to have executive strategies or similar risk escalation processes, but we do need to consider how we separate the strategic aspects of safeguarding from individual operational safeguarding and how we escalate concerns when existing responses are not working. Discussing multiple cases during one meeting is not personalised safeguarding and is not very confidential, as not all agencies need to hear about all issues in relation to all people. This strategic level of intervention assists in breaking down barriers in access to services required for safeguarding.

CHAPTER 11

Safeguarding Adults Reviews

Under the Care Act 2014, safeguarding adults boards have a duty to undertake a safeguarding adults review when an adult dies as a result of abuse or neglect, whether known or suspected, and there is concern that partner agencies could have worked more effectively to protect the adult. The Care Act 2014 introduced statutory safeguarding adults reviews to replace serious case reviews. A safeguarding adults review may also be undertaken when an adult has not died, but the safeguarding adults board knows, or suspects, that the adult has experienced serious abuse or neglect. The safeguarding adults board may also commission a safeguarding adults review in other circumstances where it feels it would be useful, including lessons from 'near misses' and situations where arrangements worked particularly well.

In the context of a safeguarding adults review, something can be considered serious abuse or neglect where, for example, the individual would have been likely to have died but for an intervention, or has suffered permanent harm, or has reduced capacity or quality of life (whether because of physical or psychological effects), as a result of the abuse or neglect.

The adult who is the subject of any safeguarding adults review does not have to be in receipt of care and support services for the safeguarding adults board to arrange a review in relation to them.

The purpose of a safeguarding adults review

It is tragic when a person dies or is seriously harmed and this could have been prevented by appropriate interventions. The process of learning about what went wrong across agencies and what the lessons are from this is called a safeguarding adults review. The purpose of carrying out a safeguarding adults review is not to hold any individual or organisation to account. Other processes exist for that, including criminal proceedings, disciplinary procedures, employment law and systems of service and professional regulation, such as those of the Care Quality Commission, the Nursing and Midwifery Council, the Health and Care Professions Council and the General Medical Council. However, if during the course of the review serious issues relating to an agency or individual involved in the case come to light, action may be needed by the relevant agency.

The purpose of the safeguarding adults review is to:

- understand what has happened and why

- learn lessons from the way professionals and agencies worked together

- identify what the agencies and individuals might have done differently that could have prevented harm or death

- prevent similar harm occurring again in the future

- improve future practice by acting on the learning

- review and improve the safeguarding adults procedures

- identify good practice as well as poor.

The safeguarding adults review should reflect the six safeguarding principles:

1. *Empowerment* – presumption of person-led decisions and informed consent.

2. *Prevention* – it is better to take action before harm occurs.

3. *Proportionality* – proportionate and least-intrusive response appropriate to the risk presented.

4. *Protection* – support and representation for those in greatest need.

5. *Partnerships* – local solutions through services working with their communities.

6. *Accountability and transparency in delivering safeguarding.*

The safeguarding adults review must result in a plain English report with clear findings and recommendations with practical, realistic and achievable outcomes and actions.

Referral process and decision-making panel/process

Any agency or professional can make a referral, such as coroners, Members of Parliament and elected members. A referral may be made to the chair of the safeguarding adults board or the community safety partnership in the case of domestic abuse.

Focus on victim, family and friends

A safeguarding adults review should focus on answers for families and friends of the adult who has died or been seriously abused or neglected. This will mean that the safeguarding adults review will have to communicate with the adult and/or their family, and in some cases it may be helpful to communicate with the person who caused the abuse or neglect. Where appropriate, the safeguarding adults review will have to arrange for an independent advocate to represent and support an adult who is the subject of a safeguarding enquiry or safeguarding adults review, where the adult has 'substantial difficulty' in being involved in the process and where there is no other appropriate adult to help them.

The safeguarding adults board should ensure that the safeguarding adults review has the appropriate involvement of professionals and organisations who were involved with the adult. It is vital, if individuals and organisations are to be able to learn lessons from the past, that reviews are trusted and safe experiences that encourage honesty, transparency and sharing of information to obtain maximum benefit from them. This will not be the case if individuals and their organisations are fearful of the safeguarding adults review.

Proportionality in a safeguarding adults review

The process for undertaking a safeguarding adults review will be determined according to the individual circumstances. There is no 'one size fits all' approach. The approach will vary due to the circumstances and other reviews that may also have arisen because of the incident.

Links and interfaces with other reviews

When setting up a safeguarding adults review, safeguarding adults boards should also consider how the process fits with any other related investigations. Potentially, the safeguarding adults review may overlap with other reviews and processes such as:

- inquest and the work of the coroner

- police investigation

- multi-agency public protection arrangements

- safeguarding adults reviews for children

- disciplinary proceedings

- domestic homicide reviews

- mental health homicide reviews.

The safeguarding adults review will have to take account of other statutory legal processes and statutory reviews. A decision will need to be made with relevant agencies about which review takes precedence. Where reviews or other legal processes cover issues of interest to the safeguarding adults review, and contain any lessons learned, these can be fed into the safeguarding adults review, thus avoiding duplication.

In the event of a death, there will need to be close liaison with the coroner's office as this may take precedence over the safeguarding adults review process. This will need to be determined on a case-by-case basis. If the person is subject to Deprivation of Liberty Safeguards, this should also be discussed with the police and coroner's office. The work of the coroner can take many months to reach a conclusion, and the safeguarding adults review may feed into the inquest.

When a criminal investigation or proceedings are underway, there will need to be liaison with the police and/or Crown Prosecution Service to decide on the timing of the review, the way in which the review is conducted and who should contribute at what stage (see the safeguarding adults review referral section for further detail).

When victims of domestic homicide are aged between 16 and 18, there are separate requirements in statutory guidance for a child serious case review, a safeguarding adults review and a domestic homicide review. Where such reviews may be relevant to a safeguarding adults review (e.g. because they concern the same perpetrator), consideration should be given to how safeguarding adults reviews (adults), serious case reviews (child) and domestic homicide reviews/mental health homicide reviews can be managed in parallel in the most effective manner possible, so that organisations and professionals can learn from the case.

In considering the type of review that should take precedence, consider the following:

- Is the person an adult and do they meet or did they meet the three-part eligibility test for safeguarding?

In situations of domestic abuse, you need to consider the following:

- Could this be an incident or pattern of incidents of coercive, controlling, threatening behaviour, violence or abuse between those aged 16 or over?

- Have they been, or are they, intimate partners/family members (regardless of gender)?

For a multi-agency risk assessment conference, was the domestic abuse considered to be a:

- visible high risk

- situation that could potentially escalate

- case of repeated domestic abuse

- situation that meets the criteria on the DASH Risk Indicator, or where professional judgement suggests there is a significant risk (the DASH Risk Indicator is a risk-assessment process in cases considered high-risk domestic abuse)?

For multi-agency public protection arrangements – in relation to a potential perpetrator of abuse, is this person:

- a person who has sexual offences convictions (registered)

- a person convicted of a specified violent or sexual offence and sentenced to at least 12 months' imprisonment (includes under hospital detention or guardianship order)

- considered to pose a risk of serious and imminent risk of harm to the public requiring multi-agency intervention? (Have they received a conviction or caution which demonstrates that they are capable of causing serious harm to the public?)

Was the person detained under the Mental Health Act 1983 at the time of significant injury or death?

The Care Act 2014 identifies that if a safeguarding adults board requests a person to supply information to it, or to some other person specified in the request, the person to whom the request is made must comply where the information would enable the board to exercise its functions, where the information is pertinent and relevant.

The guidance for domestic homicide reviews under Section 9(3) of the Domestic Violence and Victims Act 2004 identifies that:

A 'domestic homicide review' means a review of the circumstances in which the death of a person aged 16 or over has, or appears to have, resulted from violence, abuse or neglect by:

(a) a person to whom he was related or with whom he was or had been in an intimate personal relationship, or

(b) a member of the same household as himself,

held with a view to identifying the lessons to be learnt from the death.

The Social Care Institute for Excellence in its report on safeguarding adults reviews identifies that:

How we think about what causes the failure of partner agencies to work effectively to protect an adult from abuse or neglect, affects how we approach investigating and analysing these cases. It also influences the recommendations we make to prevent reoccurrence. So it is useful to give some thought to the concepts that will underpin your approach to SARs [safeguarding adults reviews]. Accident or incident investigation in high risk industries, health care and the child protection system, have all made efforts to move away from focusing too much on individual members of staff and their failings. Instead they take a much broader approach to understanding the causation of accidents which pays more attention to pre-existing organisational factors. This brings an approach to the review process, and recommendations, that focuses more on organisational learning and improvement and less on blaming and disciplining individuals. (Social Care Institute for Excellence 2015)

The domestic homicide review process reiterates this, identifying that reviews should not:

- simply examine the conduct of professionals and agencies

- be service focused or driven

- be an enquiry into how the victim died or who was culpable (coroners and criminal courts do that).

Domestic homicide reviews should:

- illuminate the past to make the future safer

- be professionally curious

- find the trail of abuse and identify the agencies who had contact with the victim, perpetrator or family

- identify which agencies had contact with each other

- highlight good practice as well as poor practice

- articulate life through the eyes of the victim (and their children)

- reflect the perceptions of those around the victim – family, friends, neighbours, community members and professionals – and seek to understand the victim's reality

- identify barriers that the victim faced in reporting abuse/neglect and discover why interventions did not work

- identify how agencies worked with the victim

- operate in the best interests of the victim

- include the consideration of coercive and controlling behaviour

- include consideration of so-called honour-based violence, forced marriage and female genital mutilation, as well as all other forms of abuse and neglect.

Section 9(3) of the Domestic Violence and Victims Act 2004 highlights:

The key is situating the review in the home, family and community of the victim and exploring everything with an open mind. It will also help understand the context and environment in which professionals made decisions and took (or did not take) actions. This would include, for example, the culture of the organisation, the training the professionals had, the supervision of these professionals, the leadership of agencies and so forth.

The guidance questions whether an adjustment could have been made to the policies or procedures to get a better outcome for the victim. This is an inquisitive approach to the investigation or enquiry and is centred on the person and their life.

There may be a tendency to exaggerate what could have been anticipated when looking back at an incident, and the Social Care Institute for Excellence report on safeguarding adults reviews warns against this hindsight bias (Social Care Institute for Excellence 2015). A forward-looking process such as considering possible alternative outcomes of events, even when the actual result is already known, is recommended in the report. Another method may be to consider 'thematic reviews'. Traditionally, thematic analysis within and recommendations from reviews have tended to focus on the minutiae of what takes place between individual practitioners, their teams and the adults who have suffered abuse or neglect. This type of review can be unhelpful and tends to lay blame with an individual, drawing the reviewer away from the wider systems.

Conversely, a thematic review of the systems in place and the systemics involved in a case can have the opposite effect. It may be possible to form a second aspect of the safeguarding adults review considering national themes within safeguarding and local themes across agencies and the local authority area, or consider the systemics involved and whether there are common failures or misconceptions across agencies. This type of thematic review element of safeguarding will not only be valuable to individual local authorities, but also to national learning objectives in safeguarding. For example, the person may have had mental health issues and be refusing medication, leaving them more open to abuse. Capacity assessments are commonly cited as an area where more could be done. Safeguarding adults reviews are repeatedly citing the same issues around the lack of capacity assessments (requiring national scrutiny about why this is repeatedly going wrong). Safeguarding adults boards may wish to consider this in relation to a theme within an organisation, or local authority area. This would require local scrutiny and auditing to determine whether this issue was specific to this case or a common theme that requires addressing on a wider scale, with the focus on improving the latter.

These safeguarding adults review considerations are illustrated in Figure 11.1.

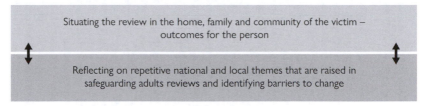

Figure 11.1: Safeguarding adults review considerations

Considering the need to reflect on national learning and put the lessons learned into everyday safeguarding practice, and driven by a desire to understand the main themes that are repeated in safeguarding adults reviews and domestic homicide reviews, I reviewed about 40 cases with a ratio of approximately 35 safeguarding adults reviews to five domestic homicide reviews to explore correlations and key themes. The result is something that I use as a tool in general safeguarding practice and which could be used to understand the national significance of the issues raised in local safeguarding adults reviews (see Table 11.1).

Table 11.1: Thematic review of safeguarding adults reviews: lessons to be learned

Guidance	Criteria	Self-assessment (including the identification of any barriers and concerns and how you have remedied them)
Identifying forms of abuse/neglect		
Local authorities should not limit their view of what constitutes abuse and neglect. Forms of abuse may include but are not exclusive to: • physical abuse • domestic abuse including honour-based crime and forced marriage • sexual abuse/exploitation • psychological abuse • financial or material abuse • modern slavery/trafficking • discriminatory abuse, including hate and mate crime • organisational abuse • neglect and acts of omission • self-neglect **A safeguarding referral should be made in cases of where the three-part test is met:** • The person has needs for care and support • The person is experiencing or at risk of abuse or neglect (including self-neglect) • As a result of those care and support needs, the person is unable to protect themselves from either risk of, or the experience of, abuse and neglect Local authorities should resist creating further thresholds for referral. The response to the referral will be established through enquiries, which can be anything from a telephone conversation to a full police investigation. This can be established at single point of contact, and appropriate responses may be anything from preventative measures, assessment and planning, information and advice through to criminal investigations and proceedings	Local authorities are coordinating an appropriate response to a referral via Section 42 enquiries. No additional thresholds are added to the three-part test	Consider the specific wording of the three-part test. Do you think that you/your local authority provides oversight and guidance to all safeguarding matters that meet this criteria? (Remember, many people referred under these criteria will not be eligible under the social work eligibility criteria.) Do you think that additional thresholds are being added to this three-part eligibility criteria? (Consider the risks to the people and the local authority in creating additional thresholds. If someone comes to serious harm as they did not meet the additional criteria but did meet the three-part test, then the local authority will not have met its statutory duties.) Does the person understand what we mean by safeguarding? Have you recorded the methods used to enable the person to recognise what you can and cannot lawfully do in the given situation? Does the person have an easy-read guide, or something in a format that will help them to understand safeguarding? Are you using language to describe safeguarding in a way that is not intimidating? Have you considered the situation and conducted a capacity assessment where the circumstances lead to doubt about the person's ability to understand? If the person is refusing support to get out of a risky or dangerous situation, have they been able to describe their rationale for this?

You do not need consent to make a safeguarding referral and share information:

- Checking out the person's consent is part of local authority Section 42 duties; there are lots of capacity assessments that may be required
- Enquiries can be made about the issues affecting the person/others, including whether the person consents to specific actions or not
- If they do not consent, this simply means that the local authority does not have their cooperation, but it does not prevent agencies from considering the wider safeguarding issues

You do need consent to safeguard the individual and to take actions in relation to their care and support, unless there is a lawful reason to do so. Enquiries should consider capacity and consent in relation to all identified needs and capacity assessments conducted by the appropriate agency risks to others (including children), public interest issues, potential crime, victim and perpetrator needs/risks explored, mental health issues, potential coercive or controlling behaviours. Safeguarding enquiries need to consider the risks to others, and the capacity of the person to make each decision that requires their understanding, signature, agreement or consent. It is about the needs or risks posed by the perpetrator. It is about considering the potential for domestic abuse, exploitation and grooming, coercion or intimidation affecting the person's decision-making ability. It is about understanding the impact of trauma on the person and whether they require mental health services and whether the person requires a statutory mental health assessment. We have a duty to protect the public and this will also need to be considered. To say that the person appears to have capacity and does not consent to the referral is not sufficient to ensure that we have a clear picture and can appropriately assess the situation while not asking questions that may destroy evidence in a criminal investigation

cont.

Section 42 enquiries

The purpose of an enquiry is to:	Have Section 42 enquiries been implemented appropriately?	Are you holding agencies accountable for safeguarding actions?
The purpose of an enquiry is to: • get a picture of the abuse/neglect/self-neglect • make sure that the person is safe • consider capacity assessments required and by whom • rule out additional or historical abuse/neglect • explore potential crime • identify any coercive or controlling behaviours • explore any mental health or substance misuse concerns • consider risks to others (including children) • determine the care and support needs of the individual/perpetrator • consider advocacy and methods of communication • determine whether a multi-agency response is required The local authority must have oversight of safeguarding procedures, but can request another agency to make enquiries on its behalf, or chair multi-agency meetings for safeguarding purposes as long as there is independence from the nature of the safeguarding incident. Information and outcomes must be shared with the local authority **The benefit of invoking safeguarding procedures:** • Duty to share information for enquiry purposes • Duty to cooperate with the local authority, and the local authority to cooperate with other agencies for safeguarding purposes • Duty to assess where there is an identified need • Duty to determine consent • Duty to provide appropriate advocacy • Duty to assess carers' needs	**Have Section 42 enquiries been implemented appropriately?** Ensure that the local authority is not applying social work eligibility criteria to safeguarding procedures prior to making enquiries	Are you holding agencies accountable for safeguarding actions? Is the best-placed person leading the enquiry? (Consider the skills and knowledge required and who has these skills, e.g. an occupational therapist, nurse, housing worker, psychologist or psychiatrist may be best placed to lead an enquiry as long as they are independent to the given situation and the local authority maintains oversight and guidance.) Are there barriers to information sharing? Do agencies recognise that they only need reasonable suspicion of abuse/neglect to make a referral to the local authority? Do agencies recognise that they only need reasonable suspicion of a crime to refer to the police?

You do not need to know abuse or neglect has occurred – you only need to have 'reasonable suspicion' of abuse or neglect. This is very important because many cases within safeguarding could constitute a crime.

The police do not need to know that a crime has been committed to investigate. Police powers of arrest identify that 'reasonable suspicion' of a crime is all that is expected. The police may arrest a person to stop the potential crime, preserve the evidence, identify the gaps in their knowledge, make enquiries to identify the gaps in knowledge and determine whether a crime has taken place. Safeguarding must follow the same principles to enable effective police-led investigations and prevent the destruction of evidence, creating equitable access to the criminal justice process for all people

Risks to others

Risks to others can include:

- fire risk
- rats, vermin, flies
- faecal matter, vomit or other bodily fluids
- toxic substances
- open wires, unsafe gas, structural issues
- oxygen tanks where someone smokes, or other medical equipment
- drugs paraphernalia (needles, spoons, knives)
- weapons
- people using the property who may target other vulnerable people
- animals at the property
- anti-social or threatening behaviour
- people residing at the property who may be a risk to those who have needs for care and support
- people who may be a risk to children residing or spending time at the property

Has the risk to others been considered?	Has the enquiry process assessed and identified the impact on animals, family members, other people and the community?

cont.

Risk assessments

Risk assessments should include:	Has the appropriate risk assessment been completed?	Do all agencies have a risk assessment that identifies when risks are increasing and considers all relevant risk factors in a consistent manner?
• historical abuse and past knowledge of the person • previous safeguarding referrals • accumulative risk • the vulnerability of the person (capacity, mental ill-health, physical disability, learning disability, autism spectrum disorder, age and frailty of the person, social isolation and the support the person has, acceptance of care and support, insight the person has into their problems and difficulties, dependent on the potential perpetrator) • type and seriousness of abuse/neglect • level of abuse/neglect • prevalence of abuse/neglect • background to incident • risk to others • risk of repeated abuse to person/others • impact of abuse on person/others • potential crime • perpetrator risks/support required • if there is anyone obstructing or preventing work with the person (family members, other people at the property)		

Carers' assessments

Carers' assessments to consider:	Have carers' needs been considered and a carer's assessment completed?	Has a carer's assessment been conducted? Is the carer aware of the responsibilities of meeting an identified need (including capacity and consent matters) – who can make the decisions? Is the carer able to understand their responsibilities? Have appropriate capacity assessments been carried out in relation to the carer's identified responsibilities?
• The carer's needs in continuing to support the person • Capacity issues relating to carer and ability to provide care • People residing at the property who may not consider themselves carers, but may still have a duty to care • Obstructive or aggressive carers/family members • If carers are meeting an identified need, then they are identified on any care and support plans as such and are informed of the responsibility to meet this need and inform services if the need changes		

Mental health and substance misuse

In assessing mental health and substance misuse consider the following questions: • Does the person require mental health assessment? • Has a referral been made? • Are there barriers to assessment? • Does the person misuse substances? • Would they engage with substance misuse services? • What is the impact of substance misuse on physical and mental wellbeing/daily functioning and increased risks? • Has there been an assessment including that of executive functions of the brain?	Have referrals for mental health and substance misuse services been considered and recorded? Have all legal duties under the Mental Health Act been considered? (Section 117 aftercare, community treatment orders, guardianships, etc.)	Has the impact of the abuse been considered? Is there indication that the person may be suffering from trauma as a result of current or past abuse? Have potential co-morbidities been explored? Have the appropriate assessments been conducted?

Capacity and consent

You assume capacity unless there is reason to believe otherwise. You should consider: The Mental Capacity Act Code of Practice states that one of the reasons why people may question a person's capacity to make a specific decision is 'the person's behaviour or circumstances cause doubt as to whether they have capacity to make a decision' (4.35 of the Mental Capacity Act Code of Practice, p.52) People often assume capacity because the person sounds coherent, despite other indicators such as serious self-neglect, hoarding, sexual exploitation or being groomed for terrorist activities. A person cannot give informed consent if they are groomed, afraid or intimidated. You may need to consider the inherent jurisdiction of the court to make decisions in some of these cases. In cases of self-neglect, the executive functioning of the brain may be affected, which means that they may sound capacitated, but when appropriately diagnosed and capacity assessed they are found to struggle with some things. If you are concerned, assess and record the findings, information, advice and support given	Are all relevant capacity assessments up to date and recorded within one support plan for monitoring?	Have the capacity assessments been effectively coordinated? Is each agency made accountable for the capacity assessments required of them during the safeguarding process? If agencies refuse to do relevant capacity assessments or claim that they cannot do the capacity assessments, have these concerns been escalated within the organisation and has training/support been offered to change this situation? Where the organisation refuses, has this been escalated to their safeguarding adults board representative and the Care Quality Commission or relevant regulator?

cont.

Capacity and consent

In determining who assesses capacity, or who is accountable for assessing capacity, you should consider the following:

- If you are the person who requires consent, agreement, understanding or a signature from the person for a proposed treatment, care provision, course of action or tenancy agreement/compliance, then you need to assess whether the person is capable of consenting by undertaking a capacity assessment
- Any capacity assessment carried out must be time specific and relate to a specific intervention or action. The professional responsible for undertaking the capacity assessment will be the person who is proposing the specific intervention or action (wherever possible), and is referred to as the 'decision maker'
- The decision maker may need to seek support from other professionals in the multi-disciplinary team, as they are responsible for making the final decision about a person's capacity
- When the person is assessed as lacking capacity, the decision maker is responsible for the 'best interests decision'
- If the person is deemed to have capacity, this should be clearly recorded along with the things that the person did/said that made the decision maker think that the person had capacity and the information and advice given
- If the person is refusing to engage with certain professionals, anyone who has access and has developed a rapport with the person should be supported by the actual decision maker to carry out the capacity assessment and best interests decision. This may mean that they give you some of the relevant and important topics to discuss and assess
- If you are the person offering care, services or treatment, then you are the person who must have consent for the care, services or treatment. If you provide care, services or treatment to a confused person who does not understand, then you do not have valid consent. To continue without assessing capacity means that you may be acting negligently. The only way forward is to assess the person's capacity to make that decision at the time that you are offering the person the service. If they are assessed as lacking capacity, then you should make a best interests decision

Capacity assessments required include:

- tenancy agreement
- tenancy support
- tenancy review
- medication offered
- treatment offered
- safeguarding referral
- assessment and support planning
- services offered (identified individually)
- finance
- aids and adaptations
- sharing of information

Local authority to ensure that safeguarding enquiries identify specifically whose responsibility it is to conduct which capacity assessments

Safeguarding principles should be considered throughout all safeguarding interventions, including capacity assessments:

- Empower the person to understand and make decisions
- Establish their desired expectations and outcomes
- Take action before harm occurs and prevent further abuse/neglect
- Make proportionate responses that are least intrusive and in the person's best interests
- Consider support/advocacy and identify someone to help the person engage in the process/provide feedback to the person
- Solve difficulties by working together across agencies
- Utilise community resources
- Ensure that agencies are accountable for their actions, knowledge and application of legal frameworks (including the ability to conduct capacity assessments and record appropriately)
- Remember that specific actions and deadlines should be given in the safeguarding plan – capacity assessments should be conducted by the appropriate agency and returned within timescales
- Ensure that the person self-neglecting understands the roles of all agencies involved in their care and support

List all the aspects of care, treatment, service provision or intervention that require the person's consent. Identify the person/agency that requires consent as the 'decision maker'. Safeguarding plans to detail the capacity assessments required and the person/agency responsible, with timescales for completion and follow-up monitoring. Once the capacity assessments are complete, then agencies are looking to see whether there may be a change in the person's ability to consent. Accurate recording supports appropriate police enquiries

If an organisation is not conducting/recording capacity assessments and comes into contact with people who may lack capacity to make some decisions, then this could constitute organisational abuse. The people who use their service have a right to make autonomous and even unwise decisions when capacitated and a right to support should they lack capacity. If this is not being determined within an organisation, then the people who use that service require safeguarding, as their right to private life may be violated

cont.

Advocacy and representation

	Does the person have suitable representation and support?
The local authority has a duty to arrange for an independent advocate to be available to represent and support the person, to facilitate their involvement in the process. This duty applies when the person has substantial difficulty in being involved in any part of the safeguarding process. Substantial difficulty is defined as the person having difficulty in: • understanding the relevant information • retaining that information • using or weighing up that information • communicating their views, wishes and feelings This duty does not apply where the person has capacity and is competent to consent to a course of action or if the local authority is satisfied that there is a person who: • would be an appropriate person to represent and support the person to facilitate their involvement (a friend or family member who is not part of any safeguarding procedures and does not have a vested interest in any potential outcomes) • is not engaged in providing care or treatment for the person in a professional capacity	Is there evidence that the person is central to any safeguarding action and that their voice or that of their advocate or family member is clear in all recordings? Have the circumstances been considered and the appropriate advocate sought (family members where there is not a vested interest in particular outcomes, independent sexual violence advocate, independent domestic violence advocate, independent mental capacity advocate or other more relevant advocate)?

Multi-agency response

A multi-agency response may be needed to:
- consider capacity issues in relation to a range of matters affecting the person and who should/can do them
- rule out additional or historical abuse or neglect
- explore potential crime
- identify any coercive or controlling behaviours affecting the person
- examine the person's mental health and how this may be affecting them
- explore any risks to others
- determine the support needs of the individual, including appropriate advocacy
- determine who is appropriate to support and provide feedback to the victim/perpetrator
- decide how each agency will facilitate the involvement of the person in decision making (safeguarding principles)

Earlier intervention assists in developing a rapport, access to community, circles of support around the person and solution-focused/strength-based rather than risk-management processes. In multi-agency meetings, consider:
- police-led enquiries coordinated alongside any required assessment processes
- (in criminal cases) the preservation of evidence
- referrals to necessary services
- involvement of services not already involved, such as domestic abuse, substance misuse, mental health services, fire service, anti-social behaviour services, MAPPA, MARAC, SARC (sexual abuse referral centre), public health, etc.
- coordination of assessment methodology
- therapeutic assessment and intervention processes
- who leads on information sharing, communication and involvement of the person
- coordination of capacity assessments
- gaps in knowledge and who will find this information
- the whole-family approach – others at risk, support offered
- animal welfare
- perpetrator risks/vulnerabilities/support and who will provide feedback
- barriers and how these will be overcome
- all aspects of the risk assessment

Has a multi-agency response been coordinated early enough to prevent the deterioration of physical and mental wellbeing?
Has a key person been identified to liaise with the person self-neglecting?

Have wellbeing principles been considered in relation to safeguarding outcomes?
How is communication coordinated?
How is risk managed?
How are capacity assessments determined and managed?
Has applicable legislation from each agency been discussed and coordinated with other legislation to ensure that the multi-agency approach is coordinated?
Has the Human Rights Act been considered to ensure that all agencies are working for the person concerned and not in an agency silo?
Does the person have access to the appropriate services?

cont.

Comprehensive and holistic assessment

Section 11 of the Care Act identifies that when a person refuses an assessment the local authority has a duty to carry out that assessment when: • the person lacks capacity to refuse that assessment and carrying out the assessment is in the person's best interests (must be recorded) • the person is experiencing, or at risk of, abuse or neglect	Has a comprehensive and holistic assessment of need been conducted with or without the consent of the individual where decision making is impacting on physical and mental wellbeing? Is there a duty to assess?	Have all agencies considered what they know about the person and the risks?

Compliance and insight

When someone is not accepting of services, explore the reasons why. What prevents the person from accepting support? Consider the following: • Harm minimisation – what can be achieved, and how much will this lessen the risks? • Has there been a negative experience of services? • How can negative experiences be changed? Be prompt, remain engaged, be on time, communicate in ways that the person can respond, do not impose actions if at all possible, work with the person and their timescales, no clear-ups before other issues explored and any clearing at the pace of the person (dependent on risks to others) • Is there someone who has a relationship with the person and are they willing/able to support services in providing care/support? • Can a rapport be developed with someone? • Has information, advice and support been offered in a way that the person can understand?	Is the person accepting of care, support and services? Is there a plan to maintain engagement/ contact? Does the person have insight into their behaviours?	

Imposed sanctions, compliance or penalties	
A person is unlikely to create change in their life when power and control are removed from them. In some cases, sanctions must be imposed, and the effects of these must be considered by professionals intervening. Consider: • eviction notices • child protection proceedings • imposed housing sanctions • criminal proceedings • debt and debt recovery • other	Are there any legal considerations or imposed compliance considerations and have these been clearly recorded?
Information sharing	
Relevant information can be shared with relevant agencies without consent when there is: • reasonable suspicion of risk to others • reasonable suspicion of crime • reasonable suspicion of public interest issues • reasonable suspicion of coercive and controlling behaviours/domestic abuse • reason to believe that the person may need assessment under the Mental Health Act Confidentiality must not be confused with secrecy. It is inappropriate for agencies to give assurances of absolute confidentiality in cases where there are concerns about abuse, particularly those situations where people may be at risk	Is information being shared across all agencies to prevent deterioration of physical and mental wellbeing and to safeguard the person?

cont.

Personalised safeguarding

The person is involved from the beginning and understands the roles and responsibilities of all parties.

The person has access to information that is shared about them.

The person is encouraged to be actively involved and lead the safeguarding process.

The person is treated with dignity and respect.

The person's values, wishes, expectations and outcomes are explored from the beginning and throughout the process by all agencies involved.

Personalised safeguarding means that when a person has capacity to make a decision they are entitled to make an unwise decision. Consider:

- Has a capacity assessment taken place and is the person making a capacitated decision (assessed and recorded as such)?
- Is this impacting adversely on anyone else?
- Has the reasoning behind this decision been explored?
- Have information and advice been offered in a format that the person understands (recorded)?

Where a person lacks capacity to make a decision, are you sure that the course of action is the least restrictive possible and in the best interests of the person? Remember:

- A safe but miserable life is no life at all
- We do not have to eliminate all risks, just minimise risk to the person as far as is comfortable for them
- Get multi-agency support, senior management support, legal support or support from the Court of Protection if the situation is proving problematic

A person is entitled to civil and criminal redress. Has this been considered and explained? Consider the Human Rights Act and whether any human rights have been affected. Consider the Equality Act and whether the person's rights under this Act have been affected

We may still need to safeguard others or consider whether the person has made an autonomous decision with all the relevant information available to support them – therefore a safeguarding referral can be made without the person's consent. After risk to others, potential crime, public interest issues and coercive and controlling behaviours have been ruled out, is there evidence of person-centred care and support planning?

Have the wishes, views and values of the person and their expectations and outcomes been identified and recorded?

Have the person's human rights been considered, including the right to a private life (autonomy)?

Has the Equality Act been considered?

Do you know the person's own narrative of their life?

What is important to the person?

What upsets the person?

What makes the person feel good?

What outcomes would the person like?

What are the person's expectations of you and other services?

What has affected the person the most?

How has the person managed in the past?

Are there any similar situations where they have felt happy about the way things went and the outcomes?

Has someone been able to engage sufficiently with the person to gain insight into their values, culture, identity and the risks that they are prepared to take in their own life?

Management support and response

When there are barriers from agencies, barriers from the person themselves, barriers in knowledge of legislation and potential responses and barriers in cooperation, and a person's physical and mental wellbeing is deteriorating, this implies that current interventions are not working and the barriers are too significant for practitioners to manage alone, even across agencies.

It is helpful to have a layer of safeguarding sitting between a safeguarding multi-agency response and a safeguarding adults review. This may be called an executive strategy/executive safeguarding/ overarching strategy. This may be chaired by a senior manager within the local authority who can look at the strategic elements of the safeguarding process to support the removal of any barriers, and feed the outcomes and actions down to operational staff and up to the safeguarding adults board for action. Individual safeguarding meetings will still be held looking at the needs of the individual or people involved and feeding information back to the senior manager

Are escalating risks taken seriously and addressed at the appropriate level of management/ intervention? Is there clarity regarding when to escalate concerns and to whom?	Is this safeguarding situation a repeat situation? Why have things not changed? What are the barriers and who can assist in breaking down those barriers? Are there operational or strategic barriers and are practitioners supported to address these? Is supervision used to reflect on difficult cases?

Defensible decision making

Defensible or justifiable decision making follows the word 'because':
- I chose this course of action because…
- I ruled this out because…

And following 'because' should be recorded the legislation used to make the decision.

In the absence of legislation, use the policy, model, method, theory or research that informed the decision. This should be balanced with what the person did or said that made you think this was an appropriate course of action, or not

Is your recording defensible (or justifiable) rather than defensive (offering reasons for failure)?	Have your actions been concluded identifying the legislation used (in the absence of legislation, then policies, procedures, models, methods, theories, research)? Have your actions been recorded in a manner that reflects the words said by the person themselves and any relevant carers (the 'I' statements or actions observed)?

cont.

Defensible decision making

Alongside attempts to enable the person to understand consequences, pros, cons and risks, alternative options and information and advice should be given. The person's expectations and outcomes should be a goal. Justify why responses were proportionate and least intrusive. What was ruled out and why?

Intervention should be justified in recording logs:

- Who is intervening?
- What is the purpose of the intervention?
- What actions were taken?
- What were the outcomes of the action?

If a professional is struggling to identify outcomes from intervention, they need to raise this during supervision.

A summary of work, progress and barriers, how those barriers have been addressed, can support defensible decision making. Consider including:

- referrals made
- appointments offered
- information and advice given
- capacity assessments
- access to advocacy
- the person's wishes, choices, expectations and outcomes
- support given to help the person recognise/understand
- duty to assess and how this has been achieved
- what was considered, what was ruled out and why
- legal frameworks used
- models, methods, theory and research used in practice
- 'I' statements of the person or indicative responses

Have your actions been recorded in a way that demonstrates what least-restrictive or least-intrusive interventions have been ruled out and why? Does your recording reflect proportionate responses?

Working with the police

The police must ensure equitable access to criminal justice and must make reasonable adjustments for people who have disabilities or mental ill-health. During the thematic review, it was noted that many safeguarding adults reviews identified the role of the police but provided little guidance regarding access to criminal justice. The access to criminal justice is an important right. Please consider some questions for your working relationship with the police:

- Are all safeguarding referrals where there is reasonable suspicion of a crime given a crime number when reported to the police?
- How many safeguarding referrals to the police in your local authority area have resulted in a prosecution?
- How many other referrals to the police may have met safeguarding criteria and what were the barriers to referring for safeguarding?
- Did the police request capacity assessments or diagnosis, or did they consider the credibility of the victim/witness appropriately?
- Of those cases that went to court, how many people had access to special measures and what were the most commonly used special measures?
- Was the victim supported to understand victim support available to them?
- Is there access to a sexual abuse referral centre in your area? How many older or disabled people have accessed this resource in the past year?
- How many evidence-led prosecutions were there in community safeguarding cases that involved domestic abuse?
- How often do police attend multi-agency meetings and share intelligence on the victim, family and perpetrator as relevant?
- How much do community safety officers and specials know about safeguarding? What training is available for new police officers in safeguarding adults and achieving best evidence (ABE)?
- Who does ABE training and is this specific to children or is there separate adult ABE training?
- Have the police discussed the points to prove and what evidence may be relevant in each case?
- How many prosecutions have there been in safeguarding cases that involve wilful neglect in the local authority area?
- If people who have disabilities and mental ill-health are refusing access to criminal justice when the majority of people in the local area say that they would report a crime, why do you think that is and how can people be better supported?
- Is there equitable access to criminal justice and civil justice in your local authority area?
- Are people who are eligible for safeguarding given individual crime numbers in your local authority area?
- Are victims of crime and their family made aware of the Witness Charter and the Victims Code of Practice? (See http://victimscommissioner.org.uk/advice/victims-code-and-witness-charter)

It is also noted that access to civil justice is rarely identified. How often are people given advice and guidance about civil redress within your local authority area?

cont.

A final safeguarding say

- A duty of care means that we must understand our professional competencies, principles of practice and the legislation that applies. It does not mean that we can impose things on people because we would feel safer, or we believe that they would be safer. No one would choose a safe but miserable life
- It is alright to have a hypothesis in safeguarding work, as long as the enquiries made can provide evidence to support or negate the hypothesis
- Social workers or safeguarding leads are not always the best placed to conduct an enquiry. If information from that enquiry is required in court, it is better to support the most appropriate professional to lead the enquiry. This may be the police in criminal investigations, a nurse where there are treatment issues, a tissue viability nurse, an occupational therapist, a housing provider or other relevant person. Consider the form of abuse or neglect and who has knowledge of the person and situation. The person must not have any vested interest or involvement – independence is important
- Safeguarding is not just about coordinating responses to risk. While this is very important, it is also important to coordinate capacity assessments, assessment of need, medical assessment and other relevant assessments. The understanding of the legislative processes being applied by each agency and recognition of any conflicting legislation should be resolved, seeking legal and court advice or referring to foundation law such as the Human Rights Act
- The principles are not just something that we say, they should be considered in every aspect of safeguarding practice, including safeguarding adults reviews
- The person's voice and the voice of people who love and care for the person are very important. Imagine that you were harmed or a crime was committed against you. After contacting the police, you want your mother, friend, partner or family member with you for emotional support. The people with whom we work are entitled to the same
- A person is entitled to criminal and civil redress. We can support people in being more credible witnesses

The scope of the review

What seem to be the most important issues to address and learn from in this case?	Are agencies required to submit reports (required for domestic homicide reviews) or will the independent reviewer conduct the whole review? If agencies are to be involved, which agencies came into contact with the victim, perpetrator and family and who is required to write the reports?	How will this review process dovetail with other investigations that are running in parallel?
Did the victim have equitable access to criminal justice?		Did the victim have equitable access to civil justice?
Is an expert required to understand crucial aspects?	How far back should enquiries cover? What is the cut-off point?	Are there any requirements around equality and diversity that may require special consideration?
Did the victim or perpetrator's immigration status impact on how agencies responded to their needs?	Were there other multi-agency forums such as MAPPA, MARAC and SARC involved?	Were there any court-imposed orders or restrictions pertaining to the victim or perpetrator?
Was the victim supported as described in the Witness Charter and Victims Code of Practice?	Did the victim have contact with specific services (if so, which services) prior to their death?	Consider any interface between domestic homicide reviews and safeguarding adults reviews.
How should family members, friends and other support networks (e.g. employers, neighbours, community services) that knew the person contribute to the review?	What are the roles and responsibilities of the agencies involved and how will they contribute to the review?	Have housing services been involved or should they be involved in the review?
Who will communicate with relevant parties: victim, perpetrator, family and other professionals?	How will the review take account of previous lessons learned: from research, previous local and national reviews?	What legislation needs to be considered and does the review panel need to seek legal advice? Consider any ongoing criminal investigation and contact the senior investigating officer.

How to choose the appropriate person to conduct the review

An independent chair is appointed to manage and coordinate the review process and produce a final overview report based on the relevant evidence. Terms of reference for the review and quality assurance must be agreed prior to conducting the review. Domestic homicide reviews have established timescales, while timescales for safeguarding adults reviews must be established as part of the terms of reference. The author of the review in some instances may be separate from the independent reviewer.

The independent chair should be an experienced individual who is not directly associated with any of the agencies involved in the review. The chair will be required to demonstrate strong analytical skills and will require a full understanding of safeguarding-related issues. The chair will need:

- a good understanding of applicable principles, ethics and values relevant to the enquiry

- strong leadership skills

- the ability to motivate people and manage the complexities of multi-agency forums

- the ability to manage strategic and operational change

- exceptional facilitation skills

- the ability to manage complex and sensitive issues in a complex and emotive situation

- good problem-solving skills

- the ability to promote reflective consideration of practice

- an understanding of learning cultures within organisations

- good communication skills to manage interpersonal matters, present topics, work with the media or other public relations, maintain a positive professional and public profile and respond to a variety of forums. To achieve this, the person must be assertive and supportive, have clear thinking, and have skills in negotiation and conflict resolution

- an ability to recognise oppression and discrimination and promote equality within the scope and operation of the review

- a strong desire to empower people, respect the right to self-determination, have self-efficacy and break down oppressive and discriminative barriers

- a clear understanding of the Human Rights Act, the associated principles and the application of this Act in practice

- the ability to successfully use technology to support the smooth running of the review while maintaining confidentiality

- self-motivation, enthusiasm, commitment, determination, a willingness to learn and approachability

- an understanding of the structure, functioning and key drivers for all public sector agencies involved, and their partners.

In some specific matters such as (but not exclusive to) forced marriage, female genital mutilation, self-neglect and sexual exploitation, the safeguarding adults board may choose someone who has more of an understanding of the particular subject matter than your average worker or particular expert in the field. On such occasions, the safeguarding adults board will need to be satisfied with the expert's:

- qualifications, skills and knowledge pertinent to the safeguarding adults review

- ability to meet all of the aforementioned criteria

- understanding of the literature or other published material available on the subject matter

- ability to translate any academic understanding of the subject matter into practical application to support practitioners in understanding the relevant lessons for practice.

An independent statement of the chair's expertise and independence should be included in the body of the report (or as an appendix) in domestic homicide cases and should be considered in safeguarding adults reviews. The statement should briefly set out the chair's career history and relevant experience and transparently demonstrate their independence from the enquiry. The chair will need to demonstrate a strategic vision linking to current legislation, case law, strategies, models, methods, theories and research. An experienced chair will be able to offer recommendations on the practical application of changes to be considered in policies and procedures and therefore practice, as a result of lessons learned.

The independent reviewer/chair will need to effectively manage the review and deter the findings being focused on the agencies themselves but rather on the following areas:

- What were the gaps in knowledge, who should have been involved and who was involved? What should their roles have been and what were the roles undertaken?

- What happened and what led to this happening (chronology)?

- What happened in practice to cause this? What could have been changed, or done differently?

- What are the commonalities with practice locally and practice nationally (lessons from other safeguarding adults reviews or domestic homicide reviews), and what is specific to this case?

- What were the barriers and how did these barriers present themselves?

- How could the barriers have been removed to facilitate improved standards of care?

Making the safeguarding adults review/ domestic homicide review process personal

The review should focus on practice and therefore learning lessons, and the quality will be significantly enhanced by placing the person, family, friends and relevant community members at the centre of the review and as key stakeholders in the contribution (see Figure 11.2).

The participation of family and friends is voluntary and the chair should outline the remit of the review and discuss expectations and outcomes with family members. Specialist advocates may be sought to support anyone involved. Feedback from and communication with family members should be delivered with sensitivity to their feelings and values. Matters of confidentiality and information sharing should be discussed and they should be able to understand the importance of their contribution to the review and how it may help others. Regular meetings and updates should be planned and aids to communication established where necessary (e.g. an interpreter or someone who has specific skills to support family members). The cultural, ethnic and religious needs of family and friends involved will need to be considered and planned for. Consideration should be given at an early stage about working with family liaison officers and relevant police personnel involvement. The 'I' statements or the expressed words of a family member or friend can be quite revealing and pertinent to an enquiry.

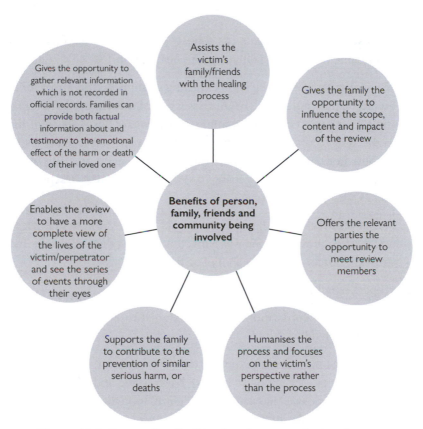

Figure 11.2: Person, family, friend and community involvement in contributing to the safeguarding adults review

In my opinion, an excellent example of person-centred reviewing was demonstrated in the domestic homicide review of Amolita (James-Hanman 2011) produced by the London Borough of Newham.

Amolita's family and friends were very involved in the whole review, which made clear recommendations for action or policy changes that addressed the issue of perpetrators abusing extended family members living abroad. The voices of services, family and friends are often recorded in the first person within the review and offer a clear picture of Amolita. Here are some examples from the report:

> 'I do believe that he had attempted to strangle her. I'm not a doctor of course but her voice was absolutely unique. You could tell that there was something very strange about her voice; it was very squeaky, very high pitched, as if her vocal chords [sic] had been damaged in some way.' (p.18)

> 'She had a very soft voice. It was almost like her voice was constricted all the time. You had to really strain to hear her.' (p.18)

> 'She participated in all the family learning sessions that we run; family literacy, family numeracy, ESOL classes and she also participated in a triple P – it's a parenting programme – the power of positive parenting. And it wasn't as a result of any referral from any other agencies to support her parenting, it was a way of her actually meeting other parents, other people and getting to know what learning in schools in the UK was about.' (p.19)

> Ms X (friend) reported that Amolita always felt like the system in place was there to prove that she was lying, it was never there to prove that she was right and therefore should be protected. (p.19)

The report concludes:

> There are no words more poignant than those written by Ms X (Amolita's friend):

> 'Blackmailed into marriage (he was rich, she was poor; he had friends in high places, her widower mother had no one and a large family to support), she was married in Bangladesh, brought to England, and abused from the day of her wedding. Enduring daily beatings, rape and broken ribs, it was only when her husband raised his hands against her daughters that she found the willpower to ignore the sometimes suffocating burden of "family honour" and finally escape. From the day she entered the police station with her three words of English to the moment she breathed her last, she tried everything she could to secure

three things: a divorce, sole custody of her children and acceptance in her community.

She died unable to accomplish even one of these goals. For to divorce a man who wants to "keep" you, and is rich enough to secure the best lawyers, one needs money (and legal aid, now demolished, is rarely enough). Nor did she have deep enough scars to convince the social workers or the judge in her custody trial of the dangers posed by the father towards her children. On top of all this, [Amolita] had to further ignore the sneers of distant family members or strangers in her community who felt they had every right to judge her for daring to "leave" her husband.' (p.30) (James-Hanman 2011)

The Home Office Quality Assurance Panel reviews domestic homicide reviews for quality and commented, 'The panel would like to commend you on your clear efforts made to engage the family and to bring out the victim's perspective in this report.' The panel also commended the author on the care and consideration offered to the children and her decision to attach a copy of the report to the children's social care records so that they could access it in later years should they wish to do so.

In safeguarding adults reviews and domestic homicide reviews the review may wish to consider the views of the perpetrator and their family and anyone to whom information may have been disclosed. Reviews must be mindful of any risks and any ongoing police investigations.

It is clear that, like safeguarding adults work itself, the work of the safeguarding adults review also requires a toolbox of methodologies, approaches and systems (Woloshynowych *et al.* 2005). Like safeguarding work, the principles of safeguarding under the Care Act 2014 and the ethics and values of safeguarding work should be applied. The person and their family and friends should be central and have a clear voice in the report.

Joint commissioning of reviews

It may be necessary to consider whether some reviews can be jointly commissioned to reduce duplication of work for the organisations and families involved. For example, a safeguarding adults review may contain elements of domestic abuse that directly contributed to the harm or death of the person, or vice versa. There may be children affected by the domestic abuse or there may be a need for a child death review or serious case review. These reviews should be combined wherever possible, with the key aspect affecting the victim being the lead review role. Remember that if safeguarding adults is about person-centred practice, then the central issue to the review should be the person and their family.

KEY POINTS

Safeguarding adults reviews should be personalised, and the voices of the person and their family and friends should be clear within the review. The processes involved in safeguarding an individual will need to be considered and key learning outcomes addressed. If an issue is raised, such as poor information sharing or lack of capacity assessments, that seems to be a key theme in safeguarding adults reviews nationally, then further work may be required to determine how much of an issue it is across agencies within that local authority area and what lessons need to be applied locally. This will require some kind of audit process or similar across all agencies involved. Safeguarding adults reviews, domestic homicide reviews and similar reviews are part of a statutory process and a statutory obligation. All agencies must recognise when to make a referral for such an independent review and should not seek to resolve the matter internally by processes such as root cause analysis.

— Chapter 12 —

Conclusion

No matter how much we want to make safeguarding a simple matter, decision making will always be as complex as human beings are. Put human beings with other human beings and the complexities increase. Ascribe roles, titles and powers to certain people and the issues are further complicated by the interaction between people. Place each group of people within a different area in society with differing demographics and the possibilities, differences and complexities are infinite. The possible definitions of safe and feeling safe alone would be vastly different.

When I started on my safeguarding journey, I quickly learned that an ego is a bad thing, that you will never know enough and that you will need to rely on the knowledge and skills of other professions. To be a good safeguarding practitioner you will need to be resilient, resourceful, inquisitive and sensitive, make people feel at ease, be a good communicator and be able to reflect on your own and others' practice, determining whether enough was done in support of the person's mental and physical wellbeing in addition to their rights. I have offered my thoughts about safeguarding adults, and I would like to hear the discussion about things that you have discovered work for you in practice. If something hasn't worked, let me know and we can analyse together why we think that it didn't, or whether it was applied in the correct way for the appropriate situation. If we can be open to criticism and the sharing of good practice, this will help to drive the safeguarding agenda forward.

In presenting the questions about how much is enough, I hope to stimulate discussion at the safeguarding adults board level about determining how much they expect from practitioners. What might you expect a GP to do and understand; what might a social work assistant be expected to do and understand; what about a domiciliary care worker, a local authority solicitor or a housing worker? Would a court expect them all to have the same understanding, or different, and if so, what does each group of people need to know? How much should a safeguarding team providing advice and guidance be expected to know? How many autonomous decisions are they able to make or how rigidly would you expect them to follow the policies and procedures, given that this is not always a good thing? How much understanding of criminology, sociology, law and psychology are practitioners expected to have to be able to lead enquiries and create defensible decisions? Is this aspirational or is it really achievable in practice? Is it a vision or a goal?

Exploring safeguarding adults board websites, I note that many cite the importance of preventative agendas and prevention in safeguarding, but look a little deeper and only a few have within the strategic plan or business plan any detail about how they are going to achieve this, how they are going to deliver training to people in the preventative agenda and how services will be structured to deliver this agenda. Safeguarding matters are increasing because more people recognise and report abuse; we need to help practitioners to recognise how to prevent abuse in the first place. Safeguarding principles should be embedded within every aspect of care and support.

The safeguarding agenda has changed and everyone is now accountable, not just for recognising and reporting abuse and neglect, but also being part of a team of people around the person, ensuring that personalised responses to abuse and neglect are facilitated. Risks to others, public interest issues, perpetrator issues and wider aspects of safeguarding need to be considered, whether or not the person wants to be involved in the process. We must also ensure that people are held accountable for sharing information, actions and responses in relation to safeguarding adults and the duties identified within the Care Act 2014. All agencies need to break down barriers to ensure the continued mental and physical wellbeing of the person.

The Care Act 2014 introduced us to some forms of abuse or neglect that are not only complex but require a variety of responses (without forgetting the needs of the person) following the abuse and neglect. Social services may cause others to conduct enquiries when appropriate. For example, domestic abuse matters may be better supported by police and domestic abuse services taking a lead, and the local authority considering the care and support needs as a result of the abuse and neglect. The impact of trauma is significant, and safeguarding work must begin supporting the person to address the trauma as soon as they are ready. Traumatic experiences do not go away without support and can affect a person's mental and physical wellbeing.

If we are to provide the very basic preventative measures in safeguarding, we must determine who the decision maker is in each event. Is the person capacitated and have we ensured informed consent, or is there sufficient doubt to warrant assessing the person's capacity? Has the appropriate person conducted the capacity assessment? Has a deadline for the capacity assessment been given, for safeguarding purposes? Have we held the agency accountable – under a duty to provide information for safeguarding purposes?

In my practice, I map all the key people involved and the risks that they have identified. I look at the decisions to be made and ask agencies to determine whether the person is capacitated to make each decision or not. I use the template in Figure 12.1 to plot my action plan.

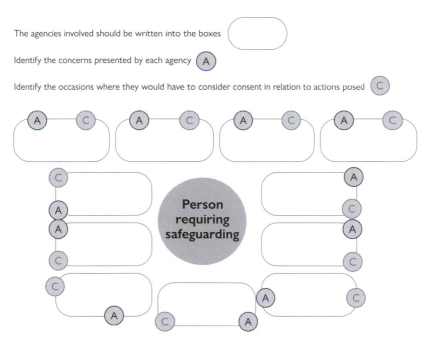

Figure 12.1: Creating a multi-agency safeguarding plan

In addition to the above, we need to consider:

- who will share information with whom and how this will be achieved (victim/perpetrator/family, other professionals)

- the legislation that applies and how this fits with the Human Rights Act 1998.

In relation to austerity measures and increasing safeguarding demands, have we established a strategically resilient methodology for the future of safeguarding?

Making safeguarding personal, and listening to the things that make people feel safe, the things that they want in their lives and empowering people to make a real choice, is very important. I have a vision that we will see the person's narrative in all preventative and protective measures in safeguarding adults. I hope that in the future I shall pick up case notes, assessments and capacity assessments and see how involved the person has been because the 'I' statements or actions taken by the person will be identified. For example, when I asked my client Mrs Jenna about what being safe meant to her, she said, 'Being safe is about having my family around me, people who love and care about me. It is about being at home with my memories, going to my local shops where people know me and using the services that I know around here.'

I will see that the person has been asked what outcomes they would like and what would make them feel safer and more secure now, and I will recognise part of their identity in their answers. When I asked Mrs Jenna what support she wanted to achieve this, she said:

> I want to know which carers will be looking after me and I want to be able to get to know these carers before they begin providing support to me. I was bullied as a child and I grew into a strong adult as a result of my experiences. I will not let myself be afraid in my own home as a result of this experience, but I need to feel that I am in control, that I can say what I want and don't want. The carers often listen to what my daughter wants for me, rather than what I want for myself. I am old and have lots of disabilities, but none that affect my thinking. I want the carers to understand this and respond to me. That would make me feel safer. This all happened because she would not listen to me.

Recording will not be process driven and there will be evidence that agencies have worked in partnership to achieve this together. There will also be evidence that families have been involved in understanding issues such as capacity and consent in order that they can prepare and plan for future decision making. We will empower people by increasing their access to services within the community, supporting self-efficacy, self-confidence and self-worth and increasing communication with and involvement of the person as the expert in their own care and services. We will ensure that the person is given the opportunity to learn and grow in understanding, and we will support this by providing information and support when a person struggles to understand. We will ensure that people have every opportunity to reach their full potential, identifying and breaking down oppressive and discriminative barriers, and we shall enable people to connect with others and their community in a meaningful way. We will measure our success by healthier, happier communities where people feel safe, families who can recognise the support provided to help them achieve this, and individuals who recognise that they were listened to and their outcomes achieved as far as is practicably possible.

All too often, crime numbers are not given in safeguarding adults police enquiries, because the detection statistics or other crime statistics might be affected by poor outcomes. Capacity, capability and the credibility of a witness for court are confused and the enquiry process is poor, affected by insufficient understanding and support from services. People are not supported to understand what can and can't happen in criminal enquiries, nor are they supported to understand how much support they can be given. Vulnerable people are targeted for abuse, groomed, exploited and neglected without equitable access to criminal or civil justice. All too often, cases are closed without consideration of the impact of the abuse or neglect on that person's physical and mental wellbeing. My vision for the future is one where the person who has a learning disability, the older person, the person subject to domestic abuse and the person with mental ill-health or autism is supported to have the confidence to get legal redress for the crimes committed against them, without fear of judgement, retribution or loss of independence.

The basics of safeguarding practice are being lost within the language used to describe the process. In addition to the criminal aspect, we need to consider the human aspect. Starting with the human rights of the person and those involved with safeguarding, my vision would be to build a framework around this:

- Article 2: Right to life

- Article 3: Freedom from torture and inhuman or degrading treatment

- Article 4: Freedom from slavery and forced labour

- Article 5: Right to liberty and security

- Article 6: Right to a fair trial

- Article 7: No punishment without law

- Article 8: Respect for your private and family life, home and correspondence

- Article 9: Freedom of thought, belief and religion

- Article 10: Freedom of expression

- Article 11: Freedom of assembly and association

- Article 12: Right to marry and start a family

- Article 14: Protection from discrimination in respect of these rights and freedoms

- Protocol 1, Article 1: Right to peaceful enjoyment of your property

- Protocol 1, Article 2: Right to education

- Protocol 1, Article 3: Right to participate in free elections

- Protocol 13, Article 1: Abolition of the death penalty.

The process of safeguarding can very quickly move away from the person or people involved. We have explored our starting point in relation to the person's outcomes, and the next key matter is the rights and freedoms of those involved. Using the Human Rights Act 1998 as a foundation act and adding into this the various multi-agency legislation in use means that we are always focused on the person/people but also that we can effectively coordinate or challenge competing legislative demands.

Where risks are escalating and agencies have got into cyclical responses without solutions and there is risk of serious harm or death, or where there is serious multiple abuse, strategic intervention should be considered to separate the strategic barrier from the individualised safeguarding practice. Safeguarding duties and responsibilities should support senior managers in breaking down barriers to services and ensure appropriate safeguarding responses. Responses will need to consider the long-term effect of abuse or neglect on the person and how that is also managed to prevent or delay the need for services. In the future, services may need to consider not only culture change but also change in the structure and organisation of services to address all aspects of safeguarding adults during times of austerity.

Safeguarding adults reviews should demonstrate the voice of the person and/or their family and friends. The outcomes that are important in safeguarding the person need to be central to the safeguarding adults review process: what were the person's expected outcomes and why were they not achieved? What did the person say that they wanted from the support provided and what went wrong? In balance with this, the systems and procedures in place to support multi-agency communication, coordination and care and support planning will need to be explored locally. Learning lessons from safeguarding adults reviews nationally can identify what kinds of things are repeatedly identified in these reviews, why the safeguarding adults board has not already addressed these matters as a result of these past lessons learned, and what needs to be considered to reassure the safeguarding adults board that these same themes will not be repeated. We can learn a lot from the domestic homicide review process and there should be more joint consideration of domestic homicide reviews and safeguarding adults reviews as we move ahead.

Moving into the future, training delivery is the responsibility of the safeguarding adults board. As a safeguarding adults board responsibility, joint initiatives should ensure that training is fit for purpose across all agencies and the level of understanding meets the expected local knowledge. For example, it is no longer appropriate for an agency to say that they are not conducting capacity assessments because they do not know how to do them. Training should be delivered by the safeguarding adults board to the extent and level that would be expected during safeguarding enquiries.

I believe that enquiries are the responsibility of all agencies involved with the safeguarding adults board and that in many cases the local authority is not the expert or is not skilled enough in the subject matter to lead the enquiry. All professionals should have the training and knowledge to be able to lead a safeguarding enquiry and chair a multi-agency meeting. This will promote effective and sustainable responses to safeguarding referrals in the future. Education resources, such as colleges, universities and community education programmes, should be supported by safeguarding adults boards to achieve high safeguarding standards and to be active partners in safeguarding matters. Training and understanding of safeguarding within teaching practice and Ofsted requirements will need to be recognised not just by the education providers, but also by the safeguarding adults board members, to ensure that safeguarding principles are applied to the thousands of people who access education in our local authority areas every year.

We need to get the basics right before we can move on to the more complex aspects of safeguarding. We need to consider the following:

- Have we identified a form of abuse that meets the criteria for safeguarding?

- Have we accurately identified the use of the three-part test without additional thresholds?

- Have Section 42 enquiries been conducted and led by the appropriate agency?

- Have the findings from the enquiry been fed back to the local authority?

- Has the risk to others been considered?

- Is there a consistent risk assessment?

- Have we considered preventative measures as well as protective measures?

- Has a carer's assessment been conducted, including carers' capacity assessments where necessary?

- Are there issues of trauma? Have we considered mental ill-health or substance misuse issues affecting the person?

- Have all the right people conducted capacity assessments?

- Have advocacy and representation been considered?

- Have we mapped the agencies involved, those who need to be involved and those who would fill the gaps in our knowledge?

- Have we considered the coordination of capacity assessments and legislative frameworks and have we ensured the appropriate multi-agency response?

- Are the assessments comprehensive and holistic enough?

- Have we considered the reasons for non-compliance and the insight of the person involved, and have they been given the right information at the right time?

- Are there any lawfully imposed sanctions, penalties or judgements impacting on the person? Are we sure of the lawfulness?

- Has information been shared appropriately?

- Have we ensured that safeguarding is personal?

- Has the appropriate management support been offered?

- Is our recording evidence led, justifiable and defensible?

- Is there equitable access for the person to civil and criminal justice?

- Have the care and support needs of those involved been considered throughout?

- Can we see the person's identity in our recording, the 'I' statements or actions of the person?

No one has all the answers in safeguarding, no one really knows 'how much is enough'; nothing will ever stay static and we shall always be changing, adapting and moving forward. I want the same as you – I want to provide the best possible services that safeguard people and create safer communities for the future. I, like you, will continue to learn and grow, and so I would like to once again extend my invitation to you to talk to me, let me know what works for you and add to this collection. Share the good practice out there and let safeguarding practice evolve from the stories of those who use our services and those who work very hard to support them.

Moving forward

This book was designed for students to study the basics and gain an understanding of the complexities of safeguarding adults. I have tried to develop some guidance, or food for thought, for safeguarding adults boards, who can accept or reject my thoughts, and I have tried to establish some standards where personalised safeguarding isn't 'a thing' but is integrated into the fabric of safeguarding and practice in care and support. I am sad that austerity has meant the demise of the more specific and tailored safeguarding training and consultancy work, but optimistic that we can find new ways to work together to transform services in preparation for the future. The training pages hope to establish a set of considerations for the standards and assessment of training provision across the partnership board, but those teaching safeguarding may also find the guidance useful in posing ethical questions and challenges regarding the balance of how much we have to do in safeguarding adults.

In writing any non-fiction book, anonymous reviewers are asked to provide feedback. I received some very useful feedback from one very helpful reviewer from an academic background who suggested I conclude with a positive message about what could be done to work through the difficulties to come during times of austerity. I must admit I smiled at this suggestion and then became fearful of how I might respond. I would not wish to alienate a potential audience by delivering my perspective on 'If I were Prime Minister of this country, this is what I would do to change the nature and culture of services', but when the challenge was put to me in writing, I could not resist having a go.

Austerity measures have a huge impact on our current ability to provide public sector services, with increasing populations of those who need care and support and increasingly complex threats to physical and mental health. We are seeing both physical and mental health conditions deteriorate to such an extent that services are overwhelmed by the challenges. Earlier intervention is required, and preventative measures that delay the need for services. Abuse and neglect, by their very nature, have a psychological effect and, for most people, an impact on their mental wellbeing. A significant cash injection into public sector services to change from crisis response to preventative earlier intervention is required, along with an increase in earlier access to mental health services not only for treatment, but also for therapeutic and psychological intervention.

Joint psychological, therapeutic and safeguarding responses that consider not only safety, capacity, consent, information sharing, lawful responses and personalised services but also the impact of the person's experiences on their mental wellbeing would ensure preventative measures to delay the need for services in the future. Creative community solutions that enable a person to maintain independence and the use of our occupational therapists' rehabilitation planning and skills to promote this independence would prevent the need for services. Community asset-based social work that does not necessarily seek to commission services, but to build local solutions, using local, sustainable resources in a creative way to meet people's identified needs and monitored closely to measure how effective these plans are, can help not only rebuild communities, but also keep people safer. Community work involving health, fire services, the police, social services, GPs, physiotherapists, occupational therapists and a variety of other professionals would ensure that people living in communities are no longer isolated. The risks associated with interfamilial domestic abuse will need to be recognised and support options provided sooner, as well as earlier responses to domestic abuse in intimate partner relationships.

This may be the vision of many public sector services, which feel that this dream is unachievable. If we don't offer our vision for consideration then our dreams stand no chance of becoming a reality. What is described above is the vision of the Care Act 2014 and we have many duties to try and make this vision a reality. The Care Act's vision is the way forward, but with austerity measures we find ourselves returning to the beginning of this book and reflecting on how much is enough. What do we expect of our services and staff? There have always been challenges and we have always found a way to meet those challenges, and we grow with each learning process. We have had community social work, therapeutic social work, family social work, individual social work – and then the process begins again only slightly differently having learned previous lessons. We have had integration, dis-integration and then integration again. All social policy has these twists and turns that help us to learn, grow and evolve, hitting similar but slightly different challenges and pressures (see Figure 12.2).

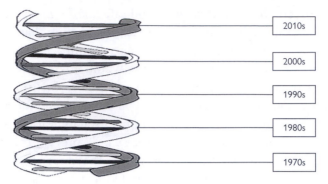

2010s

2000s

1990s

1980s

1970s

*Figure 12.2: The twists and turns of social
policy – an evolutionary process*

To speed up this evolutionary process we need to encourage creative solutions, new answers, different ways of thinking. We need to cherish our students and new employees, and give them time and attention to feel how valuable an asset they are. Listen to their thoughts without jaded ears and watch what they do without jaded eyes. Together we can analyse what we now know and how we can make things different to improve, learn from past lessons and determine a more sustainable future. A criticism of the old and jaded is that it's fine in 'theory' but in practice it doesn't work. I am prepared to demonstrate how it works in my practice and the great results that can be achieved in the most complex situations. My question to you is, how much of a difference do you want to make?

References

Adshead, G. (2000) 'Psychological therapies for post-traumatic stress disorder.' *The British Journal of Psychiatry*, 177 (2), 144–148.

American Psychiatric Association (1994) *Diagnostic and Statistical Manual of Mental Disorders IV*. Washington, DC: American Psychiatric Association.

American Psychiatric Association (2013) *Diagnostic and Statistical Manual of Mental Disorders 5*. Arlington, VA: American Psychiatric Publishing.

Assets.publishing.service.gov.uk (2011) *Reforming the law for adult care and support the Government's response to Law Commission Report 326 on adult social care.* [online] Available at: https://assets.publishing.service.gov.uk/government/uploads/system/uploads/attachment_data/file/136454/2900021-Reforming-the-Law-for-Adult-Care_ACCESSIBLE.pdf (accessed 10 December 2018).

Association of Directors of Adult Social Services (2005) *Safeguarding Adults: A National Framework of Standards for Good Practice and Outcomes in Adult Protection Work.* [online] Available at https://www.adass.org.uk/AdassMedia/stories/Publications/Guidance/safeguarding.pdf (accessed 23 January 2019).

Badgaiyan, R. and Posner, M. (1998) 'Mapping the cingulate cortex in response selection and monitoring.' *NeuroImage*, 7(3), 255–260.

Banks, S., Butcher, H., Henderson, P. and Robertson, J. (2003) *Managing Community Practice: Principles, Policies and Programmes.* Bristol: Policy Press.

Barlow, D.H., DiNardo, P.A., Vermilyea, B.B. and Blanchard, E.B. (1986) 'Co-morbidity and depression among the anxiety disorders: Issues in diagnosis and classification.' *Journal of Nervous and Mental Disease*, 174, 63–72.

Barnes, J., Katz, I., Korbin, J. and O'Brien, M. (2006) *Children and Families in Communities: Theory, Research, Policy and Practice.* Chichester: John Wiley & Sons.

Barnett, D. (2018a) *Adult safeguarding roles and competencies for health care staff.* [online] Available at: www.wiltshiresab.org.uk/wp-content/uploads/2018/08/AdultSafeguardingRolesAndCompetencesHealthCareStaff.pdf (accessed 7 December 2018).

Barnett, D. (2018b) *Self-Neglect and Hoarding: A Guide to Safeguarding and Support*. London: Jessica Kingsley Publishers.

Baron-Cohen, S. (1989) 'Do autistic children have obsessions and compulsions?' *British Journal of Clinical Psychology*, 28(3), 193–200.

Baumann, D., Dalgleish, L., Fluke, J. and Kern, H. (2011) *The Decision-Making Ecology*. Washington, DC: American Humane Association.

Boylan, J. and Dalrymple, J. (2011) 'Advocacy, social justice and children's rights.' *Practice*, 23(1), 19–30.

Bowlby, J. (1969) *Attachment and Loss. Vol. 1: Attachment.* New York, NY: Basic Books.

Bps.org.uk (2018) *Introducing the 'Power, Threat, Meaning Framework'.* [online] Available at: https://www.bps.org.uk/news-and-policy/introducing-power-threat-meaning-framework (accessed 10 December 2018).

Bradley, K., Hartmen, H. and Smith, J. (n.d.) *Provision of therapy for vulnerable and intimidated adult witnesses prior to a criminal trial – Practice guidance.* [online] The Crown Prosecution

Service. Available at: www.cps.gov.uk/publications/prosecution/pretrialadult.html (accessed 20 October 2017).

Bradley, M. (1996) 'Caring for older people: Elder abuse.' *British Medical Journal*, 313(7056), 548–550.

Brammer, A. (1996) 'Elder abuse in the UK: A new jurisdiction?' *International Journal of Elder Abuse and Neglect*, 8(2), 33.

Brandl, B. and Horan, D. (2002) 'Domestic violence in later life: An overview for health care providers.' [online] *Women & Health*, 35(2–3), 41–54. Available at: https://www.tandfonline.com/doi/abs/10.1300/J013v35n02_03 (accessed 29 january 2019).

Braye, S. and Orr, D. (2011) *SCIE Report 46. Self-neglect and adult safeguarding: Findings from research*. [online] Social Care Institute for Excellence. Available at: www.scie.org.uk/publications/reports/report46.asp (accessed 29 April 2017).

Braye, S., Orr, D. and Preston-Shoot, M. (2014) *Self-neglect policy and practice: Building an evidence base for adult social care*. [online] Social Care Institute for Excellence. Available at: www.scie.org.uk/publications/reports/69-self-neglect-policy-practice-building-an-evidence-base-for-adult-social-care/files/report69.pdf (accessed 2 March 2017).

Brenner, M. (2004) *Pacifiers, Blankets, Bottles, and Thumbs: What Every Parent Should Know About Starting and Stopping*. New York, NY: Touchstone.

Bryden, D. and Storey, I. (2011) 'Duty of care and medical negligence.' *Continuing Education in Anaesthesia, Critical Care & Pain*, 11(4), 124–127.

Capuzzo, N., Heke, S. and Petrak, J. (2007) *The Early Identification of Post-Traumatic Stress Disorder: Utilising the Trauma Screening Questionnaire in a Specialist Sexual Assault Centre*. Barcelona: The World Congress for Behavioural and Cognitive Therapies.

Carter, R. (2015) *Care Act 2014: Councils struggling with 'market sustainability' duty*. [online] Community Care. Available at: www.communitycare.co.uk/2015/08/24/care-act-2014-councils-struggling-market-sustainability-duty/?year=2015&monthnum=08&day=24 (accessed 25 July 2017).

Commission for Social Care Inspection and Healthcare Commission (2006) *Joint inspection into the provision of people with learning disabilities at Cornwall Partnership NHS Trust*. [online] Available at: https://webarchive.nationalarchives.gov.uk/20080609161229/http://www.healthcarecommission.org.uk/_db/_documents/cornwall_investigation_report.pdf (accessed on 13 December 2018).

Communities and Local Government (2008) *Communities in control: Real people, real power*. [online] Available at: www.gov.uk/government/publications/communities-in-control-real-people-real-power (accessed 2 February 2018).

Courtois, C.A. and Ford, J.D. (eds) (2009) *Treating Complex Traumatic Stress Disorders: An Evidence-Based Guide*. New York, NY: Guilford Press.

Crane, M., Byrne, K., Lipman, B., Mirabelli, F. *et al.* (2005) 'The causes of homelessness in later life: Findings from a 3-nation study.' *Journals of Gerontology B: Psychological Sciences and Social Sciences*, 60(3), S152–159.

Crosby, G., Clark, A., Hayes, R., Jones, K. and Lievesley, N. (2008) *The financial abuse of older people: A review from the literature carried out by the Centre for Policy on Ageing on behalf of Help the Aged*. [online] Help the Aged. Available at: www.cpa.org.uk/information/reviews/financialabuse240408%5B1%5D.pdf (accessed 5 December 2018).

Crown Prosecution Service (2017a) *Competence and compellability: Legal guidance*. [online] Available at: https://www.cps.gov.uk/legal-guidance/competence-and-compellability (accessed 14 May 2017).

Crown Prosecution Service (2017b) *CPS legal guidance*. [online] Available at: www.cps.gov.uk/legal/p_to_r/prosecuting_crimes_against_older_people (accessed 14 May 2017).

Crown Prosecution Service (2018) *Older people: Prosecuting crimes against*. [online] Available at: https://www.cps.gov.uk/legal-guidance/older-people-prosecuting-crimes-against (accessed 12 December 2018).

Dashriskchecklist.co.uk (2018) *Dash Risk Checklist – Saving lives through early risk identification, intervention and prevention*. [online] Available at: https://www.dashriskchecklist.co.uk (accessed 10 December 2018).

References

Davis, C. (2008) 'Women, domestic violence, "social housing" and community cohesion.' Paper presented at the Housing Studies Association Spring Conference, University of York, 2–4 April 2008.

Deem, D. (2000) 'Notes from the field: Observations in working with the forgotten victims of personal financial crimes.' *Journal of Elder Abuse & Neglect*, 12(2), 33–48.

Department of Health (2006) *Our health, our care, our say: A new direction for community services*. [online] Available at: www.gov.uk/government/uploads/system/uploads/attachment_data/file/272238/6737.pdf (accessed 26 February 2018).

Department of Health (2007) *Putting people first: A shared vision and commitment to the transformation of adult social care*. [online] Available at: http://webarchive.nationalarchives.gov.uk/20130104175839/http://www.dh.gov.uk/en/Publicationsandstatistics/Publications/PublicationsPolicyAndGuidance/DH_081118 (accessed 28 February 2018).

Department of Health (2009) *Safeguarding Adults: Report on the Consultation on the Review of No Secrets*. London: Department of Health.

Department of Health (2013) *Information. To share or not to share: The information governance review*. [online] Available at: www.gov.uk/government/uploads/system/uploads/attachment_data/file/192572/2900774_InfoGovernance_accv2.pdf (accessed 13 January 2018).

Department of Health and Social Care (2000) *No secrets: Guidance on developing and implementing multi-agency policies and procedures to protect vulnerable adults from abuse*. [online] Available at: www.gov.uk/government/publications/no-secrets-guidance-on-protecting-vulnerable-adults-in-care (accessed 27 February 2018).

Dodge, K.A., Lochman, J.E., Harnish, J.D., Bates, J.E. and Pettit, G.S. (1997) 'Reactive and proactive aggression in school children and psychiatrically impaired chronically assaultive youth.' *Journal of Abnormal Psychology*, 106, 37–51.

Domestic Abuse Intervention Programs (1984) *Power and control wheel*. [online] Available at: www.theduluthmodel.org/wheels (accessed 21 February 2018).

Domestic Violence London (2019) *What is Domestic Violence? Definition*. [online] Available at www.domesticviolencelondon.nhs.uk/1-what-is-domestic-violence-/1-definition.html (accessed 23 January 2019).

Donoghue v Stevenson [1932] AC 562.

DPP v R [2007] EWHC 1842 Admin.

Financial Conduct Authority (2017) *Protect yourself from scams*. [online] Available at: www.fca.org.uk/consumers/protect-yourself-scams (accessed 5 December 2018).

Fitzgerald, G. (2008) 'No Secrets, Safeguarding Adults and Adult Protection.' In J. Pritchard (ed.) *Good Practice in Safeguarding Adults*. London: Jessica Kingsley Publishers.

Freire, P. (1970) *Pedagogy of the Oppressed*. New York, NY: Continuum.

Frost, R., Steketee, G. and Tolin, D. (2011) 'Comorbidity in hoarding disorder.' *Depression and Anxiety*, 28(10), 876–884.

Garthwaite, K. (2011) '"The language of shirkers and scroungers?" Talking about illness, disability and coalition welfare reform.' *Disability & Society*, 26(3), 369–372.

Glasgow Homeless Network (2002) *Disempowerment and disconnection: Trauma and Homelessness*. [online] Available at: http://ghn.org.uk/sites/default/files/GHN_Trauma_and_Homelessness_Report.pdf (accessed 8 December 2017).

Gov.uk (2013) *Cross-government definition of domestic violence consultation*. [online] Available at: https://www.gov.uk/government/consultations/cross-government-definition-of-domestic-violence-consultation (accessed 10 December 2018).

Gov.uk (2018) *Discrimination: Your rights*. [online] Available at: https://www.gov.uk/discrimination-your-rights (accessed 10 December 2018).

Griffiths, R. (1988) *Community Care. Agenda for Action: A Report to the Secretary of State for Social Services*. London: Her Majesty's Stationery Office.

Hafford-Letchfield, T. and Carr, S. (2017) 'Promoting Safeguarding: Self-Determination, Involvement and Engagement in Adult Safeguarding.' In A. Cooper and E. White (eds) *Safeguarding Adults Under the Care Act 2014: Understanding Good Practice*. London: Jessica Kingsley Publishers.

Hamner, M., Lorberbaum, J. and George, M. (1999) 'Potential role of the anterior cingulate cortex in PTSD: Review and hypothesis.' *Depression and Anxiety*, 9(1), 1–14.

Harlow, H.F. and Zimmerman, R.R. (1958) 'The development of affective responsiveness in infant monkeys.' *Proceedings of the American Philosophical Society*, 102, 501–509.

Health Committee (2004) *Elder abuse*. [online] Available at: https://www.parliament.uk/business/committees/committees-archive/health-committee/hc190404-14 (accessed 6 December 2018).

Herman, J.L. (1992) 'Complex PTSD: A syndrome in survivors of prolonged and repeated trauma.' *Journal of Traumatic Stress*, 5(3), 377–391.

Home Office (1998) *Speaking Up for Justice: Report of the Interdepartmental Working Group on the Treatment of Vulnerable or Intimidated Witnesses in the Criminal Justice System.* London: Home Office.

Home Office (2015) *Controlling or coercive behaviour in an intimate or family relationship: Statutory guidance framework.* [online] Available at: https://assets.publishing.service.gov.uk/government/uploads/system/uploads/attachment_data/file/482528/Controlling_or_coercive_behaviour_-_statutory_guidance.pdf (accessed 10 December 2018).

Information Commissioner's Office (2018) *Guide to the General Data Protection Regulation (GDPR).* [online] Available at: https://ico.org.uk/for-organisations/guide-to-the-general-data-protection-regulation-gdpr (accessed 21 February 2018).

James, M. and Graycar, A. (2000) *Preventing Crime against Older Australians*. Canberra: Australian Institute of Criminology.

James-Hanman, D. (2011*) Newham Council's Domestic Homicide Review Panel: Executive summary and action plan – Amolita 2011.* [online] Available at: https://view.officeapps.live.com/op/view.aspx?src=https%3A%2F%2Fwww.newham.gov.uk%2FDocuments%2FCommunity%2520and%2520Wing%2FDomestic HomicideReviewAmolita2011.doc (accessed 14 January 2018).

Johnson, G. and Scholes, K. (2002) *Exploring Corporate Strategy* (sixth edition). Harlow: Pearson.

Jones, A., Pleace, N. and Quilgars, D. (2002) *Firm Foundations: An Evaluation of the Shelter Homeless to Home Service.* London: Shelter.

Knight, L. and Hester, M. (2014) 'Domestic abuse and dementia: What are the characteristic features and patterns of longstanding domestic abuse following the onset of dementia?' *Safe*, 2014, 10–14.

Law Commission (2008) *Adult Social Care: Scoping Report,* paras 4.270 to 4.275 and Appendix B. London: Law Commission.

Lawdon, J., Lewis, S. and Williams, C. (2014) *Making safeguarding personal.* [online] Available at: https://www.local.gov.uk/sites/default/files/documents/Making%20Safeguarding%20Personal%20-%20Guide%202014.pdf (accessed 12 December 2018).

Lawteacher.net (2018) *Osman v UK.* [online] Available at: https://www.lawteacher.net/cases/osman-v-uk.php?vref=1 (accessed 12 December 2018).

Local Government Association and Association of Directors of Adult Social Services (2015) *Adult Safeguarding and Domestic Abuse: A Guide to Support Practitioners and Managers.* London: Local Government Association and Association of Directors of Adult Social Services.

Lodrick, Z. (n.d.) *Victim guilt following experiences of sexualised trauma: Investigation and interview considerations.* [online] Available at: www.zoelodrick.co.uk/training/guilt-article (accessed 17 November 2017).

London Borough of Sutton (2007) *Summary of the Health Care Commission's investigation into Sutton and Merton Primary Care Trust Learning Disability Services.* [online] Available at: https://moderngov.sutton.gov.uk/documents/s4175/Health%20Commission%20report.pdf (accessed 12 December 2018).

Mandelstam, M. (2017) *Care Act 2014: An A–Z of Law and Practice.* London: Jessica Kingsley Publishers.

Mantell, A. and Scragg, T. (2009) *Safeguarding Adults in Social Work.* Exeter: Learning Matters Ltd.

References

Maynard, E. (2017) *What exactly does PTSD do to the brain?* [online] Very Well. Available at: www.verywell.com/what-exactly-does-ptsd-do-to-the-brain-2797210 (accessed 19 November 2017).

Montminy, D., Sarita, M., Geho, S., Holinger, P. and Doner, K. (2017) *The effects of trauma on attachment* [online] Available at: www.scribd.com/document/169323085/The-Effects-of-Trauma-on-Attachment (accessed 13 December 2018).

Munby, Lord Justice (2010) 'What price dignity?' Keynote address to the Local Government Association Community Care Conference: Protecting Liberties, 14 July 2010.

Munro, E. (2011) *The Munro Review of Child Protection: Final Report – A Child-Centred System*. London: The Stationery Office.

National Alliance to End Homelessness (2017) *Domestic violence*. [online] Available at: https://endhomelessness.org/homelessness-in-america/what-causes-homelessness/domestic-violence (accessed 15 December 2017).

National Assembly for Wales (2000) *In Safe Hands: Implementing Adult Protection Procedures in Wales*. Cardiff: Social Services Inspectorate.

NHS England (2018) *NHS commissioning*. [online] Available at: https://www.england.nhs.uk/commissioning (accessed 7 December 2018).

Office for National Statistics (2015) *Measuring national wellbeing: Insights into loneliness, older people and wellbeing*. [online] Available at: www.ons.gov.uk/peoplepopulationandcommunity/wellbeing/articles/measuringnationalwellbeing/2015-10-01 (accessed 5 January 2018).

Office of Fair Trading (2006) *Research on the Impact of Mass Marketed Scams: A Summary of Research into the Impact of Scams on UK Consumers*. London: Office of Fair Trading.

Ogden, P. and Minton, K. (2000) 'Sensorimotor psychotherapy: One method for processing traumatic memory.' *Traumatology*, VI(3), article 3.

Parry, I. (2013) *Learning Today, Leading Tomorrow. Adult Safeguarding – The Need for All Staff to Engage*. [online] Available at www.cih.org/resources/PDF/Policy%20free%20download%20pdfs/Learning%20today%20leading%20tomorrow/05%20Adult%20safeguarding%20Parry.pdf (accessed 23 January 2019).

Porges, S. (1995) 'Orienting in a defensive world: Mammilian modifications of our evolutionary heritage. A polyvagal theory.' *Psychophysiology*, 32, 301–318.

Porges, S. (2004) 'Neuroception: A subconscious system for detecting threats and safety.' *Zero to Three*, May, 19–24.

R v B [2010] EWCA Crim 4.

R v Ghosh [1982] 3 WLR 110 Court of Appeal.

Richards, M., Lelliot, P. and Baker, T. (2016) *Learning, Candour and Accountability: A Review of the Way NHS Trusts Review and Investigate the Deaths of Patients in England*. London: Care Quality Commission.

Rodriguez, C., Herman, D., Alcon, J., Chen, S. *et al.* (2013) *Prevalence of hoarding disorder in individuals at potential risk of eviction in New York City*. [online] PMC US National Library of Medicine. National Institute of Health. Available at: www.ncbi.nlm.nih.gov/pmc/articles/PMC3833068 (accessed 12 December 2018).

Rothbaum B., Foa, E., Riggs, D., Murdock, T. and Walsh, W. (1992) 'A prospective examination of post-traumatic stress disorder in rape victims.' [online] Journal of Traumatic Stress. Available at https://onlinelibrary.wiley.com/doi/abs/10.1002/jts.2490050309 (accessed 23 January 2019).

SafeLives (2018) *MARAC: Resources for people referring*. [online] Available at: www.safelives.org.uk/practice-support/resources-marac-meetings/resources-people-referring (accessed 21 February 2018).

Salman v Turkey (2000) 21986/93, Council of Europe: European Court of Human Rights, 27 June. [online] Available at: https://www.refworld.org/cases,ECHR,3ae6b6c30.html (accessed 12 December 2018).

Salway, S. and Such, E. (2017) *Modern slavery and public health*. [online] Public Health England. Available at: www.gov.uk/government/publications/modern-slavery-and-public-health/modern-slavery-and-public-health (accessed 21 February 2018).

Saxena, S., Brody, A.L., Maidment, K.M., Smith, E.C. *et al.* (2004) 'Cerebral glucose metabolism in obsessive-compulsive hoarding.' *American Journal of Psychiatry*, 161(6), 1038–1048.

Schwehr, B. (2018) *Legal View: Three Common Problems with the Care Act*. Birmingham: British Association of Social Workers.

Shareweb.kent.gov.uk (2009) *Response to the consultation on the review of No Secrets: January 2009*. [online] Available at: https://shareweb.kent.gov.uk/Documents/adult-Social-Services/adult-protection/Response%20to%20the%20consultation%20on%20the%20review%20of%20No%20Secrets%20January%202009.pdf (accessed 7 December 2018).

Simpson, R. (1996) 'Neither clear nor present: The social construction of safety and danger.' *Sociological Forum*, 11(3), 549–562.

Smith, G. and Heke, S. (2010) 'From report to court: Psychology, trauma and the law.' Workshop presented at the UK Psychological Trauma Society Third Annual Conference, January 2010. [online] Available at: www.ukpts.co.uk (accessed 2 January 2018).

Snowdon, J., Pertusa, A. and Mataix-Cols, D. (2012) 'On hoarding and squalor: A few considerations for DSM-5.' *Depression and Anxiety*, 29(5), 417–424.

Social Care Institute for Excellence (2015) *Safeguarding adults reviews under the Care Act: Implementation and support*. [online] Available at: www.scie.org.uk/care-act-2014/safeguarding-adults/reviews/files/safeguarding-adults-reviews-under-the-care-act-implementation-support.pdf (accessed 2 March 2017).

Social Care Institute for Excellence (2018) *What does the law say about sharing information? Adult safeguarding – Sharing information*. [online] Available at: www.scie.org.uk/care-act-2014/safeguarding-adults/sharing-information/what-does-the-law-say.asp (accessed 13 January 2018).

Spalek, B. (1999) 'Exploring victimisation: A study looking at the impact of the Maxwell scandal on the Maxwell pensioners.' *International Review of Victimology*, 6, 213–230.

Spalek, B. (2006) *Crime Victims: Theory, Policy and Practice*. Basingstoke: Palgrave.

Spitzer, R.L. (1984) 'Psychiatric Diagnosis: Are Clinicians Still Necessary?' In J.B.W. Williams and R.L. Spitzer (eds) *Psychotherapy Research: Where Are We and Where Should We Go?* New York, NY: Guilford Press.

Steptoe, A., Shankar, A., Demakakos, P. and Wardle, J. (2013) 'Social isolation, loneliness, and all-cause mortality in older men and women.' *PNAS*, 110(15), 5797–5801.

Stevenson, O. (1996) *Elder Protection in the Community: What Can We Learn from Child Protection?* London: Age Concern Institute for Gerontology, King's College London.

Tolin, D., Stevens, M., Villavicencio, A., Norberg, M. *et al.* (2012) 'Neural mechanisms of decision making in hoarding disorder.' *Archives of General Psychiatry*, 69(8), 832.

Tomlinson, D.F. (1993) *No Longer Afraid. The Safeguard of Older People in Domestic Settings: Practice Guidelines*. London: HMSO.

Van der Kolk, B., McFarlane, A.C. and Weisaeth, L. (eds) (1996a) *Traumatic Stress: The Effects of Overwhelming Experience on Mind, Body and Society*. New York, NY: Guilford Press.

Van der Kolk, B., Pelcovitz, D., Roth, S., Mandel, F., McFarlane, A. and Herman, J. (1996b) 'Dissociation, affect dysregulation and somatization: The complex nature of adaptation to trauma.' [online] American Journal of Psychiatry, 153(7), 83–93. Available at: https://www.traumatherapie.de/users/vanderkolk/kolk3.html (accessed 23 January 2019).

Walsh, K. and Bennett, G. (2000) 'Financial abuse of older people.' *Journal of Adult Protection*, 2(1), 21–29.

Witness Support, Preparation and Profiling (WSPP) (2017) *The Liverpool Model YouTube documentary*. [online] Available at: www.youtube.com/watch?v=gpgPM2X0CcM (accessed 20 October 2017).

Woloshynowych, M., Rogers, S., Taylor-Adams, S. and Vincent, C. (2005) 'The investigation and analysis of critical incidents and adverse events in healthcare.' *Health Technology Assessment*, 9(19), 1–158.

World Health Organization (2008) *Eliminating Female Genital Mutilation: An Interagency Statement*. Geneva: World Health Organization.

Index

Self-Neglect and Hoarding
A Guide to Safeguarding and Support
Deborah Barnett

Paperback: £19.99/$29.95
ISBN: 978 1 78592 272 5
eISBN: 978 1 78450 569 1
264 pages

Self-neglect and hoarding is present in 1 of 5 social work cases in mental health and older people's services. These cases can be the most alarming and challenging on a social worker's caseload.

A skilled, thorough risk assessment of the behaviours of self-neglect is needed in order to ensure effective care and support is available. This guide offers practical and applicable tools and solutions for all professionals involved in working with people who self-neglect. It includes tips for assessment and decision-making in the support process, and updates following the implementation of the Care Act 2014, which deemed self-neglect a safeguarding matter.

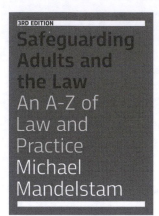

Safeguarding Adults and the Law, Third Edition
An A–Z of Law and Practice
Michael Mandelstam

Paperback: £40/$60
ISBN: 978 1 78592 225 1
eISBN: 978 1 78450 499 1
640 pages

Safeguarding Adults and the Law, now in its third edition, sets this complex area of work within an extensive legal framework and provides many useful pointers for practitioners and students. It is now in an A-Z format, enabling quick reference to a wide range of civil and criminal law, and to legal case law.

The book covers safeguarding duties under the Care Act 2014 and in particular the making of enquiries by local authorities, safeguarding adults boards, Department of Health guidance, human rights, regulation of health and social care providers, barring of carers from working with vulnerable adults, criminal records certificates, mental capacity, the High Court's inherent jurisdiction, undue influence, assault, battery, wilful neglect, ill treatment, self-neglect, manslaughter, murder, theft, fraud, sexual offences, modern slavery, domestic violence legislation, data protection and the sharing of information.

Michael Mandelstam provides independent legal training, advice and consultancy to local authorities, the NHS and voluntary organisations. Prior to this, he worked at the Disabled Living Foundation, a national voluntary organisation, before moving to the Social Services Inspectorate at the Department of Health. He holds postgraduate qualifications in law, information studies and the history of science and medicine.